WINGS

FOR

LIFE

>>

BY RUTH NICHOLS

Foreword by Rear Admiral Richard E. Byrd, U.S.N.

Edited by Dorothy Roe Lewis

J. B. LIPPINCOTT COMPANY
Philadelphia and New York

To Aunty, to H.A.S. and
to the many others herein named
who helped me so generously "along the way"

Grateful acknowledgment is made to *The Institute of Aeronautical Sciences* for their assistance concerning the authenticating of certain data.

Only in the recounting of the romantic episodes, and in the chapter entitled, "Terror at Sea," have any names been changed, and then solely for the usual courtesy considerations.

FOREWORD

Ruth Nichols is the earliest licensed American woman pilot who is still actively flying. This in itself entitles her to a special niche in aviation's Hall of Fame. But there are other aspects of the story of Ruth Nichols which, in my opinion, make her one of the outstanding women of our time.

I have known Ruth Nichols for more than thirty years. I first met her toward the end of the 1920's, when flying was a much more difficult business than it is today. Human beings were making long flights away from base and beyond the range of immediate help in order to prove that aircraft could be used for useful and peaceful accomplishments. When Floyd Bennett and I flew to the North Pole in 1926, for example, we were beyond the last outpost of civilization for thirteen and a half hours. When Lindbergh crossed the Atlantic in 1927, he would have been beyond help had he had to make a forced landing. Within a matter of one month the Atlantic was also bridged by Chamberlin and Levine, who similarly risked their lives. When the *America* flew to Paris as the first multi-engined plane to cross the Atlantic nonstop, my gallant shipmates joined me in an orderly but cold ducking in the pitch darkness of Ver Sur Mer inlet, but we were able to row ashore.

While successes were being achieved, the newspapers carried distressingly frequent accounts of pioneer aviators who disappeared or crashed on attempted flights. The process of developing the long-range aircraft of today was based on the trial and error of this period. The credit for the wonders of modern air transportation belongs to the flights that failed as well as to the flights that succeeded; to those who died as well as to those who survived.

There was a handful of women who shared in the hardships and perils of aviation pioneering. Two names that stand out, as I look back upon the late 'twenties and early 'thirties, were Amelia Earhart and Ruth Nichols.

One of the most impressive things about Ruth Nichols is her indomitable pluck. In the course of her flying career she has had six major crackups and innumerable close calls. But she always got up and tried again. In fact, her long-distance record was made while she was wearing a surgical steel brace to support a broken back.

Ruth began flying with Rogers Airlines in 1922. In 1931 between March and October she established three new international records for women—in altitude, speed, and distance. The following year she flew from Los Angeles to New York in thirteen hours and twenty-one minutes, clipping one hour off the previous transcontinental record set by Lindbergh. And it is characteristic of her that in 1955 she became the first woman in this country to pilot a twin-engine jet Executive aircraft.

There is still another aspect to Ruth Nichols' activities which has impressed me over the years. She not only did things—but she considered it her duty to use whatever influence she had to promote international understanding and to stimulate public interest in aviation. She was director of Relief Wings, Inc., from 1940 to 1949: and she subsequently became the first woman to receive the title of "World Pilot," when serving as special correspondent for the U. S. Committee for UNICEF (United Nations International Children's Emergency Fund) on a round-the-world tour.

Reading the story of Ruth Nichols has brought back vividly to my mind some of the more heroic episodes of the grand early days of aviation. It is an exciting story—the story of an outstanding woman as well as an outstanding flier.

RICHARD E. BYRD

CONTENTS

ILLUSTRATIONS

WINGS FOR LIFE

1

SKY HAPPY

It all began, I suppose, in 1919 when Father took me to an aviation show in Atlantic City as a reward for the Herculean effort of graduating from Miss Masters' School at Dobbs Ferry. The star attraction was Eddie Stinson, America's foremost war ace, who was taking up passengers in his rickety wood-and-baling-wire plane at a rate of ten dollars for ten minutes. Father bought me a ten-minute airplane ride. I haven't come down to earth since.

Dad's philosophy always had been, "Try anything once." Because he excelled in most sports, I spent most of my childhood with my heart in my mouth. My father was Erickson Norman Nichols, one of Teddy Roosevelt's original Rough Riders, sportsman, master of hounds, stockbroker, a member of New York's "400," who spent most of his life living up to his heritage as a direct descendant of Leif Ericson, the Viking hero.

When I fell off a horse, I always had to get right back on and try the jump again. When I made a flat dive from the high tower, I had to try again until I did it right. It seemed as though I was always forcing myself to tackle a terrifying job again and again.

On Mother's side, however, I come from a long line of Quakers—peaceful, Godloving people who live by fairly inflexible rules—and my beloved Quaker Aunt Polly has been my refuge and strength all through my rebellious life. Paradoxically, when I was small Aunty frequently clucked with concern over my meekness, fearing that I would be stepped on all my days.

It was with a feeling of panic that I climbed into Stinson's flimsy open plane that long-ago day in Atlantic City—panic I didn't dare to reveal before my father. As long as I could remember I had been terrified of heights. I got vertigo if I looked down from a tall building. I loathed elevators and I wouldn't have been caught dead in a roller coaster. My willingness to go up in an airplane may have been in part bravado, but there was also a determination to overcome my fear—by accepting the challenge of terrifying forces over which I believed I had no control. At any rate, I was scared stiff.

When Stinson decided to loop-the-loop for good measure, I was paralyzed with fear. My eyes were squeezed shut and my stomach was tied in a knot as the wind screamed through the struts and I felt an almost unbearable pressure on the back of my neck. When I opened my eyes we were flying right-side-up again, the breath-taking panorama of Atlantic City lay below, and the pilot was laughing.

Suddenly I felt like laughing too. What had I been afraid of? This was only air. There was none of that dizzy feeling I had when looking down from a high building. Here I was free of the earth. A minute ago I had been an earthbound caterpillar, now I was an airborne butterfly. I was free as the air itself. I wasn't afraid of *anything* any more. I wanted to go on and up forever. But the ten minutes were over and we were back on the ground. My heart, however, remained in the sky.

If Father had known what he was starting, he might never have spent that ten-dollar bill. But then I would never have found myself.

Flying has nearly killed me many times; it has never made me rich. Yet from the challenge of the skies I have reaped

World War I ace Eddie Stinson just before taking Ruth up for her first hop in a "Jenny," Atlantic City, 1919.

humanity's most treasured reward—life in its fullest meaning for myself and in relation to others.

Since the first time I sampled the clean ecstasy of flight, with the wind whistling through the wires and flimsy struts of that open-cockpit OX5 "Jenny" of World War I vintage, the freedom of the sky has been more necessary to me than food and drink, more important than the safe domesticity of marriage and children—though I wanted those too.

To the public I suppose I have often seemed to be the original "flying fool." While flying over one hundred and forty different models of aircraft, I have piloted a plane in a plaster cast and a steel corset, too impatient to wait for bones to knit from the last crash. I have frozen my tongue sucking oxygen at sixty below zero, six miles up. I have escaped twice from burning planes. I have clung to a life raft in cold, mountainous seas. I have had most of the bones in my body broken. And after each disaster there came the command from something deep within me: Get back into the air. . . .

Maybe it doesn't make sense. I have been told this so often that it has become a kind of background drumbeat to my life. Family and friends have urged me to keep my feet on the ground ever since the first time I came home in an ambulance. The only people who haven't tried to change me are flyers. They comprehend.

They would understand why recently I had to try my hand at flying a twin-engine jet plane taking off from Westchester Airport. I had been invited to look over this new executive aircraft by my friend, Olive Anne Beech, of Wichita, Kansas, president of Beech Aircraft Corporation, the jet's American distributor. I was among a small group of aviation enthusiasts who went out to inspect the new plane, a French Mauraine-Saulnier.

The French pilot was delighted when he found I could speak his language, aeronautically and otherwise. We were off with a whoosh, up in a flash and the pilot invited me to take over the controls.

Never before, even in those isolated moments of heady exhilaration during my early altitude and distance flights, have I experienced the sensation of complete and incredible freedom that came as we streaked through the upper air in complete silence—no propeller sound, no vibration, only the glorious feeling of being suspended in space.

At my shoulder I seemed to sense the presence of a gallant ghostly company—the spirit of Amelia Earhart, Wiley Post, Harry Rogers, my first flying instructor, and others of that pioneer fraternity who put love of flight above love of life.

I felt as if my soul were completely freed from my earthly body, with a new perspective on the immensity of the universe and the horizons yet to be reached.

From a great height I looked back at the adventures of my life up to now, the heavenly highs and dismal lows, the eternal struggle to go on and up again, the fears, the doubts, the uncertainties—and all at once they seemed to fall into a pattern.

After years of asking myself why I was compelled to batter my body and spirit with this insatiable urge to fly, I seemed to find the answer. In this way only could I weld the two sides of my nature—the adventurous Viking spirit of my father and the humanitarianism of my Quaker ancestors. Through flight came joy, new perspectives, and help in blazing new frontiers of the mind and heart for the people of the earth.

When finally I depart this earthly sphere for good, I should like it to be in a final burst of flight, farther and higher than any human ever has gone before, somewhere in the infinite mystery of outer space, where at least I can see where I am going. . . .

I still remember with anguish all the multiple and complicated fears of my childhood, trying to live up to the Spartan standards of a sportsman father and to conform to the rigid, and sometimes contradictory, rules of conduct laid down by a society mother, a quiet, loving Quaker minister grand-father, and a beloved Aunty.

Father had a seat on the New York Stock Exchange and, for my first dozen years, I was brought up in a high-stooped brownstone house in Manhattan, spending the summers at mountain or ocean resorts with frequent welcome stays at my grandfather's home in Yonkers, with Aunty. I was the eldest of four children—my brother Erickson Snowden Nichols and the twins, Billy and Betty—and felt a sense of special responsibility toward the younger children.

The happiest memories of my childhood are of times spent in Yonkers, with Grandpa and Aunty, to whom I could pour out my fears and loneliness. Aunty always seemed to under-stand, and after Grandpa died, "Angel" joined our household in Rye, N. Y., where we lived for several decades.

Some of my childish feelings of guilt and insecurity, I be-lieve, stemmed from poor Mother, whose own parents had been unable to fill her childhood needs. She had chosen the social world perhaps in rebellion against her plain Quaker heritage; fastidious, beautifully dressed, an accomplished hostess, she nevertheless always craved more affection than she received. Yet she always was too preoccupied with her bridge parties, teas, dinners and constant domestic problems to be aware of young children's requirements for relaxed hours of companionship. Aunty, on the other hand, appeared to have all the time in the world. How well I remember her often-repeated remark:

"Thee mustn't worry, dear. Just trust our Heavenly Father."

The words may seem unduly solemn, but my Aunt's tender smile and the twinkle in her star-sapphire eyes put blessed reassurance in them. Small wonder that we four children al-ways called her "Angel."

With the passage of every year I have grown more con-scious of Aunty's powerful influence in the motives and as-pirations of my life. To this day all our family uses the

Ruth, age thirteen, and "Aunty" in a photographer's model plane, Atlantic City.

Quaker "thee" when speaking to her, a token of our special affection and respect. In contrast, I remember the terrible epithet of Quaker children, when they wanted to vent their utmost scorn upon a playmate: "Thee horrid little YOU, thee!"

Despite her gentleness and loving understanding, Angel could be a rather stern disciplinarian. One incident of our childhood has become a family joke. This was an occasion when Angel had ordered brother Billy to stay at home when he wanted to go off on some boyish adventure, and he cried out:

"Dammit, Angel, why can't I go?"

So it was to Aunty Angel that I always turned when life presented a problem, as when, after that epic first flight in Atlantic City, I decided that I wanted to go to college and study to be a doctor.

The idea of sending a daughter to college appalled Father, who felt that a genteel finishing school was the only proper place for a well-bred young lady, whose one aim in life should be to have a successful debut and immediately thereafter a brilliant marriage.

"If thee wants to go to college, thee go," decided Angel.

And so I went to Wellesley. My parents threw up their hands at the puzzle of a daughter whose ambition was to dissect frogs and study bugs and fiddle around with smelly chemicals. This was not the prescribed course for a delicately reared subdeb, who was showing signs of flowering youth, whose too-fine brown hair, deep-set blue eyes and so-called aristocratic features were considered more of an asset than any number of college degrees.

My professors at Wellesley seem to have shared somewhat the family opinion, for they obviously considered me no mental giant. My marks were average, although I won distinction in athletics, especially riding and crew, and played leading roles in college plays. But with Aunty to cheer me on, I plodded doggedly through my classes, determined to

master the intricacies of science and Greek. And on weekends at home I loved to flabbergast the family with jaw-
breaking terms. As I launched into a learned discourse on the
taxonomy of the pteridophytes and spermatophytes, they
would shout in chorus:

"There goes Ruth again!"

I stuck it out two years at Wellesley, and then gave in to
the mass weight of family insistence that I take time out to
learn to become a lady. Father was not well, and Mother
was determined that I must have a proper formal debut,
along with its hectic social season. They painted a glowing
picture of the gay whirl of Junior League activities, a winter
season in Florida, beaux dancing attendance, theatre parties,
and the rest of it. Well, all right. If they wanted this so much,
I'd try it.

Poor Mother and Dad. Their fond plans only proved a
boomerang, for it was during the height of the winter season
in Miami that I got up into the air again. Hardly had I arrived in Florida when whom should I meet through my
brother Snowden but Harry Rogers, that gallant airman, best
of all the barnstorming flying-boat pilots.

I didn't know it then, but it was he who would shape the
course of my future life—a stocky, weatherbeaten man, whose
blue eyes had the look of piercing into the distance that dis-
tinguishes so many great pilots. He was rough, tough and
blunt—and one of the finest men I've known.

So I went to Miami to be a social butterfly and met the
man who was to give me wings of a different kind.

As soon as I could I went down to the dock, entranced by
the graceful beauty of those early flying boats. I paid for a
fifteen-minute flight, and we took off in a silvery shower of
sea foam—even more enthralling and beautiful, I thought,
than taking off from the ground. When we were up and I was
gazing breathlessly at the beauty of blue water, white sand
and green palm trees below, Rogers said casually:

"Just take hold of the controls. There, you see how easy it is? This crate will just about fly itself."

I grasped the wheel on the control-yoke, and I was sold forever—feeling the power of my own hands managing this fierce and wonderful machine, keeping this heavy craft thundering through the sky and directing her course. The exhilaration was so sharp as to be almost unbearable. I looked with shining eyes at Rogers, saw his quizzical smile and cried unbelievingly:

"It's true! It does almost fly itself!"

I marveled at the ease with which I could bank and turn this silver seagull through the sky—much easier, I observed, than driving an automobile down a concrete highway—a breeze compared to handling a high-spirited hunter or polo pony.

I had no conception then of the perils of flight instruction in those early days. I didn't realize that beginners not infrequently "froze" at the controls, that I might let the plane stall and fall off into what then meant an uncontrollable spin. I was blissfully unaware that engine trouble was always imminent, that any one of a dozen things could happen to threaten death or disaster. All I felt was the surging freedom of flight and the ease of flying.

We were hardly back at the seaplane base when I blurted out excitedly:

"How much are flying lessons, Captain Rogers?"

He grinned and replied casually:

"They come high—sixty dollars an hour."

I didn't even stop to think. After all, I had a savings account started for me in childhood, and without batting an eyelash I assigned that five hundred dollars to Harry Rogers as first payment on my wings.

Although the price was high, I couldn't have been more fortunate in choosing an instructor. To all who knew him, Harry Rogers was also one of the most popular of the early commercial flying-boat pilots. He was also the first to organize a group of barnstorming and charter hydro-airplane pilots, and he was a passionate defender of the majesty of the air.

He was at once hard-boiled and gentle, abusive and kind, shrewd and generous, crude and sensitive. He punctuated his lessons with scorching language and an occasional clout over the head. He seemed recklessly courageous, although he was always preaching safety. A favorite remark was:

"I'd rather be known as the oldest pilot than the best."

If his original idea was to take advantage of my apparent wealth, there were good reasons for it. To him I must have appeared a rattle-brained girl, flitting about on the accepted debutante rounds, whose indulgent family was well able to foot the bills. He could not know that my parents were living beyond their means; that my father's illness meant a deep cut in his income; that they had strained the exchequer to the breaking point in order that I might be properly launched in society.

A barnstorming pilot in those days had to make the most of every opportunity. For every day of booming business he might face a week of bad weather. Planes and gasoline were expensive. So whenever he ran across an air enthusiast, he became a high-pressure salesman. Regular flying lessons meant steady cash. And after the lessons there was always the prospect of selling the student a plane.

If Captain Rogers set me up as an easy mark in the beginning, he seemed to change his opinion. He recognized a kindred spirit and respected my passionate determination to fly. When my five hundred dollars was gone he continued to teach me at merely the bare cost of gasoline and oil, and often let me go along "just for the ride."

Those were singing, soaring days for me, marred by only one cloud—the realization that dear Dad's illness was chronic, and that from now on his athletic, fun-loving life must be sadly changed.

The family's social calendar took me from Miami back

home to Rye and then to a cottage at Lake George or to the Lake Placid Club for the summer. Most of my time was spent in competing and occasionally winning contests in diving, swimming, canoeing and tennis. The Florida seashore, Long Island Sound, Adirondack lakes. And on each of these bodies of water, who should always turn up but Harry Rogers?

By the end of the summer Harry and I were old friends. My love of flying was recognized as sincere, and I was admitted to the inner circle of pilots. The barnstormers in the Rogers crew rarely missed an opportunity to give me a bit more flying practice or take me along for a "ferry" trip.

When I returned to Rye, I never knew when the phone would ring and one of these pilot friends would invite me to go along on a hop to Port Washington or Garden City in order to collect some spare parts for the newest "job" Harry might be putting together. And if I live to be one hundred I shall never forget the splendor of flying back across the Sound into the gorgeous sunsets of late summer, with brilliant splashes of purple, red and yellow streaking the sky and reflecting from the water. It is such moments that keep pilots in the air.

That fall, after my year off, I returned to Wellesley. Even my family could see that my social debut had been merely an unimportant incident in an unorthodox year, and that I might as well go on with whatever strange ambition I might have.

I went back to study more science, sociology and comparative religion, but the idea of solo flight kept getting between me and my books. It became an all-consuming desire. Finally I could stand it no longer. On a Friday I went galloping up to the college observatory and burst in upon Professor Duncan.

"What kind of a day will it be tomorrow?" I demanded. "I have to know. Tell me it's going to be fine for flying!"

"My dear girl," said Dr. Duncan soothingly, "I'm sorry, but I'm afraid you'll have to go elsewhere for that information.

We haven't yet learned to predict the weather by watching the stars in their courses."

I stammered my apologies and was off to phone Harry, which I should have done in the first place. In those days, official weather forecasting was not readily available to the public. Luck was with me. Tomorrow would be fine, Harry said, guessing from the old-fashioned mariner observation.

In a dither of excitement I caught the Owl night train down from Boston to Stamford, then hung around until I could get a local to Greenwich, where Harry had moved his barnstorming business. At six a.m. I called my home, planning to make arrangements for Peter, the Irish chauffeur, to pick me up after my flight. But I didn't want the family to suspect my plans. To my consternation, Mother answered the phone.

Adopting an Irish brogue on the spur of the moment, I asked:

"Is Pay-ter there?"

"And who might this be?" demanded Mother. "And why should you disturb the household at such an hour?"

"Sure and it's Maggie, on a matter of life and death," I replied. "It's sorry I am to be callin' at the crack o' dawn, but would it be askin' too much of ye if I was to spake to Pay-ter?"

It obviously was asking too much, but my determination must have impelled Mother, and by some miracle I was connected with Peter. I told him what was going on and he entered into the conspiracy with enthusiasm.

Arrived at last at Harry's new Greenwich base, I danced in impatience for the takeoff. Harry shook hands, looked me over and decided in favor of caution. Having been up all night, in a fever of anticipation, I must have looked like a jittery mare.

"Okay, so you can solo," said Harry, "but you have to take a mechanic along, in case something happens."

In vain I protested. Harry was adamant. I know now that

he had visions of my making a forced landing with his highly prized flying boat somewhere out in the Sound, and he knew I did not have enough muscular strength to pull the propeller through for a new start. His Seagull would then drift on the rocks and perhaps be ruined.

We had a little ceremony before the start—an assortment of admonitions from everyone present, a solemn shaking of heads over the mechanic's plight and a divvying up of his personal property among his friends on the assumption that this was goodby forever.

Rogers issued his instructions: I was to taxi down the harbor, take off when clear of the traffic, make one circle out over the Sound and then come down again.

Greenwich Harbor was pretty well packed with anchored sailing craft of all shapes and sizes. I felt as you do when you're driving a new car which seems a lot longer and wider than the old one. With a flying boat it was worse.

Taxiing carefully down the harbor, I felt the tide and wind catch the hull, drawing us toward a sand bar. With a convulsive lurch I pulled clear, gunned around a yacht which I missed by inches and headed into open water.

Then my troubles were over. The takeoff was smooth and simple. It was a sparkling blue and gold day, and I had a sensation of pure joy in single-handed control over speed and space. Harry's instructions for a prompt return were forgotten in the delight of the present. I cruised around far out over the Sound, tried a couple of landings, practiced various maneuvers until the mechanic reminded me nervously that we ought to be getting back. So absorbed had I been in the all-engrossing sensation of flight and power that I came back to reality with a jolt and headed back toward Greenwich.

Now came the tricky business of evaluating tide, wind and prop blast. I knew the principles involved in taxiing a flying boat on the water. You should do it one of two ways—either very slowly, so as not to overheat the engine, or else "on the step," holding just sufficient speed to skim the surface of the

Ruth Nichols with aeronautical inspector W. R. Jones (*left*) and Harry Rogers after passing her government transport license test in a Seagull, June 4, 1927.

water. The latter often is the more efficient way, because it enables you to maintain "steerage way" through lessened resistance of the water.

I had been well coached; nevertheless I came in at just the wrong speed, fast enough to make myself believe I was displaying dexterity, but hardly "on the step." As it was, we were churning our way through a wall of water without sufficient speed for cooling the engine, so that it was badly overheated when I pulled up with a flourish before the witnesses on shore.

I stepped out of the plane to meet a scowling Harry.

"Whadda you think you were doin'?" he thundered. "Flounderin' and threshin' your way out of the harbor like a wounded porpoise! Skitterin' around the sky out of sight until we all thought you'd cracked her up. Givin' us all gray hairs! Then comin' in at a numbskull speed that probably burned up the engine! Gals! Bah!"

I stammered apologies, tried to explain. I knew even then, and I know better now, that all his blustering criticisms were based on sound reason. I could think of only one thing: Had I failed my test?

"No," growled Harry. "You soloed, anyway, didn't you?"

All was right with the world again. I flung my arms around his neck and kissed him resoundingly. "I'm a flyer now, Harry!"

He pushed me off roughly, but I caught the beginning of the familiar twinkle in his eye as he growled:

"A flyer, my eye! You've only just begun. But maybe—just maybe—you'll make it yet!"

Peter was waiting with the family car, grinning as proudly as if he had been flying the plane himself. As I climbed in, Harry called after me:

"Next thing—get your international sporting license, y'hear?"

That didn't happen until after I had been graduated from Wellesley, in 1924. But meantime I got in a lot of flying time with Harry and other pilots. Although I had soloed, Harry still considered me a pupil, and he barked instructions at me whenever he allowed me to go up with him. My chief—and only—quarrel with Harry as an instructor was that he always told me *what* to do, but he never told me *why*. Maybe he thought I was too stupid to understand theory. Anyway one of his favorite remarks was:

"For Pete's sake, don't ask me why! Do it because I tell you!"

But I remained determined to find out the reasons behind the rules.

This lack of understanding the *why* of things led to one of my first accidents. I had taken up Harry's hydro-airplane at Lake Placid one summer day, with orders to land it quickly. Not understanding the reason for the order, I came down too slowly and the hull, instead of skimming the water, sank too deeply; it felt as though the thick keel had scraped a rock. The Seagull seemed all right, so I continued back to the lock where Harry was waiting with a passenger, and said nothing.

Impatient to get off, Harry climbed in with his passenger as soon as I got out, and started to taxi across the lake. Watching from the shore, I was horrified to see that the hull was sinking. I leaped into a motorboat to go to the rescue, but Harry and his passenger were already being fished out, unscathed but dripping, when I reached them. I took one look at the apoplectic expression on my instructor's face, and kept right on going. I stayed away for two days, before I dared show my face around the base. Then I took my tongue-lashing meekly, offered to pay for repairs and was amazed but delighted when Harry grumblingly allowed me to continue making solo hops.

There was another time when he almost chucked me as a pupil. On his first flight of the season at Lake George, with many prospective passengers watching, I was riding beside Harry in the front of the Seagull. A pillow at my back cramped me, and I reached back to hand it to a boy passenger in the seat behind. But the force of the wind over the open cockpit tore the pillow out of my hand, the propeller caught it and ripped it to bits, and the feathers streamed out like smoke. People on shore thought the ship was on fire, and there was hysterical excitement before we landed safely. Then, purple with rage, Harry put both hands on his hips and proceeded to scald me with a torrent of invective, the general gist of which, highly censored, went something like this:

"Of all the half-wits in the world, you are the dumbest! You're too dumb to fly! You've ruined my whole summer business! You're a rattle-brained brat, fuzzy-headed nincompoop! Now scram before I lose my temper!"

Despite all my blunders and Harry's frequent rages, we managed to remain friends. Though he called me colorful variations of a numbskull, he did respect the sincerity of my love for flying. Gradually I became aware that he had developed confidence in my abilities, which he proved by urging me to make flying a career.

At last the time came for me to take the tests for my long-coveted pilot's license from the Fédération Aéronautique Internationale. At that time, before our own federal bureau had come into existence, this was the world's only licensing agency for pilots, its American affiliate being the National Aeronautics Association. There was no nonsense about it, either. The FAI laid down rigid rules for the tests, among which was that two observers be present.

On the morning of my ordeal, Harry and another veteran pilot, Clifford Webster, were the officials in charge. We met at one of Harry's bases on the shore of Port Washington, Long Island, and I listened carefully to the rules for the two-part test; which of course I already knew by heart.

For the first part I had to take the flying boat up above five thousand feet and keep it at that altitude for an hour, then cut my switch (not just throttle back, as is done today) and glide down with a dead motor to a landing within one hundred yards of a specified point. For the second part I had to complete a certain number of figure-eights under eight hundred feet.

There was considerable heavy-handed kidding on the part of both Harry and Cliff as I climbed into the Seagull and prepared to taxi out through the crowded harbor for the first part of the test.

For my objective they chose a yacht with two yellow smokestacks—I think it was one of the Vanderbilts'. After an hour the two officials were to come out beside it in a canoe to watch my landing.

"If you can find anything, you ought to be able to see that," said Harry, squinting at the huge, gleaming yacht with its brightly painted stacks. "Just don't go showin' off and doin' some dumb thing that'll get you lost. It's simple, see. Try to remember that. Just circle above five thousand for an hour, then spot the yellow smokestacks and come down. Nothin' to it. And for Pete's sake be careful of that Seagull!"

"Happy landings!" yelled Cliff, who was a stickler for form and one of the world's most conscientious souls. He would never stretch a point just because I happened to be a woman, and for that very reason would bend over backward to be sure he gave me no advantage.

For this test I was really alone in the Seagull, beautiful with her cream-colored wings and mahogany hull, and as I threaded my way through the crowded harbor I knew time and practice had increased my skill.

I was so eager to fulfill the conditions of the test that I actually spent most of the time above eight thousand feet. As flying boats have a low ceiling, I never had been over three thousand feet before. It was late fall, and it was cold up there. From more than a mile and a half up, all the boats in the harbor seemed to slide together into a solid mass. I began to doubt my eyes. All Harry's slurring remarks about my navigation came to mind. My frequent query "Where are we now?" had become a byword.

When time neared for descent, cold shivers ran down my spine as I snapped off the ignition switch and began the long glide. There were too many boats, how would I find a channel wide enough for the Seagull's wings, I would crack her up, I had been a fool ever to think I could be a flyer. . . .

Then as the Seagull descended, the boats in the harbor began mercifully to separate. I could see spaces of water between. Thank Heaven! But where *was* the yacht with the yellow smokestacks? I strained my eyes, but it was nowhere to be seen.

Well, I had to come down somewhere. So I selected a speck that looked like a small rowboat, near where I figured the yacht should have been. Defeated and deflated, I glided down to a smooth landing, and looked up to see Harry and Cliff in a canoe. As they paddled over to the Seagull, I wailed:

"Please don't say it! I know. I've failed. But I just couldn't find that darned yacht anywhere."

Harry and Cliff burst into loud, raucous laughter. They wiped their eyes. Then Harry gasped:

"You poor little nut! That yacht steamed out of here half an hour ago, but you landed right where it was, on the button!"

I was so weak with relief that it's a wonder I ever managed the second half of the test—flying the figure-eights under eight hundred feet. But now that I had come half-way I wasn't going to let that stop me.

I took off again and banked the Seagull through the required maneuvers, enjoying the smooth feel of the flying boat as I swung around the figure-eights.

Landing triumphantly, I met scowling reproval on the faces of Cliff and Harry.

"Wh-what's the matter?" I quavered. "That was all right, wasn't it?"

"You forgot one half of the last figure-eight," said Cliff. "You'll just have to go up and do it again."

Even Harry thought that was unnecessary but I knew better than to argue with Cliff's stern sense of duty. This time I etched each turn by a thumb nail scratch on the instrument panel and threw in an extra one for good measure.

At last the test was completed.

Harry and Cliff pumped my hand, clapped me on the back and congratulated me on at last becoming a flyer. Now I was really one of the inner circle.

When I received my official flying boat pilot's license from the Fédération Aéronautique Internationale, it represented the top achievement of my life up to then—far more highly prized than my Wellesley diploma—for it was my badge of membership in the charmed fraternity of flyers.

I later learned that this was the first flying boat pilot's license ever issued to a woman. It was written in seven languages and recognized all over the world in any country affiliated with the FAI.

2

GROWING WINGS

Did I have the right to live my own life? Probably every idealistic girl asks herself this question without finding an easy answer. My problems were multiplied by the completely divergent elements in my background, and the then unconventional urge to fly—and keep on flying. My heart was in the sky but I was trying desperately to keep my feet on the ground—a good way to grow tall if you don't break in two. If I were to hold to the high spiritual standard of a selfless life, how could I satisfy this love—which I could not feel was wrong—for a very different sort of height?

Back home in Rye, I spent most of my free time tinkering around airplane engines at Harry Rogers' seaplane base, which he had moved to Rye Beach. I came home grease-smeared but happy. Mother threw up her hands in despair at the unsettling prospect of a daughter who preferred to spend her time with "riffraff" mechanics and barnstormers rather than follow the socially accepted rounds.

I grasped any and every chance to fly, and the opportunities were frequent, for Harry's pilots liked company when they made their many hops across the Sound to Port Washington where they had a car to take them to Roosevelt Field for the spare parts Harry was always needing for some new job. Roosevelt Field was the center of all aviation in those early days. This was where you had to go to buy parts for engine repairs; this was headquarters for all the airplane manufacturers' sales agencies; this was where you met other pilots and air enthusiasts, and indulged in the fascinating pastime of "hangar flying"—swapping tales of air adventures while safely on the ground.

I loved it all—the smell of the gas and engine oil, the gloom of the cavernous hangars, the shop talk of pilots and mechanics, the spirit of good fellowship and easy camaraderie that prevailed among the members of that exclusive society of airmen.

In spite of self-questionings and the constant tug-of-war between family duty and adventure, those were glorious days. There was an added challenge in the fact that flying was still a hazardous business. All of us were aware that numerous possibilities might be fatal; routine mishaps which meant only annoyance to an automobile driver could spell curtains for a pilot.

As I look back, I realize that those early planes, top-notch aircraft of their day, were fragile, unstable, death-defying mechanisms, as different from today's multi-engine clippers as the Model-T Ford differed from a modern limousine with its automatic drive and power controls. They were romantic galleons of the air that gave way to the sleek and powerful stratocruisers and supersonic jets of today.

It had not yet been discovered that the extra wing-surface of those early unwieldy biplanes and triplanes and of the struts and wires that held them together created resistance to air speed. Perched up there at the controls, so open to the elements, so tiny an atom in the vastness of space, you had an exaggerated sensation of height and speed. The wind tore at you, shrieking and whistling, as you fought your way through it often by main strength.

Looking back, it seems amazing how many of the early pilots survived the perils of the birth of the air age—and of course there were many who did not. But all played necessary parts in the experiments that must usher in any scientific advance. As our Pilgrim forefathers tamed the American wilderness, so those pioneer pilots hacked out the air lanes in the vast uncharted skies. Theirs were the covered wagons of the air, lumbering doggedly on to new frontiers.

In the midst of my doubts and questionings I was suddenly presented with a golden opportunity to postpone any decisions about my future. I was invited to go on a world tour with one of my closest friends, Agnes Sherwood (who later became an Olympic squash player), and her family.

Yet I was torn by indecision. I felt it was my duty to stay at home. I should get a job and be near Dad. If anything happened to him, I might be half way across the world when I was needed.

But Dad was particularly determined that I must go, insisting cheerfully that he would be all right again, although both he and I were quite aware that this was only wishful thinking. Aunty added her weight to the argument, pointing out that I had all the rest of my life to take on family responsibilities, and that every young woman deserved the "grand tour." So I used all of a small legacy and off I went to see the world.

Other girls might have managed a proper, conventional and uneventful trip—but not I. My letters home read like dime-novel thrillers. They went like this:

"Dear Mother & Dad: Today I was captured by pirates in India. . . ." Or:

"Dearest Angel: Today I was accosted in a locomotive near Thibet. . . ."

Always, it seems, if there was an adventure within sight, I managed to be in the middle of it. In Honolulu I was invited to fly in a Navy bomber, and looked down on scenes of breath-taking grandeur—a primitive panorama done with bold brush strokes of riotous color. Dark green mountains with chartreuse slopes were set in fertile red fields rimmed by saffron beaches reaching out to the deep brilliant blue of the ocean. I just missed a chance to go down in a submarine, then spent a gay week in Tokyo with my college roommate,

Martha Hazell, and some of the embassy set. That week, naturally, was climaxed by an earthquake. We arrived in Shanghai in the midst of guerilla warfare, which turned out to be the start of the Chinese revolution. Here a coolie tried to kidnap me in a ricksha until I whacked him with a cane, thus convincing him that the better part of valor was to return me safely to my hotel.

Shanghai's violent contrasts appalled me—on one hand the luxurious foreign colonies and on the other such desperate starvation that occasionally one was horrified by the sight of a mother holding out her dead child in supplication for food for the living.

By the time we arrived in Calcutta, we had been cooped up so long at sea that I was itching for action. Transfer to a corridorless train for a three-day trip to Darjeeling did not improve matters. Nor did the frightening spectre of India's poverty, which appeared even more tragic and widespread than that of China. Here I saw men and women who were only skin and bones, without shelter in the cold nights and with so little clothing that it seemed impossible they would still be alive in the morning. A deep unrest began in me then and the stirrings of a determination to do something to help these people—I didn't know what, or how—I only knew that somehow, some day, I must.

These were less conscious thoughts than painful emotions, which were still easy to push aside; the high spirits of youth can accomplish wonders. My immediate goal was to find some way to break the montony of that long, dreary train ride—and so I managed to slip unobtrusively into the locomotive cab during a station stop. By some finagling I persuaded the grinning engineer to let me take over the controls, and for the next hour I had the time of my life, with my hand on the throttle, maneuvering the puffing locomotive on its zigzag track up the mountain, gleefully yanking the whistle in answer to the chattering of monkeys hanging in trees which almost brushed the cab as we passed.

And it was on my birthday, after our arrival at Darjeeling, that I reached one of the highest points of my life, a never-to-be-forgotten experience to which my memory returns again and again in times of stress or meditation.

We left the hotel at Darjeeling at two a.m. for a trek to Tiger Hill to see Mount Everest at sunrise. As insulation against the intense night cold of the Himalayas in February, I had piled on, in addition to long underwear, three layers of sweaters, a vest, leather riding breeches and a fur coat. But the fast pace of our chunky little Thibetan ponies soon warmed me up and I discarded the coat. At our rear was a single file cavalcade of sedan chairs, carried on long poles by sturdy natives. With lanterns swinging to the chant of the bearers, the serpentine caravan wound around the mountain curves like some fantastically glowing caterpillar. An hour before dawn we reached the summit of Tiger Hill, where we were served coffee in the little observatory and stamped about to keep our feet warm while waiting for the sunrise.

The sky was a black bowl studded with diamond stars when suddenly I noted a slight lightening in the east and then, as swiftly as the rise of a stage curtain, there rose out of the blackness the crystal peaks of a range of phantom mountains. One after another they emerged, alight with an ethereal pink flush, as if a celestial lamplighter touched each in turn. Then the rose turned to gold, and the snow peaks seemed to float in a sea of purple haze. All about us swirled curtains of mist, which first obscured, then revealed the breathtaking beauty of the distant panorama. It was a feeling much like flying—a sense of being suspended in space.

This celestial show, however, was only a prologue for the climax, which came when the vapor curtains were drawn aside to reveal, far distant, higher than all the rest, the shining crystal cone of *Mount Everest*—its incandescence against the purple mists, catching fire from the blazing colors of the dawn.

It was visible for only a moment, then the curtains were

drawn again. We are not permitted to retain Heaven permanently in our grasp. But the memory of that instant of incomparable beauty, as I gazed awestruck at the roof of the world, has remained with me always.

Back home and broke, with a college degree and a world cruise behind me, I faced the fact that the time finally had arrived when I really should start earning money, and so I landed the kind of eminently respectable job of which my family approved—assistant in the women's department of a New York City bank. My main job was to bring in new accounts, and through family connections I managed to pile up $100,000 worth in my brief stay in the banking world. But I found the whole business deadly dull. How could I escape? Specifically, how could I get back into the air?

One of the dismal points of my life was New Year's Eve, in 1927. I was alone in the big house at Rye, all the rest of the family having departed for various festivities which I was in no spirit to join. A new year was ahead, and what was I going to do with it? In a mood for self-analysis I confronted myself in the mirror. The girl who looked back at me was acceptably slender, wavy-haired, blue-eyed and smooth-cheeked. But the eyes held a lost, frightened look, the mouth drooped and the face had an expression of restless discontent.

What had happened to those dreams of high adventure? To the dreams of a life of service to others? The sunrise over Mount Everest had happened in another world, to another girl. My desire to secure the economic happiness of Mother and Dad was as strong as ever—and as far from fulfillment. And where was that longed-for flying career?

Already I was definitely a post-post-deb, regarded by the younger social set as rather old hat; I had not become engaged during my first season, or married during my second, nor was I now placidly raising a family and fretting over the next meeting of the bridge club. I hadn't conformed to accepted social patterns, and I had not sought a niche in humanitarian fields. I'd been the girl who was going to find freedom and a career in the vast domains of the sky. And what had I done about all these high-sounding plans? Nothing. I'd been frittering away my time at odd jobs, seizing any opportunity to avoid making a decision. I had gone skylarking around the world, I had put in a deadly boring stretch at a job, I had flown whenever I had the chance, but simply for the momentary pleasure of it. Who did I think I was, anyhow?

I definitely didn't like this picture of myself.

Just as I was ready to seek a hair shirt and put ashes on my head, the phone shrilled through the empty house. As I lifted the receiver I could hear the bells and whistles hailing the new year of 1928. The voice at the other end of the wire boomed cheerfully:

"Happy New Year, kid! I'm flying to Miami. Want to come along?"

"Harry!" I cried. "Happy New Year, Harry! Do I want to come? Does a fish want to swim? Does a bird want to fly? Of course I want to come! When do we start?"

"About day after tomorrow," said Harry. "But come on out to Rockaway tomorrow. We'll be there, tuning up."

The next night I spent at a boarding house in Rockaway where Harry and his wife, Ruth, were staying. There he filled me in on the details of the proposed flight. Though this had seemed to be a lark dreamed up on the spur of the moment, it developed that Harry had made careful preparations for the flight, and planned it as the first non-stop hop between New York and Miami. The plane was a new model single-engine seven-place turtleback Fairchild monoplane on floats, and the flight's backer was one M. K. Lee, sportsman and retired banker, who planned to go along for the ride.

On the morning of the takeoff we were at Rockaway Naval Air Station before dawn, where I talked with some of the sleepy officers on duty while Harry did some last-minute tinkering on the seaplane, which had gas tanks installed in place of the four rear seats. Just as he finished the final check-up, M. K. arrived at the base, sent his chauffeur back to town and joined us in the plane.

A winter sun struck sparkles from the water as we took off, and I felt the tingling cold even though I wore a sweater under my fur coat and had on fur-lined gloves and boots.

Harry had plotted a straight course from New York to Miami, seventy miles out to sea, so that the flight actually paralleled many conditions of the single-engined ocean crossing made the year before, when Charles Lindbergh had blazed an air trail from New York to Paris and returned to the acclaim of a hero-worshipping world. Harry's preparations included the following wire sent to Coast Guard stations along the way:

SEAPLANE 3637 MONOPLANE TYPE YELLOW WINGS RED BODY LEFT ROCKAWAY 8:05 THIS MORNING NON-STOP MIAMI KINDLY NOTIFY STATIONS TO WATCH AND PLEASE ADVISE ROGERS AIRLINES MIAMI FLORIDA WESTERN UNION TELEGRAM COLLECT OF PROGRESS.

CAPT. HARRY ROGERS

Only one station picked us up, however, as we passed over Cape May at 9:17 a.m.

The sky was clear and blue and we had a steady tail wind as we headed south, keeping a low altitude at first because of what constituted in 1927 a heavy load for our horsepower —nearly twenty-four hundred pounds. Harry had in mind a commercial air service between New York and Miami, for which this was a test flight. And I learned that Sherman Fairchild, president of the company which manufactured the plane was keenly interested in the outcome of the flight and his plane's performance.

There was still ice on the shoreline as far south as Cape

Charles. At Virginia Beach we dropped telegrams, a plane rose and circled over us and went away. At 11:05, after we had passed over Virginia Beach, Harry slid out of the seat behind the single control and told me to take over. It was CAVU—ceiling and visibility unlimited. My heart soared with the plane, and the dismal mood of New Year's Eve seemed years away. This was *life*!

Harry kept a careful log of the trip, noting change of wind, air speed, altitude and time of passing over land points. M. K. made himself useful by pumping gas with a hand-pump from an inside reserve tank to refill the plane's central fuel tank when the gauge showed near empty. Then he settled down for a nap.

At 12:45 we left the shoreline and headed for the open ocean, at an altitude of four thousand feet. I continued piloting while M. K. had a sandwich and Harry caught a nap. Over Charleston, S. C., at 3:15 p.m., M. K. took over the stick and I stretched my legs. We dropped more telegrams there.

I took over again about four o'clock, when the weather turned squally. The sun was just setting as we passed over the Florida border near Jacksonville. Then down the coast past Daytona Beach, Titusville, Palm Beach. Yes, there was Miami showing up. . . . We landed at 8:05 p.m., exactly twelve hours after our takeoff.

As we taxied up to the new Rogers Air Terminal, flash-lights popped, reporters and a crowd swarmed around—there was almost as much excitement as if this had been a trans-Atlantic crossing.

Harry, never one to overlook the values of publicity, had timed the flight to coincide with a newspaper editors' meeting in Miami. Next day we were front-page news across the country. Banner headlines blared:

"Society Flyer in Non-Stop Record Flight" . . . "Flying Deb Pioneers New York-Miami Hop" . . . "Lady Lindy in Record Flight" . . .

I was both amazed and embarrassed. After all, it was Harry's plane and Harry's flight, but the newspapermen seized on the romantic aspects of a "society aviatrix" and played it to the hilt.

These were my first headlines, and I was appalled at the probable reaction at home. I could picture Mother opening the morning paper and seeing the glaring headlines about "Daring Deb Flyer" along with pictures of her carefully nurtured daughter standing beside a plane, between two men Mother had never even met, wearing a fur coat and mittens, with her mouth open and palm trees in the background. I could see the agitated family conference over the breakfast table, with my Quaker great-grandfather's portrait looking sternly down on the scene, Dad whacking the table, poor Mother weeping into a lace-edged handkerchief, the maid scuttling to and from the kitchen in fluttery panic, my brothers laughing uproariously and my sister Bets looking dazed.

But I was more interested in what Aunty would think. I had the answer very soon for there was a telegram on my breakfast tray:

"More power to thee, child. Love, Aunt Polly."

I vowed then and there that at the first opportunity I would take her along on a lengthy air trip. It was the least I could do in gratitude to this staunch ally who always came through in the pinches.

The vague feelings of guilt that had been shadowing complete happiness were miraculously dissolved. To heck with the newspaper headlines! This was grand and it was not wrong. Angel herself had said so. I appeared to be the girl of the hour in Miami, so why not enjoy it to the utmost?

Flowers, telegrams and invitations poured in. Old friends turned up. I was squired to the beach, to luncheons, to dinner parties, to dances under the stars.

And just to cap the climax of that gay interlude, it was

there that my shining knight came riding up on his white charger.

Of course, it wasn't exactly a white charger; it was a yacht anchored in the harbor. And I was the one who came riding up, in a launch. I had been invited to a dinner party aboard the yacht which belonged to family friends who had read of my sensational arrival in Miami and of course used the occasion as an excuse for a party.

As I was lifted over the rail, I noted that the strong arms that had held me lingered longer than I felt necessary, and I looked into one of the handsomest faces I have ever seen— brilliant dark eyes and a white smile cleaving a sun-tanned face.

"Welcome aboard, Señorita!" said my cavalier, with a stiff little formal bow. "Now that you are here the sun is shining, even though it is after dark."

Well . . . and who was this smooth character?

I soon found out. Every girl present filled me in with the exciting details. He was a wealthy young Spaniard in America to dicker for American airplane distribution rights in his country, and he was a divine dancer. Above all that, he was a pilot. He bore an honored name, but to me he was Don Juan. And so from the start I called him Don.

We danced under the stars, with the tropical sky and sea for a backdrop. And when he kissed my hand as he left me at my hotel much later, I could have floated up to my tenth-floor room without bothering with the elevator.

When his voice on the telephone wakened me next morning, and when his flowers with a graceful note arrived a few minutes later, I knew I was in love.

3

GAS ON AND CONTACT!

The longer I live the more life has shown that if you just hold on long enough, there's always something wonderful around the corner. Also I have found that good luck, like bad, usually comes in bunches.

The year 1928 was a good-luck year for me, beginning with the very first minute of the New Year, when Harry Rogers' telephone call jerked me out of my evening of miserable introspection and started me on that unexpected flight to Miami. A gay cycle of exciting events followed, like a chain reaction, climaxed by the starry elation of my first serious romance.

Like every other normal girl, I had enjoyed the usual quota of athletic and social activities. But the serious side of my nature, coupled with love of adventure, kept me looking for something more than these youthful romances seemed able to offer. The young men I had known had appeared either too callow to take seriously or too dull to be interesting. Some were rich men's sons bent on spending their fathers' money as quickly and riotously as possible; others were dutiful youths learning the family business from the ground up and already set in the conventional mold of the stuffed shirt. Neither kind appealed to my romantic nature, and I held firmly in my heart the image of that dream prince for whom every girl secretly waits and hopes.

Every woman deserves at least one time of high romance,

even if she spends the rest of her life in domestic routine. Though the fire may be brief, it brings an enchantment and a brilliance that can provide a glow through all the years to come. I'm sure there isn't a woman in the world, of any age, who doesn't enjoy being swept off her feet by a gay, impetuous suitor. The evening before I was due to return to New York Harry Rogers let us take up one of his flying boats.

Just before sunset we skimmed across the water and took off in a white cascade of ocean spray. Soon we were out over the Gulf Stream, with only the vast sky above us and the lonely sea below. Sunset painted the sky a glowing pink and tinted the cloud castles, reflected from the water. We seemed to be flying through a rosy and incredible dream.

I was at the Seagull's controls and Don was close beside me, his dark hair ruffled by the wind, his eyes alight with excitement, his white teeth flashing as he laughed in sheer exuberance. His brown arm clamped tight around my shoulders as he shouted in my ear:

"You are magnificent, my beautiful flying goddess! You are an angel out of the sky! Salud, querida!"

In those days you had to shout to be heard above the shrieking of the wind in an open cockpit plane, so this love scene had to be played fortissima.

"I love you too!" I shouted back.

"We will fly on together forever!" yelled Don.

"Oh, I hope so!" I cried.

And then we both burst into helpless laughter. We were laughing, too, I think, from the pure delight of being young and in love and alone together in the limitless grandeur of space. I think I would have loved Don if he had been a ditch digger or an accountant. That he happened also to be a pilot who shared my love of speed and space, added to my delight. It was "all this and Heaven too."

I went back to New York next day to find myself still front-page news.

Sherman Fairchild, president of Fairchild Airplane and

Engine Company, whose plane Harry had used for the non-stop Miami flight, arranged a press conference for me on the roof of his office building. There a mob of reporters and photographers had assembled. Over and over I recounted the details of the flight, posed for innumerable pictures and parried questions as to my future plans.

Did I plan an Atlantic flight?

Did I prefer a career to marriage?

Was I headed toward the exploits of a female Lindbergh?

How did it feel to be a mile up in the air, going 100 miles per hour?

Was it more exciting than romance?

The questions always came back to romance—why wasn't I engaged or married? Didn't I want to be?

Through it all I kept secret the memory of that last glorious sunset flight with Don, and held to the theory that one's personal life is one's own affair and not in the public domain.

The trials of being a celebrity were fully realized for the first time when next morning's headlines screamed: RUTH NICHOLS LOVES AIR; EVADES OTHER ROMANCES.

I was furious. Just because I didn't see fit to discuss the affairs of my heart with the national press, I didn't want to be branded as either an old maid or a man-hater.

I felt better, however, when I received a wire from Don: "I don't believe a word of it. Hasta la vista, my darling. Don."

My recovery was completed after a conference with Sherman Fairchild involving a business proposition.

Until now I had feared publicity like smallpox. It was a family fetish that nice people didn't get their names in the papers, except possibly in the society columns on the occasion of an engagement or a wedding. But after my talk with Fairchild, I gained a new perspective. Publicity had a definite and important business value to the infant aviation industry. As one of the nation's few women flyers, I had become a valuable publicity asset. That the press had tagged me as "Society's Flying Beauty" and "Debutante Aviatrix" didn't hurt the situation at all. So he granted me a job in sales promotion for his company.

I jumped at the chance. Here, I realized, was an opportunity not only to start a career which might improve the family finances but at the same time would give me a part in the development of aviation which I believed even then must better the lot of mankind—though I would have been unable to say exactly how. The job seemed made to order for me. I would be the first woman executive in the aviation world, holding down an important post in a million-dollar corporation. I could thus put my love of flying to solid business use. And I would be in on the ground floor of a great new industry.

As Sherman Fairchild pointed out, I could continue flying. My job would entail frequent public appearances and speaking engagements, and if I traveled by air whenever possible, it would serve to heighten interest in airplanes as the new means of transportation.

The first speech I ever made was in Newburgh, N. Y., a few weeks later, on February 28, 1928. And I had to travel by train because Newburgh had no airport. That was the reason for the speech. Billed as "RUTH NICHOLS—DARING AVIATRIX" I addressed a civic gathering in an after-dinner speech pointing out the importance of developing interest in an airport for the town. I was suffering so badly from stagefright that I could only swallow a few bites of the dinner, but somehow I got through the ordeal and to my amazement even drew enthusiastic applause. After it was all over, I thought of a favorite remark of Father's: "You can even get used to hanging, if you hang long enough!"

In the months that followed I gradually developed the inner calm and outer poise needed for public speaking. But to this day I find that careful preparation is necessary for even the shortest, seemingly spontaneous address.

The most hair-raising part of these speaking trips was the

inevitable motorcycle escort that whirled me at break-neck ground speeds from airport or railroad station to the public hall or hotel dining room where I was to hold forth. Becoming better known as a woman flyer and as a spokesman for a new and exciting industry, I was usually given the celebrity treatment when I made an official appearance—and the motorcycle escort was a part of it.

The success of my speaking trips was pleasant but I discovered that in those days there were very few sales prospects for a $15,000 airplane. The people who could afford it still considered flying hare-brained sport. And those who had been bitten by the aviation bug usually didn't have the money to back up their enthusiasm.

So it was with much interest that I greeted another aviation proposal. After I had been with Fairchild for several months, I received a call from John S. Reaves, then a newcomer to the aviation world, who set forth a new and intriguing plan to develop interest in flying on a national scale. His idea was to enlist the support of the wealthy, sports-loving class by organizing a series of exclusive flying clubs across the country. Since planes were expensive, only the wealthy could afford them, and he proposed to arouse their interest by placing aviation in a country club atmosphere as, perhaps, the new sport of kings.

He had worked out most of the details for establishing a chain of Aviation Country Clubs, with flying regattas and inter-club competitions, to attract the sports world. The idea would be based strictly on snob appeal, the membership would be highly social and exclusive and the returns, he hoped, would be of inestimable value to the infant aviation industry in increased sale of planes and widespread national interest in flying. I was invited to join forces with Reaves and his associate, Darwin Adams, as founders of Aviation Country Clubs.

It seemed a sound plan, with fascinating potentialities. I realized that a great deal of educational groundwork must be done before the general public started buying private airplanes. Airports and landing strips must be built throughout the country to make general plane travel possible. The airplane industry was at the same stage then as was the motor car industry at the time Henry Ford turned out his first automobiles and found that there would have to be roads on which to drive his cars before the public would buy them.

Now, almost thirty years later, much the same conditions prevail. The age of the personal airplane still awaits development of a widespread network of landing strips comparable to the vast highway system spawned by the automobile industry—or the development of low-priced helicopters, or flying autos, or a combination of both. The latter are already available, but are too high-priced and too slow for popular usage. Within our lifetime we should see average families with cars so designed that wings can be attached or unfolded at a nearby airstrip. Or the solution may come with the perfection of small planes which have an overhead gyro propeller for vertical takeoffs and landings, so designed that it can either be disengaged at cruising altitude or converted for fast forward propulsion. This kind of plane already is being designed, and may make it possible for the airminded public to take off and land from its own back yard. Back in 1929 our hopes were high, our enthusiasm unbounded and our energies almost limitless.

We were faced with a monumental task—one that might have seemed impossible to less inspired zealots—in starting the wheels rolling with no initial capital or important backers. But all of us were dedicated disciples to the widening new frontiers of the air, and we threw ourselves into the work with the energy of devotees to an ideal.

Jack Reaves worked untiringly at the task of setting up the basic organization which would be a nucleus for the national body. Darwin Adams concentrated on writing the necessary brochures, pamphlets and promotional articles.

My particular assignment was to seek out both men and women prospects, and to this end I set up conferences and organized various social functions, being careful to bring together just the right socially exclusive groups.

All that summer we three musketeers worked furiously at laying the groundwork for our dream, and saw it come into reality with the founding of the first Aviation Country Club at Hicksville on Long Island. By this time, also, we had gathered together a group of outstanding aviation leaders and distinguished backers to serve as a board of governors for the national organization. They included: George Post, Earl Osborn and Jimmie Taylor, our first three members (they later formed the executive committee and the backbone of the national club), my erstwhile boss, Sherman Fairchild, Richard F. Hoyt, Charles Lanier Lawrence, Robert Law, Jr., George M. Pynchon, Jr., Clement M. Keys, and William A. Rockefeller.

The next step of our master plan was to launch the first sportsman pilot tour of the United States, with a threefold purpose: first, to tell the larger cities about the club plan, offering equal membership privileges to all clubs formed; second, to make a survey of aerial conditions throughout the country; third, to stimulate interest in flying as a sport.

All through that summer of 1928 we strenuously built up a basic organization structure, and in between times I managed to put in considerable flying. I remember one escapade that was grand fun, and a welcome relief from the summer's frantic work routine.

It was the Fourth of July, a holiday even for the most dedicated worker, and I was invited to a huge party aboard Edward Manville's yacht to celebrate the engagement of the Manvilles' daughter, Estelle, to Count Bernadotte, of Sweden. I missed the launch which was to take guests out to the yacht anchorage off Greenwich Harbor, and was inspired with the idea of borrowing one of Harry Rogers' Seagulls. I hopped into one of the flying boats and talked a pilot friend into flying me out to the yacht. We flew up and down the Sound until we spotted it, made a swishing landing and I joined the party. It was a sensational entrance.

During this summer I first became interested in land planes, and at every opportunity I "hitched" a ride in one of Harry's Seagulls, based at Rye or Greenwich, for a trip to Garden City; once there I would put in flying time at Roosevelt Field. After a number of these trips I finally soloed an OX5 Jenny, a type of training plane used during the first World War, and in due course qualified for my pilot's rating on land planes. Since that time I have flown practically every type of licensed aircraft made, including: a dirigible, glider, autogyro, land planes, seaplanes, flying boats, amphibians, monoplanes, biplanes, triplanes, open cockpit and cabin planes, single-, twin-, and four-engined planes and—most recently—jets.

By this time I was thoroughly sold on aviation as a career, with my heart set on active flying. Even at that early date I harbored a secret ambition to fly around the world, an idea that had been born during my world cruise after college.

Meanwhile, the income from my work with Aviation Country Clubs, Inc. was so small as to be negligible. I was living mostly on the income from stocks into which I had invested another small legacy as this was during the market boom, and I shrugged off Dad's repeated warnings that such inflation could not last. My financial position was as shaky as ever, a fact which failed to diminish the scope of my dreams for the future. However, my immediate objective was the Aviation Country Clubs tour, and for that we must have planes. You can't fly without wings, so I set out to get them.

It was now the spring of 1929, the stock market was still booming and money flowed freely. I outlined our plan to Frank Russell, vice-president of the Curtiss Airplane and Engine Company, who in turn introduced me to C. M. Keys, the company president. In the end I talked them into lending us two airplanes—a Curtiss Fledgling and a Curtiss Robin, each powered by new experimental Challenger motors. The sportsman pilot tour would serve as a demonstration and test for these new planes, the ensuing publicity would be valuable to the company and if there were any "bugs" in them, they would come to light. The equipment was worth about $18,000 and in addition the Curtiss company agreed to pay the salary and expenses of a service engineer for six months.

Before we closed the deal, however, I was put through a series of navigation tests about which I'm still teased by some of the old-timers whenever we happen to meet. The company, it seemed, wanted to be sure I could find my way across the country by air before they trusted me with their valuable equipment and six months of expenses.

The Curtiss men also knew that most of my piloting experience had been in flying boats, even though I was now accredited for land plane flying. So they insisted that I make a cross-country flight to test my ability to maintain a course and arrive at a destination. The objective was from Garden City to nearby Port Jervis, N. Y., a difficult place to find under low-ceiling conditions and a strong cross wind in a slow ship with small range—even for a seasoned pilot. It was necessarily a short, straight flight over terrain almost totally lacking in railroads or landmarks. From the time I left the Hudson River behind I hadn't the faintest idea where either I or Port Jervis might be. I flew such a crooked, meandering course that even Ted Winston, my check pilot, got lost and after more than two hours we returned to Garden City without ever having been within sight of our objective.

Ted was a kindly soul, however, and put so many explanations and excuses in his report that I was given another chance. This time I was to fly to Philadelphia and back.

The night before the test I sat hunched over a card table at home poring over an automobile map of New Jersey for there were no air charts in those days, while Aunty tried to help me. So confusing was the maze of lines indicating rivers, roads and railroads, however, that both of us became hopelessly mixed up, and Aunty said at last, resignedly:

"Thee'll just have to ask our Heavenly Father to guide thee, child."

It must have been divine intervention that saved my project the next day. This time Frank Ambrose, an able pilot, had me in charge, and as we were flying over New York Bay a violent thunderstorm completely blocked our path. I turned around and asked Frank:

"What do you want me to do?"

"*You're* flying the ship," he replied sternly.

I decided that discretion was the better part of valor, even though it might lose me a golden opportunity with the Curtiss company, so I turned around and headed back to Roosevelt Field. This, it seems, was exactly what I should have done, and Frank was so impressed by such a display of conservative judgment that he decided the Curtiss planes would be safe with me, and passed me on the test.

When I rushed back to report success, Reaves and Adams were jubilant. We hastened to notify the members of the board of governors, and plans were made to start the aviation tour forthwith. It was decided that I would fly one plane, the other to be piloted by Robb C. Oertel, a former manager of the Byrd Arctic Expedition who is now in charge of aviation sales for the Esso Standard Oil Company. He would also act as business manager for the tour, and would carry in his plane as passenger C. O. Bedford, Curtiss service manager.

We plunged into final preparations for the start, but my attention was somewhat divided by frequent and ardent telephone calls from Don, who protested that he was worried about my safety on the flying tour. I am sure, however, that his real concern was over the fact that I would be flying across country in company with two personable men, having air adventures in which he could not share.

Ever since that whirlwind romance in Miami, Don had remained the focal point of my emotional life, even though I was launched into the excitement of a new career. Whenever possible he had visited me in Rye or New York City, and when business took him away on trips, a constant flood of love letters, and telegrams made sure that he was prominently in my thoughts.

Naturally, I cherished every minute of this ardent courtship, carried on with all the Old-World grace which Latins understand so well, and which American men seldom seem able to grasp. I treasured those evenings when Don and I would meet at one of our favorite haunts—sometimes a restaurant with Tango music to which we danced in a dream, sometimes a quiet French café on the upper East Side, where we could be assured of a secluded table, candlelight and the proper atmosphere for holding hands.

I had never been happier than during that wonderful year when life seemed to open up in all directions, when I finally began to make sense out of my love of flying, when I was working at an absorbing job which permitted full use of my capacities and when through every day ran the tingling consciousness of being in love—and beloved.

There were bad moments, of course, when we would part in furious anger. But the quarrels only made the reconciliations sweeter. There was nothing so wonderful, I discovered, as making up after a quarrel—a fact well-known to all lovers, down through the ages.

Just before the start of the Aviation Country Clubs tour, however, the first serious cloud threatened the happy progress of our romance. Family business made it necessary for Don to return to Spain, and so we faced a tragic parting.

The night before my scheduled takeoff on the cross-country flying tour, we rode back and forth on the Staten Island ferry for hours, pledging undying love, planning our reunion. I was tearful, he was tender, promising that he would return to New York at the first possible moment.

There were certain family matters, he said, which he must clear up before we could make definite plans for marriage, a home and family. But he would overcome every obstacle. Nothing could block the path of our love. I promised I would be waiting, counting the hours until his return. He retorted that if I really loved him I would not be planning to go flying off across the country with two handsome men. He knew, of course, that I would be true to him, but what if I crashed and broke my neck? What would he do then?

I assured him that my neck was durable, that I knew perfectly well how to fly a plane. This trip was something to which I was committed, a goal toward which I had worked for a year, and I couldn't back out now. Besides, I didn't want to.

Another quarrel was brewing, until both of us realized that this was no way to say goodby, perhaps for months. And so we clung together, reassuring each other, murmuring the language of love—until I realized that I could no longer postpone going home and to bed, if I were to start an important cross-country flight next morning. A flyer always thinks of the necessity for sleep before a flight, even during a love scene.

By the time I reached home I was so exhausted from emotion that I fell asleep as soon as my head touched the pillow, instead of spending the wakeful night I was sure would follow this painful parting.

Rushing back to the field next morning, I was first delighted, then dismayed, to find Don waiting. His expression was black, his manner determined as he took me firmly by the arm and led me to his car, starting off before I had time to protest. Keeping one arm around my shoulders in a vise-like grip, he drove down a little-traveled back road, pulled the car over to the side, and faced me with fire in his eye.

"I have not slept all night, Querida!" he said. "I cannot let you go on this crazy flight. All the time I am gone I will be thinking of you, perhaps lost in a thunderstorm, crashing in flames. Or worse, falling in love with someone else."

I was thrilled at his ardor, but incensed at his peremptory decree. How dared he order me around? I was not some timid European chattel. I was a modern American girl, desiring above all else to merge for life with the right powerful male, but at the same time, I was a person whose Quaker forebears had led the movement for equal rights.

"How do you think I feel?" I cried. "You're going back to Spain, probably to make love to some boyhood sweetheart. We're not even really engaged yet. How can you ask me to give up everything I've worked for, just so you won't be worried?"

This definitely was not the correct approach to the Latin temperament. Don launched into a stream of vitriolic Spanish, only part of which I understood. But it was enough. I started to get out of the car.

He dragged me back roughly, seized me in his arms and kissed me until I could hardly breathe. I struggled to free myself. I was still deeply and honestly in love with this unpredictable man, but this was getting out of hand.

"Oh . . . Don . . . NO!" I pleaded. "We can't settle important issues *that* way . . . Let me go . . ." I ordered in my most ominously quiet voice.

Don freed me, but it took some minutes for us to regain our calm. By the time we finished exchanging apologies and reassurances and had said our goodbys again, we returned to the field to find that the fleet of six planes flying to Washington for the official start of the tour had left without me.

Fortunately George Pynchon, Jr., had waited for me and was standing nervously beside his plane as we drove up. I apologized breathlessly, and rushed to climb into my plane, which was already warmed up and waiting. As Pynchon taxied down the runway to the takeoff point, and I prepared to follow, Don stood beside my plane, reached into a pocket and pulled out a small, beautifully carved gold St. Christopher's medal suspended on a thin gold chain which he fastened around my neck, whispering:

"To keep you safe, my darling, and bring you back to me!"

I was choked with tears as I taxied the Curtiss Robin down the runway, but I looked back to see Don standing straight and bareheaded in the morning sunshine, one arm raised in salute as he called:

"Happy landings! Hasta la vista!"

4

COVERED WAGONS OF
THE AIR

Shaken by that stormy parting with Don, I stayed right behind George Pynchon's plane all the way to Washington, and finally landed right in the middle of the only mud puddle on Bolling Field, almost splashing the glittering gold braid of the reception committee awaiting me.

Major Davison, Commander of the field, drove us with the rest of our party to the Carlton Hotel, where a gala luncheon had been arranged in our honor by the Hon. F. Trubee Davison, Assistant Secretary of War.

We spent nearly two weeks in Washington awaiting the arrival of our second plane, the Fledgling, from the Curtiss company. After various production delays it arrived and we took off for the actual beginning of the flying tour, which was to take us over most of the United States on air lanes as uncharted as the covered wagon trails followed by earlier pioneers.

We were to land in cow pastures, on desert sand and dirt fields all the way across the country, for in those days there were few airports and no emergency landing fields, beacons, radio beams, control towers or any of the other aids to modern flying. (The usual pilot's telegram carried the wry code message: "Arriving G.W.W.P."—God willing and weather permitting.) Our small single-engine planes were as primitive, compared with the deluxe, instrument-laden sport-executive planes of today, as was the prairie schooner compared to a modern automobile.

Our first destination was Richmond, Va., and we took off on a beautiful, clear spring day with high spirits. I was piloting from the rear seat of the tandem, open-cockpit Curtiss Fledgling biplane, while Bob Oertel and Bedford the engine expert, were in the cabin Robin monoplane, the former as pilot. The trip was smooth, the weather fine, and we landed without incident, except that "Beddie," our service manager, didn't like the sound of the Fledgling motor, and decided to send for a new one before we got too far from Curtiss headquarters. This meant a delay of several days, which we put to good use laying the groundwork for another club and preaching the gospel of aviation.

The morning we were scheduled to leave Byrd Field in Richmond brought poor visibility and a ceiling of only three hundred feet, so we waited around for a little while—and then for a little while longer. Bob and I couldn't understand why it seemed to be taking so much longer than usual to warm up the motors, until it dawned on us later that Beddie, a dyed-in-the-wool conservative, wasn't happy about the weather and that his work on the engines was a form of filibustering.

We stopped off at Winston-Salem, N. C., for lunch, intending to make a short afternoon jump to Charlotte, as we wanted to spend the night at a nearby airport owned by Elliott White Springs, famous World War I flyer. The sky looked somewhat dubious after lunch, but we decided to push on, since Charlotte was such a short distance away.

Almost immediately we ran into rain clouds and Bob, who had the lead (we took turns at this) got lost while attempting to circle around the storm. After we were back on course, and nearing the general area of the field, we had a nasty half hour ducking thick, low clouds which pushed us down to about two hundred feet. Furthermore, Elliott Springs Air

Field at that time was not the easiest place in the world to find.

If warned in advance that a flyer planned to drop in on him, Elliott would send the optimistic pilot a diagram of the field. We had one of these, showing a triangular field, one thousand feet by six hundred, surrounded by tall trees and wires, with a check in one corner—sort of an "X marks the spot" indicating this was as far as you could go. Having finally located the field, we dodged each other around the trees, the tops of which were veiled in swirling vapor, and finally managed to disappoint the neighbors, who had gathered at sound of our motors to "see the gal crack up."

Elliott and his charming wife put us up at their lovely Fort Mill home, delighted to be able to exchange flying talk. True exponents of southern hospitality, they made our stay so pleasant that it was difficult to pull away for our next hop over the small tenant cotton fields to Augusta and Atlanta. These fields were soft and criss-crossed by irrigation ditches, making the idea of forced landings an unhappy thought. We managed to negotiate these hops safely, however, meeting with enthusiastic receptions in each place, and gaining confidence at each stop. People everywhere, it seemed, were fascinated with the idea of flying, eager to try it themselves and anxious to help us in any way they could.

We stuck to a rigid schedule, and decided that all our takeoffs should be at dawn, so that we would always have plenty of daylight to reach our next destination, even if we met with emergencies or delays. Knowing that women always get the blame for holding up any departure, I made it a point to arrive at the field before the men—the first few times. Soon, however, I learned to gauge how long it would take them to check out of the hotel, snatch a bite of breakfast and do the final engine check, and timed my arrivals more exactly, gaining a few more winks of sleep in the process.

On the morning we left Atlanta, all three of us arrived in

the hotel lobby at the same moment, congratulated each other on our promptness, grabbed breakfast and set out together in a taxi for the air field. We anticipated an easy day, as Augusta, our next stop, was only an hour-and-a-half's flight. But we had reckoned without the vagaries of the decrepit taxi. It took us two hours to get to the field, as the taxi had four "forced landings" enroute. Each time the motor sputtered and died, the driver became frantic, and Bob and Beddie would get out, tinker with the engine or run behind and push until it wheezed into life again. The short flight to Augusta seemed a breeze after our struggles on the ground.

After Augusta we headed west, and ran into headwinds which were to plague us most of the way to the coast. One of our longest hops was from Birmingham, Ala., to Memphis, Tenn. We were worried about our gas supply in the face of headwinds and decided to play safe by landing somewhere in Mississippi to refuel. There were no landing fields anywhere in that state, so we telephoned the little town of Tupelo, which we located on the map as a midway spot to stop, and were told that there was a strip of uncultivated farm land long enough to meet our specifications for a landing area. The terrain around this section consisted principally of pine woods and hills, with few landmarks. For a while we thought we were lost, but Bob stuck to his compass and we hit Tupelo on the nose.

Farmers and their wives and children had gathered from miles around to watch the landing of these new-fangled flying machines. All were curious and interested, and even the women seemed anxious to try a flight. There was a nip in the early spring air, and so they escorted us to the general store, where they built a fire in the stove and offered us our choice of the stock. Since most of the merchandise was in the nature of dry groceries, we lunched on potato chips and candy.

With our new-found friends cheering us on, we took off without mishap, fuel tanks filled with automobile gas which

had a low octane rating and gave Beddie a cause to worry more than usual about his precious engines. We headed straight for Memphis, where we stayed only one night before taking off for Little Rock, Ark., a short flight across the Mississippi River. After we left the Memphis airport, which had real runways and was pure luxury in those days, we were over the river in a matter of minutes, and I was amazed to look down at a solid sheet of water stretching away as far as the eye could see. It was a season of serious floods on the Mississippi, and there certainly could be no emergency landings around here. Since I was in the lead, I decided to gain added safety in altitude, and took the Fledgling up to four thousand feet like a kite. I knew the Robin was faster than my plane and could easily overtake me, so I didn't worry about Beddie and Bob.

After about thirty minutes, however, I scanned the sky behind me and could find no orange-colored speck. Alarmed, I circled back and scoured marshes and flooded fields for miles around, but there was no sign of the other plane. Bob and Beddie must have turned back, I decided, or else they had come down in some place impossible for me to find. There seemed to be only one thing to do—continue to Little Rock. With a tail wind, I made excellent time. I landed and was making frantic inquiries when, five minutes later, in glided the Robin. *They* had been scouring the sky for *me;* apparently we had been playing Blind Man's Buff in the air. They had lost sight of me, it seemed, during my fast climb into the glare of the sun and were afraid I might have had engine trouble and crashed out of sight beneath the muddy flood waters.

From Little Rock to Tulsa we flew along the Arkansas River, whose shores, though often marshy, offered occasional possible landing areas. This, in my opinion, is one of our country's most beautiful flights, with pine-clad mountains rising on either side of the lazy, meandering river. There was a stiff wind and tornado warnings had been issued, keeping us constantly on the lookout for the black bowl-shaped mass of cloud which heralds the approach of a twister.

In Tulsa we were delighted to find several large airports and open country all around. Even in this early period, flying was put to practical use in this section. Many oil millionaires took to the air with enthusiasm, as they had found planes a convenient method of scouting the oil fields, while the flat topography of the country made flying a joy. Here, we felt, was an ideal location for a strong link in our projected chain of Aviation Country Clubs.

From Tulsa across northern Texas we passed over terrain that was a pilot's dream—it was one big landing field. And with the exception of a strong gale which kept us hangar-bound for a short time, after a brief stop at Shreveport, Louisiana, we had days of perfect visibility.

At Dallas we were joined by another member of Aviation Country Clubs, Charles Taylor of Little Rock, flying a new Command-Aire. He had just started flying and wanted some cross-country experience. So we welcomed him to our caravan, and this keen-witted, good-natured southerner proved a happy addition, keeping us in gales of laughter along the entire route to Los Angeles.

All the way across Texas, as far as Midland, flying conditions were so ideal that often I didn't have to touch the controls for an hour at a time, and with an habitual glance for a rare plane, I was able to read frequent chapters in a navigation book I kept in the cockpit, or to think about Don —what was he doing, where was he, and who was he with?

Passing over Ranger enroute to Midland late one afternoon I looked down at the flat plains of mesquite and greasewood, saw a lone cowboy as a moving speck on the lonely desert, and was seized with a longing to find a horse when we landed at Midland and to have a limbering canter over the plains at dusk. Days of sitting in the cockpit of the Fledgling hadn't afforded much opportunity for exercise, and I felt the need for action. It was very disappointing, therefore, when I found, after many phone calls, that there wasn't a piece of horseflesh available within fifteen miles of Midland. "Wild West, indeed!" I muttered disgustedly as I prepared to go tamely to bed.

Midland and Pecos are the jumping-off places for the Guadalupe Range and the desert. After so many days of easy flying over flat country, it was an abrupt change to encounter mountains again with their problems of rarefied air and turbulence. From Pecos to El Paso is only one hundred ninety miles, but the mountain range between is eight thousand feet high, and on this occasion we were fighting forty-mile headwinds to boot. Battered by unpredictable air currents, our under-powered planes struggled valiantly and we finally managed to scramble over the top of the pass. On the other side, however, we were met by the hot blast of the desert, the overheated air causing convection currents which in turn created air pockets and down drafts that tossed the planes around like leaves in the wind. Some of the drops were so sudden that my motor cut out twice, and I began to think it might be necessary to walk. Each time, however, I managed to get it started again by adjusting the fuel mixture control, and we fought our way onward, through heat blasts and miniature whirlwinds of sand and alkali dust, to land at El Paso with only a half gallon of gas left in the Fledgling's tank.

This had been a long and exhausting day. We had been in the air since early morning, with only a few hours sleep the night before, so we decided we needed some diverting relaxation, and after landing at El Paso about four in the afternoon we had a late lunch and then went sight-seeing in Juarez, just across the border, to have a quick look at Mexico.

Nothing seemed to dampen the high spirits of Charlie Taylor, and his uproarious accounts of his feelings as he tried to push his plane over the Guadalupe Range that afternoon soon had us all relaxed and laughing.

"I've handled some rough broncos in my day," said Charlie, "but this confounded plane can out-buck any of 'em. I was about ready to trade her in for a harp and a pair of angel wings when blamed if she didn't take the jump, nice as you please!"

After an early evening of laughter and fun, we returned to the field to work on the motors until close to midnight, while strong gusts of wind were blowing sand under the hangar doors kept open due to the heat. When finally we straggled wearily into the hotel, who should be waiting for us but an alert reporter? There ensued an hour's interview during which I parried such questions as "How do women compare with men in flying?" Or—"What would you do if your husband didn't want you to fly?"

Other days were equally full. There were frequent formal luncheons, at which we would outline our plans for Aviation Country Clubs, meet with committees, and help set up a framework of organization. Evenings were occupied by studying whatever maps were available for the next day's flight, writing up logs, keeping up with correspondence—and, on my part, washing out stockings and underwear.

By sticking to an agreed routine, we managed to keep going. We found it necessary to catch up on sleep every three or four nights, keep our diet light and have at least one day a week of exercise.

One of the most beautiful parts of our cross-country tour was flying over the Arizona desert. Here are colors and scenes of breathtaking grandeur that must be seen to be believed. I will never forget the savage magnificence of flying across the desert at sundown, seeing the jagged mountain peaks change slowly from rose quartz to cobalt blue and violet, with the desert sands stretching in yellow waves at their bases in startling contrast to the blackened lava flows. At such a time one stands in awe at the power of the Master Artist whose invisible hand paints a landscape of such bold and primitive color.

It was after such a flight that we landed one evening at Tucson. Hot and tired, but still dazzled by the beauty through which we had passed, I accepted gratefully the invitation of a tall young Arizonan to drive out to the Papago Indian Reservation, some distance from town, and nestled beside the protecting mountains. We arrived at an old alabaster mission just as the vesper bells were ringing. Against the muted colors of the sunset afterglow, a procession of black-robed monks and nuns wound slowly up a rocky hill overlooking the valley. On one side of the summit was a sanctuary of the Virgin Mary, and from all directions there converged gaily, though poorly, clad Indian men, women and children to kneel by the shrine in simple reverence which would have been a credit to any Friends Meeting. Then their voices lifted in the haunting melody of ancient hymns which floated out over the valley, a celestial accompaniment to a never-to-be-forgotten scene.

The next morning we faced the last day of our westward flight and the completion of the first half of our tour. And this leg of the trip offered violent contrasts, as we flew over seared deserts and emerald irrigated valleys, lofty mountain peaks and the sand dunes of the American Sahara.

We stopped for lunch at Yuma, surely the hottest spot on earth. Arid sands, sizzling enough to fry eggs, stretched in all directions, with the only vegetation an occasional dried-up sagebrush. Yet just north was the winding Colorado River, its banks a lush green border of tamarack, eucalyptus, pepper and bougainvillea trees.

After departing from Yuma we cruised across unending white sand dunes. On and on over the sea of sand we flew by compass, our eyes strained to keep in sight the hairline highway to the left, our one link with water and transportation. And then, like a mirage, the vivid green carpet of the Imperial Valley lay below us, in striking contrast to the blue of its Salton Sea.

We were flying at eight thousand feet altitude, in order to

scale the towering Sierra Nevadas, the last barrier before the Pacific coast. I noticed the "revs" dropping due to ice forming in the carburetor from the moisture in the atmosphere, and exploded it out by leaning the mixture. Banking around jagged crags, dodging through box canyons, I felt a sense of awe and also a strange comfort in the impregnable strength of these lofty peaks. Lesser hills might be razed, desert sands might be irrigated, but here were rocky bastions too great to be changed by the hand of man. Even while concentrating on the problem of climbing over the peaks, I was conscious of the exhilaration of the moment, when all my senses seemed sharpened and I was able to savor the winelike quality of the high, thin air, drink in the beauty of the brilliant blue glacial lakes set like jewels in the mountains, and pay reverence to the Divine hand which had set them there.

Finally we cleared the last peak and saw in the distance the silver Pacific. Then and there I vowed to myself, never again to come west by train, and so far I have kept that promise.

We spent a hectic, exciting and highly rewarding week of concentrated work on the coast, meeting with committees, making public addresses and actually getting two Aviation Country Clubs started, in Los Angeles and San Francisco.

Father had come out to Los Angeles to meet me, and I flew him in the Fledgling to San Francisco, a beautiful flight over winding coastlines and redwood forests. This was a proud moment, for up to now Dad had looked on my flying with tolerant amusement, refusing to believe I could be serious about an aviation career. But when he sat in the open cockpit ahead of me and looked down on the scenic wonders below, when he noted that I knew how to keep the plane in the air and how to follow a course, his old adventurous spirit rose up, and for the first time I think he understood and shared my love of the air. After we had landed smoothly at San Francisco, he patted my shoulder in approval and pronounced one of his highest terms of praise: "Good girl."

h Nichols and her famous Lockheed Vega plane, *Akita*

WINGS FOR LIFE

hals

Keystone Photo Service

Just before taking off from Los Angeles on another leg of the Forty-six-State Aviation Country Club tour: Ruth Nichols and her Curtiss Fledgling, flight engineer C. O. Bedford and executive pilot Robb C. Oertel with Curtiss Robin, 1929.

Following our week of high-pressure work, the three men of our party and I decided we deserved a weekend of rest. So as soon as we had put Father on a train, we took off for Monterey where we spent two days of swimming, sunning and complete relaxation.

For the trip back to San Francisco I had what was then the unique privilege of riding in an Army aircraft which flew in a five-plane squadron with such perfect precision that I have never forgotten it. I was amazed at the takeoff in formation, when it seemed to me the slightest shift in wind current or change in a motor's r.p.m. would cause a collision. We climbed swiftly into the clouds, where the leader flew on instruments, but all the other pilots concentrated on watching the wing tip ahead. The landing was made with the same precision, impressing me with the amazing technique which had already been developed by our military pilots.

This was quite a contrast to an earlier flying experience I had had during our stay in Los Angeles, when I had taken time out for a flying-boat trip to Catalina Island, to see the home of my childhood's favorite western author, Zane Grey. The owner-pilot of the hydro-airplane seemed to regard the craft as a plaything, and amused himself by chasing seagulls close to the water on the return trip. After watching these antics for a while, my hair stood on end, for several times we were on the verge of a power stall or a dive into the Pacific. Although there was no control wheel on my side of the cockpit, I discovered I could operate the ailerons by pulling the chain on the yoke, so I suggested with a casual laugh that he let me try flying the boat by that means. The idea of piloting the plane without any control wheel appealed to his sense of humor, and so I was able to keep him diverted and the plane under control until our trip was safely ended.

Our flight westward was merely a warming-up period for the pinnacles of wonder that were to be ours on the trip back, over the majestic northwest. This time, too, we had a new companion in adventure, Margaret Perry, another young flyer who lived in Beverly Hills and who wanted cross-country flying experience. Later, as Margaret Perry Cooper, she became the first woman to own and operate an airport and flying school.

Margaret joined us in San Francisco, just for our coastal leg, flying her small Walter-motored Spartan plane. And if she wanted flying experience, she got a double portion of it over the snow-capped mountains of Oregon and Washington. (It must not be forgotten that flyers in those days operated their under-powered planes without benefit of air maps, flight weather forecasts, or radio facilities.)

Our armada of three planes took off from San Francisco, following the Sacramento River country, where the mountains are always crowned with snow and the valleys warm enough for orange groves. Almost at once we ran into difficulty approaching Corning, California, on the first leg of our flight northward. This was one of the few times during our six months' flying tour when weather conditions were not ideal. We had to climb a rather long, high range of mountains which were hidden by huge billowy clouds. It was a question either of playing hide-and-seek between the ravines, with sudden blockades of fog or cloud, or of climbing over the entire cloud bank. We decided on the latter course.

At eleven thousand feet we looked down on an unearthly panorama of white puff-balls, with snowy peaks poking through at intervals, and overhead a sky of deep and brilliant blue. In the distance, like a lodestar, was Mount Shasta. We flew above a frosty fairyland of delight, but occasional breaks in the clouds revealed frightening jagged cliffs which made me decide firmly that if my motor conked out here, I'd use my 'chute.

We finally arrived safely at Portland, and from there to Seattle flew over a green carpet of valleys and low hills, with a stage-curtain backdrop of three towering volcanic peaks visible off to the right—Hood, Adams and Rainier.

After Seattle we all felt a need to get away from *people,* whom we had been meeting in such large numbers, and so we decided to take a detour through Montana.

Here we would find the solitude we craved, the great open spaces that are nature's landing fields, and mountains that are friendlier than the jagged Sierras and desolate Rockies. That flight was a constant delight, reaching its climax when we landed one evening in a flat sagebrush valley completely encircled by high mountain pinnacles.

Near Missoula we found a picturesque dude ranch where we had four perfect days of glorious rides, an overnight pack trip—and continued peace. After this respite we started off with renewed vigor for new cities to vanquish in our campaign for sports flying. A brief gas stop at Idaho Falls was the first in order.

The plains of Utah contributed nothing to break the monotony except an occasional lava bed and the Three Peaks Volcanos. Because of a delay in Ogden we didn't reach Salt Lake City until after dark. My motor was apparently objecting to months of running time and was sputtering in protest, so that I was unusually tired when we finally sighted Salt Lake, only to find that no floodlights had been turned on at the field. Precariously we felt our way over high tension wires and managed to locate the field with the help of border lights, landing on solid ground just as my engine gave its last gasp.

Some carburetor adjustment soon put the motor in good humor again and we traveled in fine style through Wyoming and Colorado, with fast landings and slow takeoffs. The fields near the Continental Divide are at an elevation of about seven thousand feet, where the air is so thin that landing fields often must be a mile long.

Although strong tailwinds made the air bumpy, the weather on the whole was remarkably good throughout the trip. It was not until we were over Kansas that we encountered anything like a serious storm. Here we ran into what at first looked like a mild local thunderstorm but which turned out to be a violent cyclonic disturbance. My idea was to skirt the black cloud bank—which I soon found was a mistake.

Trying to circle the storm, I was caught on the edge of a line-squall, which today's aerology teaches all student pilots is apt to be the most violent part of any wind storm. Without warning my plane shot up four thousand feet, motor full on and nose down. Then at the top of the updraft the plane was spilled over, like a raft on top of a giant wave, fortunately right side up, for I might have found myself, like some other pilots, in an inverted spin. I was able to descend with the plane under control, and as rapidly as possible I veered from those angry black and white cloud vampires, and noted that the Robin had followed the same tactics. We set a course due north, flying a hundred miles out of our way, pursued for half the distance not only by the usual sand twisters but by a black, funnel-shaped tornado. This was one instance in which it was better not to look back, but to concentrate on finding a safe landing ahead. Had I seen the black funnel on my plane's tail, I'm afraid I might have been turned into a pillar of salt, like Lot's wife.

After this somewhat rugged experience we reached once again the pilot's dreamland of perfect flying country, with flat open stretches as far as the eye could see, no trees, no wires, plenty of section-lines to follow instead of having to depend on maps and compasses. A plane can "sit down" almost anywhere between Kansas, Omaha, Iowa and the Dakotas with the comfortable assurance that human habitation is nearby.

From Fargo, North Dakota, we turned east again, whizzing with strong tailwinds over Minnesota's thousands of small, sparkling lakes. What a country for flying boats! Not having flown one of my original pets for more than a year, I felt a sudden longing to have this faithful Fledgling sprout pontoons, so that I might skim to a landing on one of those larger jewel-like ponds.

The rolling hills of Wisconsin came next, and then, after we reached Illinois and Michigan, there was a month of flying over middle-western farm lands—Ohio, Indiana, Missouri, Kentucky. Then northeast across West Virginia, Pennsylvania and on to Albany and a whirlwind tour of New England.

The final trip down the Atlantic coast seemed far more beautiful than it really was, because at its end lay the Long Island Aviation Country Club and the triumphant finish of a successful pioneering tour.

In this six months of flying over all kinds of terrain and in all kinds of weather, I felt I had developed from a fledgling into a full-grown pilot. We had flown twelve thousand miles without a forced landing for either ship—a wonderful record for the two Curtiss planes and a tribute to C. O. Bedford's mechanical skill. We had landed in forty-three out of the forty-six states over which we had flown, including ninety-six cities, had sold the idea of flying to thousands of people, had made hundreds of speeches and left a nucleus of Aviation Country Clubs in ten more cities: Washington, Memphis, Los Angeles, San Francisco, Minneapolis, Milwaukee, Buffalo, Louisville, Pittsburgh and Cincinnati. This was in addition to the clubs started in ten cities before the tour. And there were now club members in thirty-one cities throughout the country.

The future of sports flying looked bright and the era of the personal airplane seemed near. Probably the history of personal flying would have been much different if the stock market had not stepped in.

Hardly were we back on the ground after our successful tour when financial catastrophe struck the nation. The crash of October, 1929, wiped out fortunes overnight and ushered in the start of America's worst depression.

Few people would be able to afford to fly airplanes for a long time to come. The era of social and sports aviation had to be filed under unfinished business.

5

POWDER PUFF AIR DERBY

What chances we took in those pioneer days of flying! What narrow escapes we had during takeoffs and landings on the many rough, short airfields of the twenties! Yet at the time, we did not think of ourselves as particularly daring. We could not know of the swift advances to be made in the next few years in the science of aerodynamics or the new safety devices that would be developed. Most pilots of today would shudder if called upon to fly one of those early planes under the conditions which we considered routine.

The air age arrived with such speed in the early thirties that many of us have forgotten the hazards that faced a pilot in his precarious flying crate in the days just before commercial airlines started their regularly scheduled service across the country. Yet anyone of middle years today can think back to the time when regular air travel was unheard of, when people discussed airplanes as miraculous new experiments which might change the customs of man at some far-off future time. Speculation about air travel then was at much the same stage as are our discussions of space ships and trips to the moon today—fascinating conversation, but not to be taken seriously.

Actually the age of routine space travel may be as imminent today as was the era of regular air travel in the early twenties. I fully expect to fly to the moon before I die. And I hope I shall be permitted to pilot the space ship.

When, in the midst of our return flight during the Aviation Country Clubs tour, I received an invitation to compete in the Women's Air Derby, I was delighted. This would be an exciting break in the monotony of daily conferences, speeches and committee meetings. Bob and Beddie agreed it would be a fine idea, *if* I could get hold of a fast plane. My Fledgling was a tried-and-true old friend, but its plodding pace could not compete with the far higher-speed aircraft that would be entered in the race.

The "Powder Puff Air Derby," as it was immediately dubbed by headline writers, was to be from Santa Monica, California, to Cleveland, where the women pilots would join up with others competing in the National Air Races, under the management of Cliff Henderson. I did some high-pressure telephoning and succeeded in arranging the loan of a plane from the president of the Rearwin Company. Although it was a stock job, it was fast for that era, and in comparison with the Fledgling.

There were nineteen women pilots entered in the race, of whom thirteen were in the so-called heavy airplane class. At that time there were only nine licensed women transport pilots in the country, of which I was one. In addition eleven women held limited commercial licenses, ninety-two were accredited as private pilots and there were a number of student pilots.

These one hundred and twelve licensed female pilots were widely scattered around the country, with usually not more than one to a city. Most were working girls, close to half of them were married, many to pilots, and a number had children.

Among the band of petticoat pilots with whom I would be competing were such storied figures as: Amelia Earhart, whom I already knew through our preliminary work in organizing a women pilots' group; Margaret Perry, our gay and stout-hearted companion on the Aviation Country Clubs tour of the northwest; Thea Rasch, outstanding woman pilot of

Germany; Mrs. Keith Miller of Australia—or "Chubby," as
all of us soon called her; Phoebe Omlie, another veteran
woman pilot, who had graduated from stunt flying at county
fairs to partnership with her pilot husband in a flying school
at Memphis; Ruth Elder, who had tried a trans-Atlantic hop
two years previously as a passenger in the plane piloted by
George Haldeman, and who had dunked in the ocean; Louise
Thaden, the wise-cracking Valkyrie who was to become one
of my best friends; Gladys O'Donnell, fine pylon racer of
California, and the ill-fated Marvel Crosson, a pretty girl and
popular flyer who was to crash fatally in the mountains of
Arizona before she reached the starting point. Formidable
opposition, but I was confident that with a good plane I
could give them a run for the money.

The sportsman pilot tour had reached St. Louis when I
began preparations to enter the derby, working out a schedule that would not delay the tour more than was absolutely
necessary. Bob and Beddie waved me off as I took a hurried
departure for the west, in the sleek red plane whose motor
sang sweetly.

"Give 'em heck, kid!" shouted Beddie.

"Bring home the bacon!" yelled Bob.

How I wished for the mechanical know-how of Beddie
before I reached Santa Monica and the starting line! Exi-
gencies of weather, business arrangements, financing problems and too little time have always plagued racing pilots
except for those rare cases in which unlimited funds and time
to spare happen to coincide. The result too often has meant
a compromise on perfectionist attention to last-minute checking.

However, the sleek red Rearwin plane was a joy to handle
after so many months at the stick of the lumbering Fledgling.
I reveled in her speed and slid light-heartedly across the
Kansas sky. I felt like a queen bee, speeding gaily and regally
through space, but when I approached Wichita, making
knots on a long power descent, suddenly the motor quit cold.

With only three hundred feet of altitude, there was neither time nor distance to be choosy about a landing spot. My mind sped as follows: Only small fenced-in areas on all sides. . . . Must stall-in over fence of tiny pasture dead ahead. . . . Better slip and fish-tail. . . . Creepers! What a floater! Running out of field and the wheels haven't touched yet. . . . Full brakes, she'll turn over. . . . Better just hit the fence head-on and pray. . . . Duck! Please, God, You take over now! . . .

Ri-i-i-ip! . . . Jolt! . . . Silence.

I lift my head. I'm still alive! The plane is right side up—in the next field.

God and Aunty *had* taken over.

The plane had skimmed over the ground at such speed that it had sailed across two three-foot ditches and broken through two high fences, carrying the wire and fence poles with it. I jumped out to inspect the damage. Wings, landing gear, motor—all intact. Only a few tears in the fabric on the underside of one wing. It just wasn't possible, but there it was.

"Thank you, God!" I whispered. "And thee too, Angel Aunty. . . ."

Weak with relief and still awed by the miracle, I hurried down the road and thumbed a ride to the Wichita airport, seeking the services of a mechanic. There I met a fellow pilot who offered to come back and help me out of my difficulties. As we pushed the Rearwin into the next field, after pulling down a fence to clear the way, he remarked:

"Gal, you sure must live right!"

I discovered with embarrassment that the motor had quit merely because it was out of fuel, and that all the time I had had a full reserve tank of gas. That was what came of hurrying too much. If only the factory mechanics had briefed me on cockpit and flying details!

By working all night, mechanics were able to repair the torn wing fabric. I took off again next morning, and made Tulsa and Dallas without mishap. The third day was a long hop from Dallas to El Paso, mostly over fairly flat plains of Texas, but with the formidable Guadalupe Range at its western end—one of the country's most difficult areas for planes with limited horsepower and brief cruising ranges.

I stopped to refuel and reconnoiter at Pecos, the jumping-off place for the mountains. There were three possible courses; I could follow the canyon railroad, I could fly above an oil pipe line which had been laid across the mountains, or take a straight compass heading for El Paso. I decided on the railroad, as the longest way round but the safest way there, since it also offered a few possible spots for forced landings.

Heading for the mountains, I kept the railroad as a guide-line below, and just as I reached the first high range there loomed ahead one of the blackest thunderstorms I'd ever seen. Lightning flashed and the rain came down in sheets. I turned south to fly around it, but another thunderhead blocked my course. Dodging desperately around each new cloud mass, I lost the railroad completely and found myself in the middle of the mountains, with no landmarks and no possible landing spot. It was too late to turn back. Storms hemmed me in behind and ahead. Lightning flashed around the plane as I was buffeted between five storm formations. I thought, it's like "The Charge of the Light Brigade":

> "Cannon to right of them,
> Cannon to left of them,
> Cannon in front of them
> Volleyed and thundered . . ."

The black clouds around me looked indeed like "the jaws of Death," and "the mouth of Hell"—and there was only one of me, not six hundred.

Just one thing to do—open her wide, dodge and run. Saw-tooth mountain peaks flashed by only a few feet beneath as I tried desperately for altitude, clearing some of them by inches. Then, dear Heaven, a green river-bed showed up ahead. I didn't know where it was and I didn't care. Anything to get away from those murderous peaks.

With a prayer of thanks for another deliverance, I turned to follow the river, having figured out that it must be the Rio Grande, and if so would lead me to El Paso. Then another mysterious hazard developed. The plane became more and more tail-heavy. I couldn't understand it, since the stabilizer was all the way forward. Finally I was forced to fly with the stick pushed almost against the instrument panel, to keep the plane flying level. Just as my arm muscles were ready to quit, I sighted the little town of Juarez, Mexico, right across the border from El Paso.

I managed to land as a new and larger storm broke, and as I taxied the plane down the crude runway I noticed that my feet were slipping on the rudder bar. When I braked to a stop at the hangar and looked down into the cockpit, I saw oil, thick as the bilge of a boat. Wearily, I crawled over the side; there was more oil dripping all the way down the fuselage to the tail. Examination of the motor showed that the vibration caused by the long period of "open gun" throttling while trying to outrun the storms had broken the overflow line, so that the entire five gallons of oil in the tank had leaked down into the pointed spinner, causing the tail-heaviness I had been fighting for the last half-hour.

Again, mechanics worked all night, cleaning out the oil-soaked fuselage, installing a new oil line and welding the cracks which had sprung open in the tank itself. They had the plane ready in time for my takeoff at seven the next morning.

The new day brought a pilot's boon—calm blue skies and a brisk tailwind which sent me whizzing light-heartedly to Douglas, Tucson and Phoenix, with time enough—if lucky—to make Los Angeles the same afternoon. That would give me two days to rest and tune up the motor.

So I stopped at Phoenix only long enough to refuel, skipping lunch in order to play follow-the-leader behind a tri-motored transport plane which I had been told by a pilot at the airport had a cruising speed similar to the Rearwin's. It was scheduled to leave for Los Angeles fifteen minutes later. I soon saw that I could not keep up with the transport if I traveled at normal cruising speed. By advancing the motor's revs so that the air-speed indicator showed 145 m.p.h., I was able to keep an even distance from the lead plane, but when it gained altitude I found myself slipping behind. By now it was apparent that the motor was not turning out its usual power, and also that the transport plane was much faster than I had been told.

I had been flying with throttle wide open for some time, which can be done without overheating above a certain altitude, when I noted, ahead and to the right, another dreaded thunderstorm. This one was bigger in its solid formations than any I had yet encountered, and I didn't know what to do. For an hour and a half we had been flying over stretches of desert with no recognizable landmarks and no habitations, the transport plane was leaving me farther and farther behind, and though I was pushing the Rearwin to the utmost it was impossible to catch up. The transport, far in the distance, seemed to be trying to circle the storm by taking a more southerly course. I wondered if my fuel supply would be equal to the extra mileage, and what I would do if I lost sight of the lead plane completely. It was a nightmare.

Now, the black cumulo-nimbus clouds covered half the sky, lightning bolts flashed jaggedly—and then, one of my periodic glances at the instrument panel jolted me upright— the oil pressure gauge read zero! This was the end. In a very few minutes the pistons would "freeze" and a forced landing in this trackless and mountainous desert became inevitable.

Sacrificing altitude, I made one last desperate effort to get within sight of the transport plane by diving, thereby obtaining a final burst of speed, so that the pilot might at least see that I was forced down and send help. I made it to within a half-mile of the lead plane, rocked my wings in emergency signal and then headed toward a flat-topped mountain, too small for a landing. To the left was a ragged peak, but as I precariously banked around it I came within sight of a wide valley which looked as if it would offer a pilot a chance to walk away from a crash. Maybe I could make a landing in one piece. . . . Maybe I could keep the motor running, tape together the broken oil line, ride out the storm on the ground and then take off again. Maybe. . . .

With my heart in my mouth, I glided down the remaining four thousand feet, desperately searching the horizon for some sign of civilization. At a thousand feet I sighted a cabin in the distance and beyond that what seemed to be a hairline logging trail—a new hope, a new lease on life. At least I wouldn't have to walk fifty or a hundred miles across the desert to reach the railroad and help. Now I had a fighting chance. I concentrated on making a right side up landing, if possible, and thereby save the plane. There appeared to be a reasonably clear space ahead, but when a half-mile away from it the motor froze tight, from no oil and overheating.

Now there was no choice. I had to land right then. I pulled the nose up and squashed in at minimum stalling speed, dodging the sagebrush hummocks. Again, I had by some miracle, managed a perfect landing, with only one small scratch on the wing fabric.

For a few minutes I just sat, leaning my head back against the cockpit headrest, and uttered another prayer of thanks. Looking at the sky, I realized how good God was—even the huge storm was veering off to the north away from my valley.

Sagebrush and sand stretched away in all directions. Maybe someone was living in the cabin I had spotted during the long glide. It must be about three miles away. I had brought along ropes for a possible stakeout at some field where there was no hangar space, but had neglected to bring a sledge hammer for pounding in stakes, so the ropes would be useless. I climbed out of the cockpit and surveyed the situation. The plane was undamaged, except for the broken oil line, but the propeller was immovable. There was nothing to do but start walking and try to find help.

I hooked on the cockpit covers, tied a tarpaulin around the engine and pulled out my old knapsack, containing emergency supplies, which I always carried with me. These included a three-day supply of compressed food, water, an automatic pistol, matches and flashlight. I hoisted the sack on my back with the straps over my shoulders, grabbed up my worn leather jacket and set out on foot across the desert.

I headed in the general direction in which I thought I had seen the cabin from the air, and sure enough, very soon it was within sight, and very evidently deserted. . . . But in the opposite direction I saw another, newly ·painted. Someone *must* be living there.

This bright, beckoning cabin seemed very near. But the desert plays strange tricks. The longer I walked, the farther away it seemed. Maybe it was only a mirage. I stumbled wearily over hard-caked sand and around quicksand and mud holes left by recent rains. Cactus bit at my ankles while rattlesnakes and a gila monster slithered out of my path. The sun beat down with almost unbearable heat. I narrowly avoided a tarantula. Was I nearly there? The water in my canteen was almost gone. Was this to be my epitaph . . . She almost made it?

Then suddenly the cabin was right in front of me. It was no mirage—it was real. I could even see the movement of a window curtain, as if someone peered out at this strange apparition with long hair, helmet askew and coveralls flapping in the hot wind. I broke into a trot for the last few yards, lurching onto the door-step and feebly pounded on the door. No answer. I looked again. No window curtain. The movement I thought I had seen was another mirage—a trick of light and shadow. This cabin was deserted, like the other.

When the full import of the situation struck me, I sank down on the step with my head on my knees. Never, before and only once since, have I felt the terror of nature's vastness and the individual's desolate loneliness. Why had I ever embarked on this harebrained adventure? Why had I ever thought I could fly? Why was I not married to Don, who would protect me? Where now were all the high hopes and bright promises of the future? What good was all my frantic striving, if I was to end as a heap of bleached bones on the limitless sands of a desert?

Through the desperate silence I seemed suddenly to hear a quiet, staunch voice, Aunty's voice, far away in Rye, New York, where there were wide lawns and green trees and soft beds and loving people. Across the miles, as clearly as if by radio-telephone, I heard her say:

"Lift up thine eyes unto the hills, from whence cometh thy help."

I lifted my eyes—and saw, far off, below the foothills, the same line that I'd spotted in the Rearwin's glide—only now it was wider. It must be a highway, and beside it was another house. Unbelieving, I staggered to my feet and stumbled on. Maybe it was another mirage. Maybe I was suffering from hallucinations. The straps of the knapsack cut into my shoulders and my eyes burned. As I at last approached the little building and saw that it was real, I heard with incredible joy the barking of a dog. A door opened and a brown-skinned angel in a soiled calico dress stared at me suspiciously. At least she looked like an angel to me, although her black hair was greasy and her face forbidding.

Weakly I leaned against the unpainted board walls of the cabin and grinned.

"Have you got a telephone?" I asked.

"No sabe."

I pantomimed the act of cranking an old-fashioned wall telephone, holding a receiver to my ear and mouthing words. A light of understanding dawned in the woman's eyes, and she smiled suddenly, shook her head and pointed toward the highway, waving her arm in a gesture that I interpreted as meaning that there was no phone for many miles. Then she opened the door wider and waved me in.

It was a one-room shack, with a bed in one corner and a stove in another, orange crates nailed to the wall in lieu of cabinets, and an occasional chicken sauntered through the room. She offered me a tin cup of tepid water from a pail, which I drank gratefully.

Strength renewed, I sat on the floor and considered the situation. How could I get word to the family that I was safe? They didn't even know I had entered the air derby. They thought I was still in St. Louis or Cleveland organizing Aviation Country Clubs. But soon they would see the head-lines . . . "GIRL FLYER CRASHED IN DESERT" . . .

There was no answer as I couldn't get far over unknown miles of desert. Best to rest a while until I could perhaps better face the situation. Through gestures I indicated to my now amiable hostess that I was tired, stretched out on the floor and promptly went to sleep. It seemed only a few minutes when I was awakened by the noise of a missing engine.

A clattering jalopy was coming down the path-like road. I jumped up and waved frantically until the car stopped. It was occupied to overflowing by four beaming Negroes, the two women resplendent in "town" clothes. They welcomed me aboard and somehow made room for me. They were headed for the nearest town, where there was a railroad. A train that came through every twenty-four hours was due at eleven p.m. When we got there it was only six. Maybe I could get help, go back and tow the Rearwin nearer the railroad and still catch the train for Los Angeles.

Again my guardian angel was on the job. A good Samaritan in the form of a tall, tanned engineer offered his help. He too was waiting for the train, returning to Los Angeles after an inspection tour of his mining properties, and seemed glad to have something to do to help pass the time. He managed to borrow a car, picks, shovels, ropes and lanterns and we set out for a two-hour drive back across the desert. When we reached the plane we attached tow ropes and tried to pull her through the sand. But it soon became apparent that it would be impossible to get her to the railroad intact. Too many sagebrush hummocks barred the way. So we staked her down securely and my benefactor drove me back in time to catch the train.

I sent off telegrams at the next stop, accepted a piece of apple pie from the station-mistress, and arrived at Los Angeles the next morning much the worse for wear. I had removed my coveralls, and my dress was torn and streaked with dirt; long runs were in my stockings from wading through sage and cactus. I must have presented a startling sight to the engineer's wife, who was at the station to meet him. She offered me the hospitality of a bath and a rest, but I realized that there might still be time to rescue the Rearwin and enter the derby, so I excused myself, with heartfelt thanks, and made a dash for the Curtiss Wright Flying Service.

Here, after lengthy argument, I finally prevailed upon the men in charge to fly a new motor out to the desert in a tri-motored Ford plane. It took all day and most of the night to locate an available plane, tune it up for a flight and equip it as a flying garage. It was three-thirty in the morning by the time we finally took off with a crew of three mechanics, the pilot and myself.

As the brilliant stars paled in the sunrise, the pilot turned to me and remarked casually:

"I suppose the boss told you this ship mustn't be landed on anything but a regular airport or a marked emergency field?"

My heart sank. After all this effort, after the agonizing trek through the desert and my frantic efforts to rush repairs, was I doomed to failure after all? I decided to hedge. Once we sighted the plane, I was sure I could find a safe landing spot. It was a difficult job to locate the small plane from the eight thousand foot altitude the pilot insisted on maintaining, but at last I spotted it, a tiny red speck in the desert. So again I summoned all my powers of persuasion to induce the pilot to circle lower and try a landing. Why he finally gave in I'll never know. Maybe it was from sheer exhaustion. But finally the big plane glided to a smooth and perfect landing on the packed desert sand, about a mile from the Rearwin.

Now the problem was how to transport the heavy new engine from one ship to the other. The pilot said flatly it would be impossible to taxi the big transport plane over the sagebrush hummocks. But when the mechanics looked over the distance they would have to lug engine and tools, they decided maybe the ship *could* taxi over after all.

The pilot may have been stubborn, but he was skillful. It was an inspiring sight to see the big mother plane, with a roar of first one engine and then another, wind like a polo pony around the obstacles and finally nose up to the stricken, would-be racer.

Again we faced a problem—how to lift the fifteen-hundred-pound motor off the Ford and onto the Rearwin's motor mount. As the mechanics argued, I suggested meekly that maybe they could suspend a block and tackle from the Ford's center motor. At first horrified at the idea, the pilot again gave in, and the feat was accomplished with no harm to the big plane.

We worked all day, using the wings of the Ford as shelter from the sun. We had brought along sandwiches, fruit and a barrel of water which diminished with astounding speed. We struggled until dark to change an oil tank which wouldn't fit inside my motor mount, then went at it again at dawn. I learned that had rubber connections been installed in the oil lines and had the tank itself been hung in an adequate sponge rubber harness to give flexibility, neither would have crystallized and broken under the strain of vibration. I'll always be grateful to those mechanics who worked so doggedly and with such skill. By noon we were ready to fly.

Taxiing in and out among the sagebrush, we finally

found a clear stretch of sand, and both planes managed a takeoff. This time I took the chief mechanic as a passenger in my plane, just in case of more trouble. I knew the poor man had no faith in a woman pilot, and in addition he had neither helmet nor goggles, but he gamely agreed. I'm sure it was not a happy trip for him, but it was for me, for the new motor purred sweetly—and we arrived at Clover Field in Santa Monica twenty minutes before the air derby's final registration deadline. We had made it!

Again—no time for further tests on the new motor; just last minute hurried checks. No time for anything, really, but desperately needed sleep. Bright and early, we were all at the starting line. We jammed our feet on the brakes, gave the engines full throttle, holding tensely until the starter's flag dipped. Then each plane jumped into the air, and the Powder Puff Derby had begun. I knew that I couldn't open up the engine to top speed until it had been broken in at cruising r.p.m., just as you must drive slowly at first in a new car. I would be far outclassed by faster planes at the start— but at least I was in the race!

That conscientious (though still shaken) mechanic, had done his work well, and the motor hummed sweetly as the Rearwin climbed and then leveled off for the flight eastward. I started at sixteen hundred r.p.m. and each day advanced the throttle fifty revolutions, so that by the time we reached Texas she was turning up eighteen hundred with very little vibration.

Knowing the country from previous flights, I was able to cut a few corners in navigating; when we reached Abilene I was in third place, even though most of the other ships were faster. Now was the time to "pour on the coal."

At Columbus, Ohio, I felt the motor had had sufficient time to warrant changing the pitch of the propeller to two thousand, also to advance the throttle. I had this attended to the night I landed, and the next morning went up for a short test hop. Never had the motor run better—smooth as

The remains of the Rearwin after its collision with a tractor on the runway at Columbus, Ohio, one hundred miles short of author's goal in the Powder Puff Derby, August 27, 1929.

butter, just the right revs, no slippage. Elated, I turned back toward the field and glided down for a landing.

Heading into the wind, I ruddered toward the center of the runway, since the rest of the field was being graded and was too soft for use. Out of the corner of my eyes I saw a tractor at the right edge of the landing strip, and just as the wheels were about to touch the ground a side current of air caught the plane and carried it to the runway's edge. The wing struck the tractor and my racer did a double cartwheel, finally landing on its back, leaving me hanging by the seat belt upside down in the wreckage.

A workman rushed over shouting:

"Are you hurt, Sis?"

"No," I cried, "but get me out, *quick*, before the gasoline explodes."

He hauled me out unscathed, the plane didn't catch fire; in this case switching off the ignition had avoided a fire—but that was the end of the race for me.

Heartsick, I surveyed what had been a sleek plane, now lying helpless as a squashed beetle, with its wheels in the air.

After all the months of smooth flying and no mishaps during the Aviation Country Clubs tour, this ill-fated race had brought me two forced landings and a crackup.

6

THE 99's—
AND CHANGING COURSE

If my early adventures in the air had given me nothing else, they still would have been worth while for all the friendships they brought with other women pilots of the day.

One of my earliest friends in the sorority of the air was Amelia Earhart, whose career paralleled mine in many curious ways. Certainly both of us lost our hearts to the romance of flight after our first experience with it. Again and again, Amelia and I planned the same flights at the same time, each without knowledge of the other's intentions. And, an even stranger coincidence, we had both been interested orginally in medical and social service careers.

I first met Amelia by correspondence:

> 76 Brooks Street
> West Medford, Mass.
> September 15, 1927

My dear Miss Nichols:

May I introduce myself as a fellow F.A.I. and prepare you for a letter concerned with aviation?

Because your picture has been appearing lately in Boston papers, I make you the victim of an idea which has been simmering for some time. What do you think of the advisability of forming an organization composed of women who fly? I wrote to the N.A.A. for a list of F.A.I. women and find there have been issued twenty-one licenses. Many of these pilots are not active at the present time, some no longer live.

I should judge there are about ten who are really engaged in aeronautics, but how to reach them I do not know. The N.A.A. files are out of date and checking up obscure notices in newspapers is not satisfactory.

If you think the idea worth pursuing, won't you let me know your ideas on the following?

Should women who are connected with aviation in remote capacities (stenographers, factory workers, etc.) have certain membership?

Should there be a distinction between active F.A.I. and non-active?

Should women who are active in the aeronautics industry be entitled to memberships and how?

Personally, I am a social worker who flies for sport, and am on the board of directors of an aeronautical concern. I can not claim to be a feminist but do rather enjoy seeing women tackling all kinds of new problems—new for them, that is.

I hope to hear from you.

Very sincerely yours,
(Miss) Amelia M. Earhart (signature)

This was the beginning of a long friendship, including two years of planning the formation of a women pilots' organization which finally came into being in the fall of 1929 as the "99's."

I replied promptly to Amelia's letter, expressing my interest in her suggestion and offering some of my own ideas. More than six months passed, however, before I heard from her again. This time the letter was typewritten:

DENISON HOUSE
93 Tyler Street
Boston, Mass.

April 24, 1928

My dear Miss Nichols,

How sorry I am that I didn't answer your letter more promptly. Had I done so, you probably would have felt it possible to communicate with me, somehow, when you were in Boston, a short time ago. . . .

Despite a lost opportunity for informal conversation, let us take up the feminine end of flying with action in view. I propose we

make three grades of members in the organization talked of—
Honorary, consisting of F.A.I. inactive flyers, like Katherine Stinson; Active, of Transport or Private Operators and perhaps, those
actively in administrative capacities in recognized aeronautical
concerns; and an Associate, or any women who would like to
boost aviation.

To have a purpose is sometimes a deadening thing, but I think,
to boost aviation is behind all thought of mine and probably of
yours. I think, to that end, we ought to write to all on the N.A.A.
list of license holders, and make some definite statements of
organization and purpose. (This part will take a month, at least,
for many addresses are incorrect, and may have to be traced
through the state chapters.) Then, after we get a society organized, send notice to the N.A.A. of our existence, and tell something concrete about our plans—which would have to be determined in accordance with the results of our letters.

What think you? As to organization, let us have a governing
committee of three, you and I and one of the Honoraries. I think
we have to be autocratic about officers, at first, in order to start
something. One of us should be chairman, and a secretary and
treasurer may be elected later.

I am writing these details in order that you may have something to criticize, not as rules to be followed as put down. Won't
you write me your idea of a letter to be sent, if you approve of
the plan? When an idea strikes me, I have very little control, and
I fear you will suffer from another broadside like this, if you
don't answer soon. Is this full warning?

By the way, Denison Airport Corporation, of which I am a
Director, has recently been appointed Boston agent for Fairchild.
Do you think that circumstance will help us get together?

                    Sincerely yours,
                    Amelia M. Earhart (signature)
P.S. I chanced upon a write-up of you in SILHOUETTES the
other day.

My reply offered certain suggestions, endorsed her ideas and
expressed my warm wish that we might meet soon.

When I finally did meet Amelia, the first thing that struck
me was her amazing resemblance to Charles A. Lindbergh—
a resemblance that has been remarked upon by many people.
It was this striking likeness, so the story goes, that won

Amelia the opportunity for her first trans-Atlantic flight Lady Winston Guest had planned to make the flight herself, but was dissuaded by her family, and so offered to underwrite the first trans-ocean flight by a woman. Perhaps whimsically, she asked her friend, George Palmer Putnam, to find "a girl who looked like Lindbergh." Putnam made inquiries of Capt. H. H. Railey, who observed, "There's a girl always showing up around Boston Airport who looks a lot like Lindbergh." He introduced Amelia to Putnam, who eventually fell in love with her and later became her husband. Putnam in turn recommended Amelia to Lady Guest, and she became the first woman to fly the Atlantic as a passenger. Later Amelia made the same flight solo, continuing to pile up "firsts" until her tragic disappearance during her Pacific flight in 1937.

Through occasional meetings and continued correspondence we worked out the framework for a women pilots' organization. But both of us were busy, and so it was some time before our plans became reality.

It was after my return from the Aviation Country Club tour and my ill-fated entry in the Powder Puff Air Derby, that the "99's" was born. I had seen Amelia in California at the start of the Derby, along with a number of others who were to be charter members, and we had made plans to get together in New York as soon as possible to complete the organizational preliminaries.

In October I had a telephone call from one of the girls in the Curtiss Wright organization, saying that a group of women in the company were thinking of forming a women's flying club, and what did I think of the idea. I told her that Amelia and I had been working out plans for such an organization for the last two years, and suggested that we all meet to discuss possibilities.

At that time Curtiss Wright had a women's department that included: Neva Paris, Frances Harrell (Margalis), Margery Brown, Fay Gillis, Betty Huyler (Gillies), Opal Kunz and Clara Trenckman (Studer). All except Clara were pilots.

Betty Huyler, Clara Trenckman and I met for lunch a few days later and agreed it was high time the long-discussed group got going. Soon afterward a pre-organization meeting was held at the home of Opal Kunz. This time Amelia was present, but a previous commitment kept me from attending. It was agreed that a letter be sent out to all licensed women flyers asking them whether they wished to join a national women pilots' organization, and inviting them to attend an organization meeting at Curtiss Airport, Valley Stream, Long Island. The letter was signed by Neva Paris, Frances Harrell, Margery Brown and Fay Gillis.

At that time the licensed women flyers in the United States numbered just one hundred and ten. The only existing organization for women pilots was the Skylarks, made up of women who flew in the first all-women's air derby; but this was not a national organization and was limited in scope.

Twenty-six women from six states turned up at Curtiss Airport on November 2, 1929, for the organizational meeting. Thirty-one others had sent in their approval of forming such a group by mail, telegraph and telephone. Neva Paris presided at the meeting, Fay Gillis acted as secretary and Wilma L. Walsh was appointed to act as treasurer. It was decided that the organization should be kept as informal as possible, with a governing committee composed of pilots from different sections of the country.

One of the chief subjects of debate at that first meeting was: "What shall we call ourselves?" Some of the suggestions, recorded in the scrawled notes of the meeting, were: Lady Birds, Angel's Club, Gadflies, Homing Pigeons, Lady Buzzards, Sky Scrapers, Cloud Chasers, Moon Calves, Spinners, Bird Women, Licensed Women Flyers, Air Dames, Queens High, Breezy Birds and Climbing Vines. None of these seemed quite to fill the bill. It was Amelia Earhart who suggested that it might be a good idea to choose a number rather than a name—the number of charter members. This motion met with unanimous approval.

Several women flyers had been licensed since the announcement of the meeting went out, and addresses had been lacking for others, so a committee of two—Amelia and Neva Paris—was appointed to send a new letter to all then licensed women pilots inviting them to charter membership. The total of acceptances, plus the original twenty-six at the first meeting, would be the name of the organization.

At the next meeting on December 14, held at the home of Opal Kunz, eighty-six names were announced. This number was increased to ninety-nine when a number of letters bearing a much earlier postmark arrived with acceptances, having been held up in the mails.

So was born the Ninety-Nines, a group that has attained worldwide fame, has become international in membership and is still the top organization of women pilots.

At first we operated informally, without a full set of officers. The original organization provides for a national secretary, a national treasurer and a board of governors representing eight geographical sections. Louise Thaden was appointed to hold temporary office as national secretary until permanent officers were elected.

The first permanent president of the "99's" was Amelia Earhart, elected at the national meeting in Cleveland in 1931, at the time of the National Air Races. She held office for two years, and was a constant inspiration to the members. At that same meeting, I was appointed chairman of the Constitution Committee. In 1938, the year after Amelia's loss on her world flight, I had the sad task of serving as chairman of a committee to decide on a memorial for our first president. We established the Amelia Earhart Scholarship Fund for Advanced Flight Training which still continues to assist one deserving pilot a year.

National meetings were held annually during the National

Air Races, at which time nominations were made for new officers. During the course of "99" history, I headed a good many executive and program committees, but the necessity of earning a living left little time for wider service.

Soon after its organization, the club started publishing the first magazine devoted exclusively to women pilots, "The 99er." Directed at its inception by Amelia, it continued for some years under the editorship of Clara Trenckman, who also published the Curtiss Wright "News Letter." Published monthly, the magazine constituted a strong bond among women flyers, listing the activities and achievements of women in aviation and reporting flying events in the various sections of the country.

The goal of The Ninety-Nines, Inc., is and always has been to benefit women in aviation in every way possible. Some sections established funds to aid members to keep up their flying. Others established trophies for outstanding achievements among women flyers. One raised money to buy a club plane for the use of members. Today the All-Women's Transcontinental Air Race is one of its chief national projects.

Many newspaper articles around that time rather ghoulishly discussed the supposed rivalry between Amelia and me. I have no hesitation in stating that they were exaggerated or slanted or untrue. Both of us were intent on flying careers. Both of us went out after every record we could get. Both of us had strong, deep, active interests in humanitarian affairs. We remained good friends throughout all our competitions.

After her marriage to George Palmer Putnam, Amelia became a Rye neighbor, and as a result it was easy to visit each other on the spur of the moment. We were united by a common bond of interest. We spoke each other's language— and that was the language of pioneer women of the air.

I suppose, after Amelia's marriage to Putnam, I may have felt a few twinges of envy that she was able always to obtain the latest and finest planes, while I had to search for backers for any flight I undertook. But I know, also, that there was no bitterness in my envy. I liked and admired her, and I believe she felt the same way about me.

That Amelia always seemed to manage to beat me to the starting line in record flights that both of us were planning was simply the fall of the cards. I felt then, and I feel now that the achievements of any flyer, man or woman, advance the science and the understanding of aviation, and so are of eventual benefit to all civilization.

Both Amelia and I had crackups and successes. We both won a lot and lost a lot. But we were privileged to have places in the starting lineup of our country's women flyers, and each of us fulfilled her destiny as she saw it.

If Amelia could be here today I am sure that she would join me in saying that the joy is in the race itself, not alone in the victory—and that once you have experienced the exaltation of space and speed in flight, no matter who wins, it's *mostly* velvet.

7

OPEN THROTTLE

Colonel Clarence Chamberlin, first pilot to fly from New York to Germany, strolled casually into my life in the spring of 1930—and became the second great mentor of my flying career. The first, of course, was swashbuckling Harry Rogers, who taught me to fly. The lanky, dry-spoken Chamberlin was as different from Rogers as night from day. Easygoing and almost diffident in manner, he regarded life quizzically and greeted almost any situation with a disarming grin.

I was still working for Aviation Country Clubs and helping Jack Reaves launch aviation's first magazine devoted exclusively to private flying, *The Sportsman Pilot,* when Chamberlin called me up.

"I've just built what I consider is a very efficient airplane," he drawled. "It's an eight-place cabin monoplane, but so easy to fly that I'd like the public to know even you can handle her."

Well! That was not a very flattering way to present an offer, I thought, but then I heard Chamberlin's contagious chuckle over the phone, and I decided to listen.

"I've thought up a good stunt," he continued. "We'll take up a parachute jumper, and when he steps overboard you'll cut the throttle and show that the plane will descend more slowly than a man can float down by parachute."

It sounded like fun, as well as a chance to fly a new plane, so I agreed. The experiment was a success, doubly so because our jumper decided to play a trick on us by opening *two* parachutes. But I was able to hold the Chamberlin Crescent with throttle closed to a slower glide, so that we were still airborne after he had landed.

Chamberlin was pleased, and asked me to cooperate on another "first." This was a midnight flight to Chicago, to make the first air delivery of New York newspapers to that city. Accompanying us was Captain James Fitzmaurice, Irish trans-Atlantic pilot who was one of the crew aboard the first plane to make a westward air crossing of the Atlantic. Although he made no comment at the time, Chamberlin later released the following statement about our flight which was published the next day in the *N. Y. Evening Post*.

"She has an uncanny feeling for drift and held her course much more accurately, for instance, than I do. We started out at night for Cleveland. After she had flown for half an hour I saw she was so good that I went to sleep and didn't wake up until we had arrived. At any minute she could tell exactly where we were. She not only is a fine pilot, but has the rare gift of common sense, the kind of horse sense that means everything in an emergency."

This was the first and, as far as I can remember, one of the very few words of praise Chamberlin ever uttered about my flying. But from then on we regarded each other with mutual respect. More and more frequently I sought his advice, and finally worked up enough courage to tell him about my longstanding ambition to make a round-the-world flight. Chamberlin promptly quashed the idea. "That flight," he said, "would be much more dangerous than a solo Atlantic flight." Even if I carried a crew, he pointed out, I would be sure to run into trouble with a multi-engine plane, which he felt still left much to be desired. "Why not a solo hop?" he added.

The suggestion of a solo trans-Atlantic flight intrigued me, but I asked:

"What about ice and blind flying?"

"Fly high like I did," he replied, "and you won't have either problem."

So was sown the germ of an idea which was to lead me through many new adventures, the excitement of new highs and the heartbreak of record lows. From time to time we discussed the possibilities. Chamberlin was always optimistic, and I gained confidence. I felt that speed would be an essential factor in the success of such a flight, since it would cut down the hours of endurance necessary for both engine and pilot. We considered various types of fast planes with long cruising range and agreed finally that a Lockheed Vega was the best on the market at that time.

As always, I was driven by a compulsion to make my flying career pay off before too long in a large hunk of solid cash for the benefit of my family. Thus could I square things with my conscience, which kept twinging with guilt complexes because I was following a life which gave me such keen joy, when perhaps I should be settling down either to some solid and more lucrative business, or to a service dedicated to humanitarian needs. An Atlantic solo flight might, I dreamed, resolve my dilemma.

Sometime before this I had maneuvered Aunty into taking a long flight as I had promised I would. Harry Rogers had suggested that I pilot one of his Seagulls back North in the perennial migration of his hydro-airplanes between Miami and Long Island Sound. Aunty was persuaded to accompany me, more in the self-sacrificing role of chaperon than for pleasure. She looked distrustfully at the big cream and mahogany flying boat as I helped her into the cockpit, and settled into her seat with a grim do-or-die attitude. It was a sparkling blue and gold morning, and we taxied across the harbor slowly.

"Just like a boat ride," remarked Aunty.

Then, after we were in open water, and rocking the hull onto the step in order to release the water suction and form an air cushion, we took off in a shower of foam and soon were cruising above the Florida coastline. I looked at Aunty and saw that her eyes were bright and her cheeks pink with excitement. She peered at the blue water and the toy boats far below, took a deep breath and called out, over the motor's roar:

"I don't know what keeps this thing up, but whatever it is, I like it!"

After that experience, it was easier for her to understand my obsession with flying and when I began to talk about a flight that might replenish the family coffers, she listened with some concern, but also with sympathy and interest. Once she said, positively:

"If thee thinks thee can do it, *then try*."

Also, she understood the moments of loneliness which usually coincided with the arrival of a letter from Spain. Don had been gone nearly a year and gave no hint of when he might return. . . .

Meanwhile, Chamberlin had suggested that I give up my work with Aviation Country Clubs, which appeared stalemated by the stock market crash, and assist him in the sales department of the Crescent Aircraft Company. I would receive a regular salary and obtain further experience in handling a large airplane besides.

This seemed a sound plan, and I accepted gratefully. So began a new phase of my airborne career, that was to lead me eventually into constant competitive flying and record attempts.

My new job offered me frequent opportunities for flights, learning more and more about heavy airplanes. On one occasion I made a flight to Washington, carrying as passengers Otto Merkel, managing director of Lufthansa, German Airlines, Mrs. Chamberlin, Earl Dunlap, engineer, and Zeth Hunter, mechanic. There I had the novel experience of demonstrating the plane to the world famous naval Commander,

Jack Powers, and other officers for possible government purchase.

When a plane was sold, I occasionally was called upon to ferry it out to its new owner. One such flight was to Dennison, Iowa, a trip which gave me an opportunity for several detours to visit friends enroute and also to fly the plane in a local race. When he heard of this meandering course, Chamberlin was at first annoyed, but his native good humor came to my rescue, and I escaped with an amused reprimand.

After finally depositing the plane with its owners, I went on to Chicago to enter the Mrs. Robert R. McCormick Trophy maximum speed race for women. Since I was so near, I figured, this was too good a chance to miss. Matty Laird, manufacturer of fast planes, generously agreed to let me fly his new racing Laird, powered by a Chevrolair motor and clocked around two hundred miles per hour. In those days, that was a record speed for a small plane. It seemed even faster to me, after piloting a 90 m.p.h. Bird and a 125 m.p.h. Crescent.

Apparently Matty got cold feet just before the race started, for he came dashing over as I was climbing into the plane, grabbed a bystander and said:

"Give me a dollar. I'm selling you the plane before a witness, in case you get killed during the race. I don't want any comeback from your family."

Although I had had no time to get the "feel" of this plane, and had had no experience with such fast planes, I wound it around the course and made what I was told was a perfect landing, without the motor quitting, which I later learned it had done on all previous test hops. I did not fly a good race, partly because I was unfamiliar with the plane and partly through lack of practice in making pylon turns. Actually, I almost met disaster at one of the pylons, when one of the other girls in the race cut in too close. The only way I could avert a collision which would have meant death for us both was to jerk the control stick back in a vertical turn, thereby fouling the pylon. The other pilot either had not seen me, or else misjudged her relative position, because naturally if she had hit me it would have been curtains for her as well as for me.

That near-tragedy was enough. I decided closed-course races were not for me. This is one type of air race in which the cards seem stacked against you, for no matter how skillful a pilot you may be, you never can tell, in a close, civilian race in which there always may be amateurs, what other contestants are going to do. This has been demonstrated several times in men's races, when one plane has cut off another's tail.

Though I flunked the pylon race, I placed first each day in spot landing contests during the same series. Flying the Fledgling in and out of small fields on the forty-six state sportsman pilot tour had been invaluable experience for short and varied landings.

In the late summer of this same year, 1930, I was invited by American Airlines to be one of the passengers on the inaugural flight of their coast-to-coast "through" service. Up to that time transcontinental air passengers always had had to do their night traveling by train, picking up a plane again the next morning. Now it was to be possible to fly all the way.

The flight was scheduled to start from Atlanta, but since I couldn't make train connections in time, I left Newark Airport at dawn in a Ford tri-motor piloted by Earl Ward. Thus, inadvertently I became the first woman passenger to make a "through" flight from New York to Los Angeles.

The importance of that flight for me, however, was a half-hour stopover in Cincinnati, which allowed just time enough to discuss new flight plans with Powel Crosley, president of the Crosley Radio Corporation and owner of several airplanes. He was at the field when we landed in Cincinnati and described in glowing terms his new Lockheed Vega plane, "The New Cincinnati." I suggested that it might be a good idea if I used the plane to try for new transcontinental altitude and speed records as publicity for the Crosley company. Crosley seemed interested, and we parted with plans for further discussions.

It took another two weeks after my return from the west coast to finish selling Crosley on the idea, and to arrange for slight changes in the plane. I won't soon forget my first flight in that beautiful, speedy ship, out of Crosley's own small private field, which was surrounded by telephone wires. Since the plane had a single cockpit, permitting no co-pilot to go along for the usual check flight, I had my hands full manipulating all kinds of new and unfamiliar gadgets. One of these was a stabilizer, which had to be pumped rapidly to readjust the center of gravity just before a landing. Trying to keep my left hand on the throttle while working the pump and managing the control stick with the right, switching my eyes from the complicated instrument panel to the shortening distance of the telephone wires bounding the field was like trying to pat your head and rub your stomach at the same time.

Also the engine sounded so powerful that it took me quite a few flights before I felt confident that it would not pull itself right out of the plane.

I decided to try first for an intercity speed record between Cincinnati and New York. I started out one beautiful clear morning, after checking the New York weather reports with Chamberlin by telephone and ascertaining that conditions were ideal there. The sensation of power and speed was wonderful as the Vega roared through the sky with ceiling and visibility unlimited. Everything was fine and I knew I was making record speed until I reached the Ohio River and the first range of the Alleghenies. There, following the river, was a solid bank of fog about five thousand feet high. I flew above it for about ten minutes, hoping to find a break, but there was no such luck. I felt it would be stupid to continue flying "over the top" without radio, since I might hit a mountain peak or overshoot New York without knowing it. So I circled back and decided I would try to get through underneath the ceiling.

As I passed over the first two ridges, I had a comfortable ceiling, but then the clouds dropped and I had to follow winding valleys north and south in order to see where I was going. The further I went the worse the weather became, and I had turned in so many directions that I had very little idea where I was. Suddenly I found myself bottled up in a small valley with no means of exit even from the rear. The clouds were closing in so fast that I realized I must land— but quick.

There is no worse feeling for a pilot flying over land than being forced down in the mountains, with quickly lowering and swirling gray blankets of fog making visibility almost nil. Added to this was the realization I had only had two previous practice flights in a fast landing plane.

Suddenly the flank of a mountain materialized dead ahead, and in a cold sweat I kicked the ship into a vertical turn, praying that a wingtip would not catch a cliff or a tree, or that I wouldn't crash into a mountain on the other side. Having made the hairpin turn without a stall, I could only try to get down as fast as possible, and hope that I would be in one piece. As I banked, one wingtip almost touched the ground, and the other was invisible in the thick fog above.

Somehow I managed to get the wheels down and the Lockheed went bumping over a rocky field, crashed through a wire fence and came to rest with its nose buried in the ground, its tail in the air. But I was safe, the plane did not catch fire, and when I was able to clamber shakily out and reconnoiter I found that the only damage seemed to be a bent propeller.

This was a fine way, I told myself bitterly, to start out to win fame and glory for myself and the Crosley company. What would Powel Crosley think of me? How could I tell him I had banged up his beautiful new plane on the very first hop? How would he ever be willing to trust me with it again?

I plodded across the field toward a tiny settlement I had glimpsed briefly through the curtains of fog on my way down. It consisted of a general store and half a dozen ramshackle houses. But at least the store had a telephone—the kind you crank, fastened to the wall. By the time I had succeeded in putting a call through to Pittsburgh and had persuaded a mechanic to come out and get me and the bent propeller, the entire population of the village, numbering about two dozen, had gathered open-mouthed to stare at this strange, tousle-headed creature who had fallen out of the sky to disturb the peace of their remote valley.

Suddenly I had a wonderful thought. I remembered that my friend, Louise Thaden, was living in Pittsburgh with her husband, and I put in a call to her.

"Where are you?" came the unsurprised voice of Louise. "I'll come and get you."

It seems that pilot friends frequently found the Thaden home a handy place to wait out a storm over the Alleghenies, and Louise took the most unexpected arrival in stride.

"Don't bother, the mechanic will drive me out," I replied, and a day later I was installed before a crackling fire in the Thaden living room, relating my misadventures. The next morning I faced the unwelcome task of returning to the mountain settlement and my crippled plane.

Louise, who always was too big-hearted for her own good, offered to drive me out and stay with me until the Lockheed was repaired. I'm sure she regretted it when, after considerable difficulty, we located the tiny village. The general store, which dispensed groceries, drugs, dry goods, hardware and the United States mail, also had the only available sleeping accommodations—a spare room adjoining the family's own living quarters over the store.

The storekeeper's wife chatted volubly as she led us upstairs to a barren cubicle with splintery wood floor, no rugs, a cracked pitcher and bowl, an ornate iron bed with a sagging mattress and no curtains or shades.

This, our hostess told us, had been Grandma's room. It was fortunate for us, she went on, that Grandma had passed away last week or we would have had to sleep on the floor in a corner of the store. With the pride of a conductor of a sightseeing tour, she pointed to the unwelcoming bed.

"Yes ma'am," she proclaimed, "that there's the very bed poor Grandma suffered and died on!"

When our landlady had departed, Louise and I with one accord tiptoed over to the bed and lifted the covers. There was no question that the sheets had been slept on for some time since their last laundering. Had it been by the late lamented Grandma? We shivered in unison, hastily replaced the quilts and got out into the open air as fast as possible.

We ate supper with the family, such as it was. We didn't get much, since we had not been warned of the technique of outreaching the others at the table. Afterward the lady of the house handed us a flashlight and said:

"It's out back. Take the left-hand path and go around back of the woodshed. And you better bundle up and put your rubbers on."

Our outdoor excursion completed, we climbed to the damp room that was to be ours for the night. We decided unanimously not to occupy Grandma's sheets, and so lay down on top of the covers, wrapped in coats and sweaters and huddled together for warmth. After trying fruitlessly to dodge the lumps in the mattress, we decided that undoubtedly it was the bed that had finished off Grandma.

The next morning I took Louise out to the rocky little field where the Lockheed sat disconsolately. She looked over the terrain dubiously and remarked:

"You'll never get her out of here."

"I got her in, and I'll have to get her out," I retorted.

After long argument and a crossing of his palm with

silver, I finally persuaded the farmer who owned the pasture to take down a section of fence separating it from the adjoining narrow field. Several little boys, thrilled at being allowed near a real airplane, eagerly helped roll some of the largest boulders to the sides of the field. Then we paced off the pasture and finally decided on the least unlikely path for a runway, reasonably clear of stumps and boulders. Louise pointed out a dead tree near the end of the field, and advised me to shut off the throttle and stand on the brakes if the wheels were not off the ground by the time my wingtips passed it.

Shortly after noon the mechanic returned with the repaired propeller. It took only a short while to screw and bolt it on. But farmers and their wives and children crowded around the plane. Even the schoolteacher had declared a half-holiday in honor of the impending takeoff, so that the children need not miss the excitement. Louise and I were worn out answering questions. The standard opening remark of the onlookers was:

"Ain't never seen one of these hyar things clost up afore. They buzz around up thar right smart, but this is the fust one ever druv in hyar."

With the propeller installed and the pasture reasonably cleared of the largest impediments, I was faced with the moment I had been trying not to think about all day. It was up to me to get this thing out of here.

Louise describes the takeoff in her delightful book, "High, Wide and Frightened":*

"The engine sputtered and missed fire when Ruth ran it up. After playing with it for several minutes she shut it off, climbing through the hatch out of the cockpit.

" 'She's turning 200 r.p.m.'s short on both magnetos and 600 shy on the left mag,' she told me.

" 'Probably fouled plugs,' the mechanic surmised. But to

* From "High, Wide and Frightened," by Louise Thaden, The Stackpole Company, Harrisburg, Pa.

get to the nine rear spark plugs meant virtually dismantling half the airplane, so Ruth decided against it.

" 'Maybe you can burn them off,' I suggested to Ruth.

" 'You get in,' she said, 'and see what you can do with it.'

"But I had no better luck.

" 'I wouldn't attempt taking off with the engine like this!' I squalled down to her through the open cockpit window, propeller blast making my eyes water. 'You'll need everything it's got—and if it should quit, or rev down on takeoff, you'll pile up sure. I'm not even certain you can climb fast enough to clear the ridge ahead with the engine turning the way it is.'

" 'Get down and I'll run it up again,' was her only answer.

"I don't know how nervous Ruth was, but I've never been more choked up with anxiety.

" 'It doesn't look good to me,' I was telling the mechanic when Ruth throttled the engine and leaned out the small window.

" 'I think I'll try it,' she called.

" 'Okay,' I answered. 'It's your neck and your airplane, but if it were me, I wouldn't risk it.'

" 'I think I can make it. Thanks for bringing me down.'

" 'I enjoyed it,' I said, trying to grin. 'Good luck. But wait until I get some of these fellows, we'll give you a push to give you a faster start.'

" 'Now when I yell,' I instructed them, 'you fellows stop pushing and run like the devil so the tail surfaces won't hit you as they go by. If you can't get out of the way, dive for the ground and lay there.'

"As the Lockheed weaved down the field, I swallowed hard several times, and forgot to breathe.

" 'She's not going to make it!' I yelled to no one in particular. But she did, and I watched, still trembling until the plane was a tiny black speck in the sky."

When I finally made it back to Roosevelt Field, I was greeted by a bunch of newspaper reporters and Colonel Chamberlin. The reporters kidded me about my forced landing, and Chamberlin announced that the weather was just right for the start of an east-to-west transcontinental trip—tomorrow.

I hadn't bargained for such a fast schedule as this, but Chamberlin pointed out that it would be a good idea to take advantage of good weather before winter set in. So I put aside my plans for a few days of rest and some recreation, and again made hurried preparations for the flight. We spent the rest of the afternoon with mechanics making last-minute adjustments.

One of these mechanics was the man later to be known as "Wrong Way Corrigan," who flew to Ireland after announcing that he was bound for Los Angeles. Several years later, just before his famous "wrong-way" flight, I was chatting with him beside the plane in which he had made a twenty-nine hour flight from the west coast to New York. Believing him to be a young amateur flyer, I cautioned him about his plans for a return flight to Los Angeles, urging him to take along my parachute.

"You know," Corrigan said, "I worked on that Lockheed of yours the morning you took off for your transcontinental hop in the fall of 1930."

"Shades of yesterday!" I cried. "Are you the one I've always wanted to get my hands on, who greased my throttle so heavily it creeped back right after my takeoff? I was so strapped for money I didn't dare dump nearly four hundred precious gallons of gas, so I landed again at Roosevelt at ninety-five miles an hour!"

"I remember that landing well," grinned Corrigan—"how you slipped over the wires to get in the nearest edge of the field, and even then had so much momentum from your overload you had to ground loop at the other end of the runway. But, honest, I only assisted one of the other mechanics."

That first takeoff on the morning of November 24th after my return from the adventures in the Alleghenies occurred as related by Corrigan. I had barely gained altitude when the throttle slipped and I realized I would have to go right back and try to make a landing. This was another of the many close shaves that have marked my aeronautical records, but even with the ground loop, I managed to get out of this one without damaging either myself or the plane.

I took off again a few hours later and fought a thirty-mile head wind as far as Columbus, where I had to land to get a short-circuit repaired. The next morning brought the first blizzard of the winter, forcing another day's stopover. The second day the wind still was blowing like fury, but I decided to push on, even though only my time in the air was being counted toward the record, as Mr. Crosley expected me back within a fixed period. I had rough flying, with snow and icing conditions, just out of St. Louis, but passed safely through it and continued to Wichita. The next day I made poor time to Amarillo, Texas, and waited another day before going on to Albuquerque. Storms and head winds were slowing down my record attempt.

I finally landed at Burbank Airport on December 1, 1930, seven days after my start from New York. But the elapsed flying time, as clocked by officials, was only sixteen hours, fifty-nine minutes and thirty seconds, which beat by eight hours the time of Chubby Miller, the Australian girl flyer, who had been handicapped by a slower plane.

After a week's rest, I left Los Angeles on the return flight, to try for the west-to-east transcontinental record. This one made a much better showing, although the weather was bad. But I was able to fly high now, with the wind on my tail.

Weather reports at that time still were not as accurate as they are now. I started out with unlimited ceiling and visibility. Then I began to glide through sun-walled chasms of cumulus clouds, flanked by golden massed castles of myriad sculptured designs. How majestic is nature's aerial architecture, I reflected in awe. But soon the yellows faded into white and the density as well as the contours of the clouds changed, so that far to the right I could see dark-streaked nimbus clouds with their low, rolling masses denoting a low-pressure area in which both snow and ice had been reported.

By the time I had reached Sante Fe, I had had to climb to twenty thousand feet to stay above the solid cloud mass. Then an air bubble appeared in my aperiodic compass, deflecting the needle; the earth-indicator compass already had quit, so I had to depend on the magnetic compass, which I knew had a twenty-degree deviation at certain points.

I stayed at the high altitude for about half an hour, too busy navigating, switching gas tanks, adjusting the mixture and so on, necessary at high altitude and low temperatures, to bother much about oxygen. I did not realize it was growing increasingly difficult to think clearly or exert the physical strength needed to pump the alemite gun which sprayed grease into the rocker arms.

At times it looked as though the clouds licking at my wheels would envelop the whole ship and bring it down with ice, since I was already at the maximum ceiling for the load of gas I was carrying.

For two hours I flew like this, barely clearing the thick sea of clouds, with visions of a parachute jump on some lonely, rocky mountain. Since I was flying a great circle course far off the beaten track, I would have had little hope of rescue if the plane had been forced down. Then at last the clouds began to break, I had my first glimpse of the ground over Raton Pass, and clear weather over Oklahoma.

I landed at Wichita seven hours and one minute after the Los Angeles takeoff, amazing airport officials who were expecting a "woman's record"; they told me I was only one hour behind Frank Hawks' time on his three-stop record flight from Los Angeles to New York.

I took off before dawn the next morning, to beat the storm moving into Wichita, and at once got into two hours of as nasty flying as I have ever experienced. I was forced down to three hundred feet by low-lying clouds and fog, flying, contrary to the manufacturer's advice, with a wide-open motor, making over two hundred miles an hour, and it was difficult to check landmarks, because of the poor visibility. I clamped down on a wad of chewing gum and roared on, putting my trust in Providence and my sense of direction. Then the windshield wiper broke and rain streamed in torrents across the glass, reducing visibility to almost nil. I managed to outrun the storm before reaching St. Louis, and just as clear skies opened up I had a sudden reaction of nausea and dizziness. The strain of yesterday's long drag at twenty thousand feet plus the tension of today's high-speed hedge hopping was catching up with me.

"Come on, you never have passed out," I rebuked myself. "Pull yourself together and fly right!"

I prayed, I thought of Aunty, I chewed more gum and pinched myself for about a half hour before I began to get back to normal. Across Ohio and the mountains of Pennsylvania the towns whisked by so fast that I couldn't believe my computed ground speed, which showed nearly three hundred miles an hour.

By now I was flying at fifteen thousand feet, near the average person's limit without oxygen, and was feeling very gay, with a strong tail wind pushing the plane along.

I sang, I whistled, I thought of Don, somewhere in Spain, but instead of feeling sad about our separation I was filled with optimism, and I pictured a gala homecoming to Aunty and the rest of the family in Rye as I streaked over the last lap, landing at Roosevelt Field six hours and twenty minutes after leaving Wichita. This made a total flying time from Los Angeles of thirteen hours, twenty-one minutes. I had beaten Frank Hawks' time between Wichita and New York, though not his coast-to-coast record of twelve hours, twenty-five minutes.

As I climbed stiffly out of the plane after taxiing up to the hangar at Roosevelt Field, I grinned happily at Mother, Aunty, Chamberlin and the officials, and was driven home jubilant but so tired I was barely able to reach a bed to collapse into. They had to wake me up to show me the headlines in the next morning's papers:

RUTH NICHOLS SPANS NATION; BEATS TIME OF LINDBERGH

8

CAVU

Ceiling and visibility were unlimited for me at the start of 1931, destined to be the most eventful year of my life up to then. Everything, as flyers say, was CAVU.

Colonel Chamberlin was giving me technical assistance and guidance in the step-by-step development of a flying program which would lead with increasing build-up for the first woman's takeoff on a solo Atlantic hop. My transcontinental record flight in December of 1930 had been the first of a carefully planned series of other records which were to follow, all forming a build-up for the big Atlantic try.

We planned a preparatory program punctuated by successive women's world's records, which not only would give me excellent experience in handling the Lockheed Vega under all conditions, but also would provide the publicity necessary for obtaining backing for the Atlantic flight. We agreed that the Lockheed would be the ideal plane in which to make the ocean try, after some adjustments had been made, and we were counting on being able to talk Crosley into giving me permission to use it for this ambitious venture.

It was a lucky day for me, I realized, when I first met Clarence Chamberlin. Seldom, if ever, have I known any pilot so prolific in ideas, enthusiasm, experience and know-how. He had that superb flying "feel" with which great pilots are born, plus a practical engineering background and the sort of personality that kept everyone around him keyed up to a high pitch of enthusiasm. There were plenty of laughs interspersed with the serious work of plotting my future course.

Clarence initiated some completely original, excellent ideas for redesigning certain features of the Lockheed to which I added several of my own, which I had been developing for some time. At times we agreed, other times there were stormy battles over a feature that I insisted must go into the plane but which he felt was impractical. Often he won, but there were a few points which I felt must go through, and on these I stood my ground.

We decided to prepare the plane first for a record altitude flight, and this meant stripping it of every possible pound of weight not vital to its operation—all extra seats, upholstery, door handles and even the back-rest behind the pilot's cockpit. In addition Chamberlin's draftsmen had designed a new, light-weight and streamlined type of landing gear which we were trying out on the Lockheed. Today I shudder to recall that the gear had a safety factor of only 3:1—that is, if the plane landed heavily with a weight equal to three times its own, the gear would collapse. Since then standard government regulations have required a landing gear safety factor nearly twice that ratio—but at that time we knew that certain serious chances had to be taken. We were limited both as to money and time, since in those days there were only two optimum months in the year to fly the North Atlantic. Therefore certain chances *had* to be taken. When the gear had proved its advantage of added speed and when we knew it could carry the heavy load if handled gently, that was enough for us.

Our program for high standards in this flight did not stop with the plane—it extended also to my physical condition. I must be in top form if I were to stand up under the rigors of the next few months. And so I started watching my diet— a task I found harder than bucking the assorted problems of

International News Photos

Welcoming crowd at Floyd Bennett Airport greeting Ruth Nichols during preparation for a record flight. Spring, 1931.

a transcontinental flight; I have always been addicted to hot fudge sundaes.

In addition I instituted a program of early bedtimes, daily setting-up exercises and a regular schedule of sports, such as squash, handball and horseback riding. On weekends I took off whenever possible for some place where I could ride or ski and keep my muscles toned up. One weekend, I remember, was spent in the snows of the New Jersey hills, where airplanes and dog teams met only a hundred miles from New York City.

These were days of heady excitement and high joy, suddenly climaxed by Don's unexpected return from Spain. During the long months of his absence he had written regularly, always renewing his protestations of devotion—but letters, though they may be comforting, are not likely to keep a girl happy for long. One evening as I was leaving the Crescent Aircraft hangar at Jersey City where I had been tinkering with the Lockheed, Don came dashing up in a taxi just as I started to get into my Stutz coupé.

In greasy coveralls and cap, with a smudged face, I am sure I did not look like any man's dream of romance—but Don swept me into his arms nevertheless, and somehow managed to make me feel as fragile and feminine as if I were attired in a perfumed cloud of white tulle. He didn't say, "You look terrible, Toots!" like an American beau. Instead he lied gallantly: "You are more beautiful than ever!"

After I hastily repaired my appearance as best I could, we drove for hours through the New Jersey hills, across Bear Mountain Bridge and eventually back to Rye, filling in for each other the long span of our separation, in the immemorial fashion of lovers, recounting the pattern of events since last we met.

As I look back, I see that most of the accounting of events of the past months was done by me, and that Don's reference to his stay in Spain was very brief indeed. The press of family affairs had kept him there until now, he said. But the gaps in his narrative went unnoticed. The important thing was that he was back, we were together again—my handsome, impetuous Don Juan. And most wonderful of all, my heart glowed at the pictures he painted of how many children we would have, where we would live and travel together when our present professional commitments were completed.

There were many test hops in the days that followed, to try out the new landing gear and to familiarize myself with the plane's new flying characteristics and gadgets. Landings with the thin gear had to be pinpoint-perfect, and I had to bring the plane down on the small Jersey City field as if I were landing it on eggshells. The little improvised airport was only a thousand feet in one direction and little more in the other, with, of course, the usual obstacles of telephone wires and tall buildings on three sides and the bay on the fourth. Since we had removed all passenger seats in preparation for the altitude flight, Don could not accompany me on these hops, but frequently he was waiting anxiously on the field as I landed, congratulating me on the flight or warning me to be careful and please not to break my precious neck. This sort of thing, as any woman knows, is heady wine.

Day by day more equipment was stripped from the plane, to lighten its four thousand pound weight as much as possible.

Finally, on March 6, 1931, the airplane was ready, the weather was passable and barograph, paper forms and officials were on hand. The newspapers had been notified and one of them, much to the amusement of some of my cynical friends, carried the headline, "RUTH NICHOLS TURNS ANGEL TODAY." I had no wish to become an angel just yet—life was too much fun. There was nothing angelic about my appearance when I was finally ready for the flight. To prepare for the sub-zero temperatures I would encounter at high altitudes, I wore long underwear and four sweaters, ranging in hue from rose through lavender to blue. On top of all this conglomeration went a reindeer flying suit, lent me for the occasion—picturesque but, as I was to learn, not very warm. Finishing touches were a pair of gaily beaded reindeer boots worn over two pairs of skating socks, mittens to match, a fur-lined helmet, a plaid wool scarf and finally a parachute.

Before the flight could get started I had to pose for a seemingly endless series of news pictures. Every pilot hates this procedure before a record try; some are even so superstitious that they refuse to permit photographs before a hazardous flight. But knowing the publicity would be valuable for my future plans, I naturally complied with the photographers' requests.

The day was bright, windy and bitterly cold, even on the ground. One friend present for the takeoff, stamping his feet for nearly three hours at the airport, vowed it was only fourteen degrees above zero. Weather maps showed the clockwise circulation of an approaching high-pressure area.

At last the photographers were satisfied, I had obeyed the final request for "just one more," last-minute instructions and good-luck tokens had been received, and I was ready for the long-anticipated takeoff.

When I gave the 600 horsepower engine full gun, it was 12:31 p.m. I pushed the throttle beyond the safety notch for normal takeoffs and felt the bite of a special ten-foot-six propeller we had just installed. The plane practically leaped off the ground, jumping off in the astounding space of 92 feet. The swift acceleration of speed and altitude felt, as one pilot put it, like "a kick in the pants."

In one minute flat the plane had attained an altitude of 2200 feet, as rapid a rate of climb as could be made by any of the small military pursuit planes of the day, and they were built to carry only a pilot and no heavy load. And the little pursuit planes of 1931 did not have the weight of this seven-place Lockheed.

I made one turn over New York City and then headed due

west, knowing that since the winds were blowing at sea level from that direction, they would be much stronger when I gained altitude. All winds north of east seem to change in a counterclockwise direction, the higher you go up to a certain point. All winds which are south of east at the surface veer clockwise. After you go above fifteen thousand feet, winds are usually from the west, because of the rotation of the earth. If, therefore, surface winds are blowing from the west to start with, the wind remains from that direction but increases its velocity the higher you fly.

I had crossed Newark Bay and headed over Elizabeth and the Orange mountains of New Jersey, a distance of about fifty miles, when my altimeter registered ten thousand feet. I was amazed to find that I appeared to be standing still, as far as ground speed was concerned. Although the plane was capable of doing two hundred miles per hour in level flight, and I had the throttle wide open, it seemed to be making no headway. However, she was still climbing, so I didn't worry about where we were going—except up. I realized we must be bucking extremely strong headwinds, and concentrated on the problem of the moment, which was to gain maximum altitude. Soon we passed through a layer of cumulus clouds which blotted out most of the landmarks.

From then on the Vega climbed steadily. I turned on a heater which had been installed by faithful, competent Bill Hartig, foreman of the Crescent Aircraft Company, and was fairly comfortable in all my layers of clothing until we reached about twenty thousand feet. I was too busy to think much about the cold, anyway, since there were many dials to watch and valves to adjust with varying altitudes, in addition to keeping an eye on the compass and the stubborn movement of the altimeter.

After twenty thousand feet I had turned on the oxygen, feeling no need for it previously. Today we know oxygen should be turned on at lower altitudes. My method of taking the oxygen was simple—I merely put the tube in my mouth.

I noted it seemed uncommonly cold and glanced at the thermometer fastened to the wing, in which the steel oxygen flask also was strapped; it was a common household thermometer, registering only down to forty-five degrees below zero, and it had hit bottom some time before. I recalled that Weather Bureau officials had told me I would find temperatures of sixty below at that altitude, and conceded they were right.

The powerful Wasp engine of the Lockheed roared smoothly, as I sat alone in a cold sparkling void of brilliant sun and blue sky, with a thick layer of white cotton clouds below. I was filled with exultation except for a passing regret that the cloud layer obscured the view, because if it had been clear at that height, I could have seen from Philadelphia to the tip end of Long Island. God was in His heaven and all was right with the world.

As the plane climbed steadily higher I became more and more conscious of the intense cold—especially in my tongue. I was sucking oxygen direct from the steel tank in the wing, where it did not have even the slight benefit of the cabin heater. I tried moving my tongue; it seemed to be a solid chunk of ice. I removed the tube from my mouth for a moment, and this brought some relief, but I knew this was dangerous business at such an altitude, for if I didn't maintain a steady flow of oxygen I might black out. Flyers know that you can lose consciousness very suddenly if you breathe in the rarefied air at high altitudes.

This, you must remember, was before the days of modern pressurized cabin planes, in which the oxygen content of the air is kept constantly stable no matter how high the plane flies. There was available at that time a mechanical valve which would release just the right combination of air and oxygen, but this equipment cost more than two thousand dollars, and I couldn't afford it.

I had to keep constantly alert in order to watch the dials

and adjust the valves, and I had to keep shifting the oxygen tube in and out of my mouth as I bent down or reached back to make some necessary adjustment. Soon I noted that my movements became slower and slower, and that the slightest exertion—even of bending forward to reach a pet-cock or turn a knob—made me giddy. My tongue apparently was frozen stiff, since it had lost all sense of feeling.

"Well," I thought irrelevantly, "it's a good thing I don't have to make a speech."

It was now thirty-five minutes since the takeoff, and three Pioneer altimeters, agreeing closely, registered twenty-eight thousand feet. The rate of climb now was falling rapidly, so that the big propeller and super-charged engine were able to pull the plane upward at only about a hundred and fifty feet per minute, in the rarefied air. I had gradually been adjusting the stabilizer for nose heaviness. I was hauling the stick back against my belt with both hands, but then the climb stopped completely and I couldn't for the life of me keep the plane's faltering nose up.

The plane was trembling at what seemed to be its peak, when as a last resort I turned on the oxygen tank connected with the carburetor. Instantly the engine speed picked up two hundred revolutions and the plane struggled laboriously higher and higher, foot by foot, until the altimeter indicators were quivering at 30,350 feet.

I felt a soaring sense of elation as I kept the four-thousand-pound plane literally hanging on the prop, pulling the stick back into my stomach with both hands and every ounce of strength I could muster. I guess I was somewhat light-headed from my erratic oxygen intake, my frozen tongue felt like a large ice cube, but what did I care? I was higher than any woman ever had flown before. I knew I had established a new record.

The sky above me had turned a darker blue, as it does at great heights. Pilots who since have climbed high into the stratosphere report that the sky becomes almost black even at midday, because of the lack of air particles from which the sun's light can reflect.

Suddenly the engine's staccato drone coughed apologetically, then quit cold. I was shocked, as my reserve of five gallons was not scheduled to be used except at the end of the homeward glide. Although I could have glided all the way down, I wanted the engine to stay with me, since I did not know how far from my home airport I might be, and if my altitude record was to be official, I had to land at the point of takeoff.

I fumbled frantically to turn on the five-gallon reserve, but before the engine could take hold the plane had dropped like a stone five thousand feet. My eardrums felt like bursting and my head was aching from effects of the change of pressure. I felt dizzy and the slightest movement required great effort. But instinct directed me to push the throttle open to what was at that altitude a high cruising speed, and the faithful Wasp engine responded with a roar. From habit I then eased back slightly on the throttle after the engine caught, as is usual in a glide.

But at this altitude the propeller had to turn over rapidly in order to drive enough wind over the wing for control and lift, even in a descent of three thousand feet per minute. This, incidentally, was just twice as fast as doctors consider comfortable for average ears. My eardrums were still not consistently normal, but even hampered by my frozen tongue I was able to swallow and hear the click in the inner ear indicating the equalized pressure which would stave off permanent harm. I had to get down in the shortest time possible, before that precious five gallons of gas gave out.

The clouds were still solid beneath me, and as I wondered where I was I remembered a famous altitude story told on himself by Shorty Schroeder after he had set a new record:

"As I attained higher altitude than ever reached by man before, I began to wonder what would happen after I passed beyond the effects of the earth's gravity—whether I would fall down between the planets, and which one I would eventually meet up with. Well, when my altimeter showed 35,000 feet, I decided that was plenty high enough. So I nosed the plane over, dived five thousand feet, looked out the side of the plane and saw nothing. I dived another five thousand feet, looked all around—and still saw nothing. After the next five thousand feet of drop, with no earth in sight, I said to myself, 'By Jove, I've missed it!' "

With my heart in my mouth, as it has been so often since childhood, I dived through the floor of clouds, almost afraid to see what was beneath, and as we broke through the last cumulous layer I peered fearfully over the side. Beneath me was open ocean! Yet the last time I had looked I was over the Jersey mountains, heading West. At this point I was struck by the realization that the westerly winds must have carried the plane slowly but surely backwards, as our sharp angle of ascent had reduced the present air speed to something like sixty miles per hour. Later I figured that at one point I had been bucking headwinds of over one hundred miles per hour so that, in effect, I must have been sliding backward at the rate of forty miles per hour.

This posed a problem. What if I had to ditch before reaching shore? How far would that remaining five gallons of gas carry with such a large carburetor gulping huge quantities of gas, even at gliding r.p.m.? What if the engine quit over the skyscrapers of Wall Street? Where was I, anyway?

I remembered the morning's newspaper headline "RUTH NICHOLS TURNS ANGEL TODAY" and I thought, "Well, maybe they're right; but before I get fitted for angel wings I sure am going to stretch this glide to shore." . . . Soon I saw New York's skyscrapers dead ahead. Then in a few minutes more, as we were passing over Manhattan's canyons, I prayed, "If she's going to quit, God, please let me at least make the river." This was before CAA regulations prohibited passing over the city at low altitude.

It didn't seem possible, but due to freak headwinds and steep rate of climb I had been flying a two hundred m.p.h. plane due west for an hour and a half and ended up right back where I started from! This phenomenon later was the subject for one of Robert L. Ripley's "Believe It or Not" cartoons.

Then I saw with exquisite relief the blessed outline of Jersey City Airport—on the nose!

I saw the smudge fire which had been lighted to give me the exact direction of ground wind—a welcome sight since I had no brakes and the general wind was coming the short way of the airport. I realized that I would have to come in over the wires, and that, with my gasoline down to the last few drops, I did not dare risk even one turn of the airport. So I slipped her in over the wires, said another brief prayer and trusted in my guardian angel to halt the plane before she rolled off into the bay.

The guardian angel was on the job, and the Lockheed came to a smooth stop with several hundred feet to spare. An excited, shouting crowd immediately swarmed around.

These are the moments a flyer lives for.

One of the mechanics climbed up in order to help me out of my parachute. As I stood up, the crowd pushed forward. I couldn't talk when at last I climbed stiffly out of the cockpit—my tongue was still frozen. I couldn't walk very straight, either, but that didn't seem to matter, with Walter Ward, N.A.A. official, on one side of me and Clarence on the other. Walking and talking are two of man's most vital functions, but they can be supremely unimportant at times.

I hardly noticed the pain as my tongue was thawing out by the means of time, conversation and hot coffee, while reporters and photographers crowded around and Willda helped me to peel off the successive layers of oddly-assorted clothing with which I had prepared myself. Ward had removed the barograph from my plane, and informally com-

Ruth is congratulated by Willda and Clarence Chamberlin after her feminine world record altitude flight, Jersey City Airport, March 6, 1931.

puted my altitude as over thirty thousand feet. He pointed out, however, that the exact figures would have to be verified by the Bureau of Standards at Washington and later accepted by the F.A.I. The official record, as finally accepted by the F.A.I., was twenty-eight thousand eleven hundred forty feet. The difference between this and my altimeter readings was due to corrections in atmospheric pressure, which at high altitude can give the altimeters a false reading. This, however, established a new world's altitude record for women, breaking that previously established by Elinor Smith.

Before we left the airport, the afternoon papers were on the street announcing my new record of "six miles up."

There was only one flaw in this great day. Don had not been there to see my triumph, as he had been obliged to go to California on a business trip for his company. But his telephone call that night made everything right. Being a pilot himself, he understood the importance of this day and let the toll charges mount while I recounted the giddy elation of hanging "on the prop" six miles high and my fear before I broke through the cloud floor. His final "Adios, mi Chiquita" provided the perfect period to a perfect day.

After the altitude record flight, there followed the usual aftermath of radio appearances, after-dinner speeches and endorsements of various products. I released helium-filled balloons for a charity campaign in New York. I was given a test hop in a new type of low-wing aircraft which had just been check-flown by Colonel Lindbergh an hour earlier, and thereby gained the privilege of my first meeting with Anne Lindbergh, who has since remained in my memory as one of the most charming and delightful people I have known. I set a new inter-city speed mark between Newark and Washington, tying the existing record set by Frank Hawks. I was interviewed on the subject of correct styling and pricing of women's flying clothes. It was all exciting, and all ephemeral, as I prepared for the next assault at the world's speed record for women.

At present I held two women's trans-continental speed records (East-West and West-East) and the world's feminine altitude record. But in discussing flight plans still another record for the Vega seemed advisable, before I started serious preparations for an Atlantic solo flight.

The transcontinental flights had demonstrated the Lockheed plane's load-bearing ability and the pilot's endurance. I had shown the altitude which the plane would reach. Now the logical sequence was to focus attention on speed, leaving out wind variables. There was also the possibility of providing disinterested contributions to aviation research as well as to personal prestige and business gain. The long distance performance had shown the dependability and load-carrying ability of the plane. The altitude flight would contribute to future comfort and safety for passenger flights, in which planes would be able to fly *over* the weather. But *speed* was the real "raison d'être" for an airplane—the ability to get there "fastest with the mostest."

In preparation for the speed record, Chamberlin had designed further improvements to the landing gear, which in tests showed twenty-six miles per hour added speed. Also the original horsepower of the motor, owned by Crosley, had been increased by Pratt and Whitney in redesigning it to include high-compression pistons, a Hornet B carburetor and a larger blower. With its new improvements the Lockheed was rated at six hundred horsepower.

At that time the only established official international three-kilometer speed course in the United States was located at Detroit. So I flew the souped-up Lockheed out there reveling in her power and speed. Arrangements previously had been made with NAA officials to have their electrical timing apparatus set up there by five o'clock the morning after my arrival. The early-morning time was set because there is less difference at that time between ground and air surface temperatures, and therefore less interference from ground convection currents.

I planned to retire early, in order to be fresh and rested for the early takeoff, but the usual Detroit hospitality prevented this. A dinner party and dance delayed bedtime until after midnight. I left a call at the hotel desk for three a.m. Normally, I need nine hours' sleep to be at my best, so when the phone shrilled and I rolled out of bed after only two hours' sleep, my morale was at low ebb. It took an hour to reach the airport by taxi, but I arrived just as the first dull gray of dawn was seeping into the darkness. And then I was told that the timers could not be ready for at least another hour and a half.

This was definitely annoying. The delay might necessitate a postponement of the record try because of rough air, likely to develop after sunrise. That would mean additional expense of timers' fees, extra gasoline and hotel costs, increased danger of landing on an experimental gear and the possibility of a crackup.

I was disgruntled, but realized that a display of temperament would not alter the situation, so I merely plopped my parachute down on a long table in the hangar, used it as a pillow and went to sleep for two hours.

Meanwhile a barograph was installed in my plane to record the altitude, since F.A.I. regulations required that the initial dive be started below one thousand feet at a point a mile back from the course, and that after crossing the three-kilometer starting line, the plane level off below five hundred feet. A pair of big sheets, snatched at the last minute from the bed of one of the flight observers, was used to mark the course.

After my informal nap, I took off from Grosse Isle Airport at 6:50 a.m., with Harry H. Knepper of the NAA present to check my time. I circled down-wind for a few miles, gaining altitude. Then I dived with wide-open throttle, in order to achieve the maximum speed at five hundred feet where I leveled off and held that altitude for the measured three-kilometer stretch. It was difficult to keep the plane steady, straight and close above the surrounding trees because of the bumpy air which had developed, as usual, after dawn. But by keeping both hands and my knees gripping the stick I kept her from getting away from me. After passing the second bed sheet, marking the end of the run, I pulled back the throttle and allowed the plane to zoom up to a thousand feet to gain altitude for another power dive and to lose momentum for a turn which would get me exactly back on course. As when a tight 180-degree turn is made at high speed, a pilot can black out from centrifugal force. Then I repeated the previous performance of diving at full throttle to five hundred feet, again holding the Vega at that exact altitude on the down-wind leg.

I made two round-trip runs, required in order to offset any help from the wind. On both I noted a drop in engine revolutions, sometimes as much as three hundred r.p.m., so that I had little hope of having broken any record. But when the time was clocked, officials found the following readings: Those against the wind were 191.036 m.p.h. and 202.80 and those with the wind were 221.825 and 226.80 m.p.h.

The record was accepted officially as 210.685 m.p.h., thereby surpassing by twenty-five m.p.h. Amelia Earhart's record of 181.157 m.p.h. made the year before.

So now the Vega and I had flown higher and faster than any other woman in the world. The time seemed ripe for the climax of all these efforts, the solo flight across the Atlantic.

On the way back to New York from Detroit, I flew down to Cincinnati for a talk with Powel Crosley. I had won the records for which I had borrowed his plane. Now I had to talk him into letting me use it for the trans-Atlantic try.

Would he do it? What if he said no?

My hands were clammy and my heart was pounding when at last I was ushered into his office. And his opening remarks made my heart sink. A male industrialist was speaking, and he said he did not wish to take the responsibility of risking the life of a woman.

I argued desperately. I pleaded. I pointed out the injustice of making different rules for women than for men. I recounted all the difficulties and the desperate efforts entailed in establishing the three records I now held, for his plane. I guess I managed to talk him and his associates down, for in the end he spread his hands, smiled and said:

"Young lady, no man could hold out against such arguments. Go fly the ocean if you must, with my blessing!"

9

ATLANTIC TAKEOFF

April, 1931.

Commerical aviation over regular routes was just trying its shaky wings, depending principally on air mail contracts for its bread and butter, carrying a few passengers at a loss, flying castoff planes of World War I. The first CAM (Contract Air Mail) routes had been started five years earlier, in 1926—New York to Boston, Chicago to St. Louis and Chicago to Dallas. Then in 1929 the first transcontinental route, part air, part rail, was pioneered, and took fifty hours. I had a grandstand seat for the great show which might be called "The Birth of the Air Age," but of course I didn't half realize the importance of the dramas I witnessed. I had accepted as a routine lark the opportunity to go along on the first commercial coast-to-coast "through" flight in the summer of 1930, and considered the lumbering Ford Tri-Motor transport plane the last word in passenger comfort, even though it could barely make enough altitude to clear the mountains, carried the most primitive kind of instruments, bounced like a roller coaster in bumpy air and took more than twenty-four hours for the trip. In addition the clanging noise of its non-insulated metal fuselage earned it the name "Tin Goose."

I left Cincinnati with Powel Crosley's consent to use his Lockheed for a solo Atlantic hop.

"Go fly the ocean if you must," he had said. And I knew I must.

Now that I had the plane, nothing would stop me. It did not even occur to me that I didn't have to take this chance—nobody was forcing me to risk my neck in a flimsy plane and gamble my life on its single motor. Nobody but myself.

I couldn't wait to get back home. There would be many obstacles to hurdle before I could actually take off on my adventure—chiefly financial ones. I would have to find backers for the flight. Many changes would have to be made in the plane to increase its fuel capacity and cruising range. There would be long days and nights of grueling work—and I was bursting with impatience to get started.

When I landed at the Jersey City field, I hardly gave the Lockheed time to stop before I leaped out and went tearing across the field in search of Clarence. When I found him I gasped out my great news.

Breathless as I was, I managed to describe, somewhat incoherently, my interview with Crosley.

"I can do it! I know I can! I've got the plane and the rest will be a breeze!"

It was then the middle of April, and we settled on June for the Atlantic takeoff. That was when the weather was best. And that would give us from six to eight weeks to re-design, overhaul and tune up the plane, assemble maps, charts and equipment and—most important—line up financial backing.

I think Chamberlin was almost as excited as I was over the prospect, for he had a warm, generous interest in furthering a fellow flyer's career. He already had won his laurels. Now he was eager to help me win mine.

Also prominent in my cheering section was Don, who managed to appear at the field at frequent intervals, insisting that I knock off work long enough to have dinner at one of our favorite spots or take a drive through the Jersey hills to clear the gas fumes out of my lungs. These occasions meant a great deal to me, though, looking back, I can see that we disagreed on so many points that it could not have been pleasant for him. In any case, off he went to Spain again, before my takeoff.

Although the Lockheed-Vega would seem primitive compared to the high-speed multi-engine planes of today, at that time it was the answer to my dreams, the last word in aircraft. It even had a closed cockpit! I wouldn't have to fly with the wind shrieking in my ears and the rain in my face. This in itself seemed incomparable luxury. The plane was a single-engine high-wing cabin monoplane with an over-all length of twenty-seven feet and a wing-spread of forty-one feet.

In addition to the removal of the six passenger seats in the cabin to install extra fuel tanks, many hours were spent trying out different groupings of dials on the instrument board for easy quick reading. He also spent a lot of time designing feed systems and locations for the various cabin tanks and testing the great six-hundred horsepower Pratt and Whitney supercharged Wasp engine. I promoted a set of expensive spark plugs from August Goldsmith, President of the B. G. Corp. Then Clarence promoted from the Hamilton Standard Propeller Company a new adjustable-pitch propeller, which we installed. This was a prop specially designed for a large single-engine plane, to provide a faster takeoff with a heavy load and adjust to cruising speeds with more economical gas consumption for longer range and safety. There have been many improvements in this propeller since then, and the one installed in the Crosley Lockheed was, I believe, the second one ever manufactured; it is now in the Smithsonian Institution. We managed to secure two of the newest navigation instruments from Elmer Sperry, a real pioneer in aeronautical instrument design and head of the Sperry Gyroscope Company. These were an artificial horizon and a directional gyro. I insisted on three altimeters and two compasses besides the gyro, one of which was an earth-indicator compass. Other navigation instruments were installed—about thirty in all.

The total fuel capacity, with all the extra tanks, was five hundred and seventy gallons of gas and twenty-five gallons of oil, with an estimated cruising range of over three thousand miles. This meant that at most I could fly for nineteen hours, averaging thirty gallons of gas per hour. As my original plan was to make the ocean takeoff from Newfoundland, I would have enough fuel to make the Paris flight in about fourteen hours, thereby giving me ample reserve fuel. I would use more gas at the beginning of the flight, with a heavy load, and less as the fuel load was lightened and as I flew at high altitude, permitting a leaner mixture.

It was agreed that after my takeoff, if I did not sight land in seventeen hours, I would throttle down the engine from one hundred seventy-five to one hundred twenty-five miles an hour, thus using only fifteen gallons of fuel per hour and giving me four hours more fuel instead of only two.

My top speed at sea level, making no allowance for wind, was two hundred ten miles per hour. It was planned that when I reached cruising altitude of eight thousand feet I would fly at an average of two hundred miles an hour without wind, and would count on a twenty-mile tail wind.

This was considered reasonable by dear old Doc Kimball, head of the U.S. Weather Bureau in New York, an expert of his day on trans-Atlantic air conditions. He was to notify us when a high pressure area had developed just south of my course, which would produce the tailwinds on which I was counting, as well as good weather during the full moon, which would help to provide a night horizon line, so that I would not have to depend entirely on my instruments for night flying.

The preparations, the test flights, the checking of charts and maps went on endlessly, so that I practically lived in the hangar. On the rare occasions when I got home to Rye, I met mixed reactions from my family. Mother at first was horrified

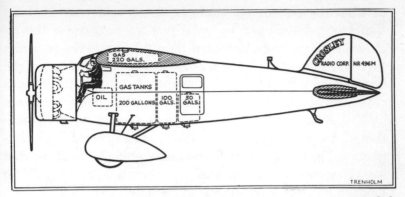

Diagram of Lockheed Vega showing fuel-tank disposition.

Cockpit of Lockheed Vega in which author made her
transatlantic solo attempt, June 22, 1931.

at what she considered wild plans, but when she realized that I was determined to make this try to conquer the air over the Atlantic, she accepted it, and I think even basked a little in reflected glory. As the news of my prospective ocean hop seeped out around the neighborhood, excited friends constantly were calling up to find out if it actually were true.

"Yes, Ruth is bound and determined to do this desperate thing," Mother would say, settling herself beside the telephone. "I just don't know what we are going to do about that girl. I've tried to reason with her, but it is no use. These modern girls think nothing is impossible. . . ."

Dad issued the expected words of caution, but I recognized the glint of adventure in his eyes, and I am sure there was a wistful note in his exhortations.

The twins, Bets and Bill, took it all in stride. Bets looked on my aerial escapades as strictly a nuisance, since she so often had to wait for me wearily and in deep boredom at an airport, to drive me home. Sometimes she used to drive out to Roosevelt Field to meet me as I landed from a cross-country flight, and sometimes to Armonk if I could wangle a ride back from Jersey City. Since I never could tell exactly when I would land after one of my check rides, Bets spent many hours sitting in the car just waiting. To her, flying was merely a tiresome business.

It always seemed strange to me that some of the excitement of those early days of aviation didn't rub off on Bets, but it didn't. She had no interest in learning to fly, or even in going along as a passenger, although I often urged her to try it, and even offered to teach her to fly. Bill was always eager to fly and when practical I took him on flights so he could get some instruction. Both Billy and Betty were absorbed in youthful activities of their own set, considering themselves briefly in love with first one dating companion and then another, engaging in the normal social rounds and having very little time to waste on worrying over an elder sister's career.

My brother Snowden never was much impressed by my aerial adventures. After graduation from Princeton he had tried his hand in Wall Street for a brief time, but now he was determined on an Air Force career. To him aviation was a responsible business, and he considered my escapades somewhat frivolous, I think, even though I was five years older.

So, as usual, it was to Aunty that I turned to share some of my hopes and dreams. I shall never forget the night I came home after the flight from Cincinnati and Crosley's final consent to my Atlantic try. After the jubilant celebration on my arrival at the air field, I came home to break the news to the family. I rushed up the steps, bursting with the glad tidings, to find the house apparently deserted. Mother and Dad had gone out for the evening, the twins were off somewhere on dates, Snowden was away. I shouted from the front hall, "Isn't *anybody* home?" And then Aunty appeared at the top of the stairs.

I went bounding up to tell her the wonderful news, sure of her answering enthusiasm, but for once Aunty didn't respond as I had hoped.

We went down to the porch where we sipped cool ginger ale while I recounted my triumph with Mr. Crosley, described in detail the Lockheed plane, and explained my imminent plans to fly the Atlantic. I told her about Chamberlin's help and encouragement, and how lucky I was to have the benefit of his knowledge and experience. I told her how I hoped to make enough money from the flight to give Mother and Dad financial security. I talked on and on, and Aunty continued to sip her iced drink. At last I ran down, and Aunty still was silent.

"What's the matter, Aunty dear?" I finally asked.

"It's such a big ocean," said Aunty, "and such a little plane."

"But I won't be flying for more than nine hours over water," I said quickly. "It's already been done, and I'm sure

I can make it. We have it all figured out. It's what I've been hoping and dreaming for so long . . . if I can just do this, I'll feel that all my work has been worth while. I've got to do it, that's all!"

Aunty looked at me for a minute, then she smiled.

"Well, if thee must, thee must." She brightened. "Besides, I've been wanting to visit my brother in France, so I guess I'll go over and wait for thee."

This was wonderful—even more than I had hoped. To have Aunty waiting on the other side, to be able to share my triumph with her, to take her on a trip through France—oh, we would have fun! It never crossed my mind that I might not get there.

Aunty observed prudently that we would have to be very careful about breaking the news to Mother and Dad. As we talked her cheeks grew pink, her bright blue eyes sparkled and we became fellow conspirators. As I have done so often, I realized how lucky I was to have such a confederate, and wondered what I would do at any crisis without Aunty's staunch support.

I tried to tell her a little of how I felt, and as I talked it occurred to me there was one more thing I wanted to do before I left for my big try. I wanted to become a member of the Society of Friends. Mother and Dad had raised me as an Episcopalian, but the strongest influences in my life had been of Quaker origin—the understanding guidance and example of my Grandfather and Aunty. These were the people I admired most, and I wanted to be like them. I explained all this, haltingly, and Aunty nodded briskly.

"Thee already is a Friend by heritage and the desires of thy heart," she said. "We'll ask Clement Biddle tomorrow to take the necessary steps for thy membership in Purchase Meeting."

After due consideration by a committee of Friends, who are never impressed by public prominence but rather by demonstrated motives, I was accepted as a member of the Purchase Meeting. Quakers have no formal creed and they have many strong divergent beliefs. However, their unifying basic convictions are in the power of goodness and the efficacy of love, with the earnest endeavor to live by these truths according to each individual's "inner light." They believe there is something of God in every single human being, no matter how cruel he may be. This has been demonstrated frequently in war work by the American Friends Service Committee, when dealing with sadistic military leaders. Each individual Friend interprets truth as best he can—often with surprising results.

One of the high moments of my life was when, as a member, I attended Purchase Meeting with Aunty and sat in silence, her hand in mine, feeling such a sense of peace as I never had experienced before.

Once her mind was made up, Aunty moved with characteristic speed and precision. She made her plans immediately to sail for France, where she would visit her brother, then living in Brittany, and wait for my arrival. She also arranged for me to take a letter from Purchase Quarterly Meeting to be delivered to the Society of Friends in England. Aunty planned to sail about a month before my estimated time of arrival in Paris, so that she would have time to visit with her brother, perhaps do a little sightseeing and be in plenty of time to greet me.

We had a quiet family dinner party in Rye the night before she left. Thanks to Aunty's serene attitude, Mother and Dad were now reconciled to my flight, and refrained from any foreboding remarks.

Mother and Dad drove Aunty to the pier with her luggage, but I had other plans. Pleading pressing business about the flight, I said goodby on the steps at Rye, and as soon as the family car disappeared down the road, I telephoned Harry Rogers, who still had his seaplane base nearby. I told him I

wanted to give Aunty a real sendoff, and he agreed enthusiastically, having been one of her ardent admirers ever since
her first flight in one of his Seagulls.

So it was that, as Aunty's ship steamed down the bay,
Harry and I in the Seagull circled the liner. In his determination to be recognized, Harry flew so low it looked as though
we'd hit the ship's smokestack, but we missed it by inches
and continued to circle until we saw Aunty excitedly flutter-
ing a white handkerchief at the rail.

In the days that followed I threw myself into the final
preparations with redoubled vigor and a warm feeling in my
heart. The Lockheed Vega was being tuned and groomed
with more loving care than is lavished on a champion horse
before a big race. She was painted white, with gold wings—
and now she had to have a name.

After long arguments and hundreds of suggestions, I decided on the name *Akita,* a word used by the Indians of
South Dakota meaning "to explore" or "to discover." It sym-
bolized an appropriate purpose and also had the musical
sound that fitted the graceful beauty of the white-and-gold
plane.

By now most of the obstacles had been overcome. We had
obtained financial backing for the flight. Among the sponsors
were Columbia Broadcasting and Paramount Newsreel Com-
panies, William Horlick, Van Raalte Hose and Westclox, Mr.
and Mrs. John Dunlop, Mrs. Frederick W. Guest, Mrs. Ogden
Reid and Mrs. Katherine Buckley Woodruff.

After the Wasp engine had been overhauled through the
generosity of the Pratt and Whitney Aircraft Company it
still sounded rough. Chamberlin's mechanics couldn't seem
to locate the trouble, so I flew *Akita* up to the Pratt and
Whitney plant at Hartford, Conn., for a last-minute examination. Factory experts could find no reason for the excessive
vibration, and called in representatives of the Hamilton Propeller Company to see if the trouble could be with the pitch
of the new prop. They worked on the plane for days, and

even Colonel Art Goebel of trans-Pacific fame took it up for a test hop. This was the same Colonel Goebel who was the subject of one of Chamberlin's favorite anecdotes.

As Clarence tells it, Goebel once invited him to take a test hop in a new plane he had just built, and at the same time urged an innocent bystander at the airport to come along for the ride. The flight turned out to be a series of aerial acrobatics designed to prove that the plane could fly upside down, right side up or sideways, and the passenger, taking his first flight, was not only violently air-sick but scared out of a year's growth. When finally the novice stumbled out of the plane he is reported to have said: "Never accept a ride when a trans-Pacific pilot is showing a trans-Atlantic pilot what his plane can do!"

Goebel and all the other experts finally decided that *Akita's* vibration was not serious enough to cause any real damage, except to the instrument board. So it was decided to yank out the instrument panel and try to cushion it more thoroughly at the same time checking the instruments for accuracy. This meant further delay, each change meant a test hop, and I began to feel that I would never get off.

Between factory sessions I was instructed in blind flying and checked out on an Army plane, by special permission from officers at Mitchell Field. I also studied celestial navigation with Giles Stedman, a trans-Atlantic ship captain notable for a number of shipwreck rescues. And in between all these sessions were the frequent talks necessary for raising funds, as well as the innumerable press interviews and posing for news photographers. My mail grew to voluminous proportions, with letters pouring in from all over the country wishing me luck, offering advice or asking to go along as passengers. I was learning that the preliminaries to an ocean flight are an exhausting business.

Finally *Akita* was checked out on her last tests, nobody could think of anything more to do to her, and I returned to Jersey City for a final hop. There Clarence met me with the news that his friends, Colonel and Mrs. Henry Breckinridge, had invited us, with Chamberlin's wife, Willda, to have dinner at their apartment and discuss flight plans with Colonel Charles Lindbergh and his wife, Anne. The opportunity to receive advice from the most famous solo Atlantic flyer of them all, the first man to fly alone from New York to Paris, was an honor that left me breathless. I accepted with the speed of lightning.

After dinner, Lindbergh, Chamberlin and I withdrew to the library to discuss details of my proposed flight. Lindbergh felt that any Atlantic flight was still highly dangerous, warned me of all the things that could happen, and advised looking before I leaped. I insisted I had looked, and still intended to leap. Clarence and I told him all the preparations that had been made for the flight, described the engine, the new prop, the fuel load and cruising range. We went over fuel consumption curves, considering various r.p.m., altitude and load conditions, plans for coping with ice, drift, etc., and "Slim," as his pilot friends called him, listened carefully. In the end he approved of the general technical plans, but advised one more important piece of equipment—an emergency radio set. My heart sank at the thought of raising additional money to buy it and learning how to use it in the last-minute rush, but I realized that this was sound advice.

The evening ended on a note of high hope and good wishes from the world's most famous flyer. Anne Lindbergh pressed my hand warmly as we left and wished me the luck that rode with "Lucky Lindy."

On the way home Willda, Clarence and I discussed ways and means of installing a radio set, and we all agreed that we should accept Lindbergh's judgment in the matter. Luckily I already knew International Code, then used instead of radio telephone, but I was doubtful of my ability to learn the mechanics of the equipment on such short notice. This was equipment to be used in case of a crash or a forced landing at sea, and meant setting up a seventeen-foot mast for an aerial in a rubber life boat amid possibly heavy seas. It was a chilling prospect, but we decided it must be done. We managed to get some makeshift equipment together and to have the radio installed.

One hot afternoon in the first week of June Chamberlin received the report that good weather was expected in the next thirty-six hours, and we decided to pack everything aboard *Akita* and take off from the Jersey City Airport for Floyd Bennett Field, where my start was to be made. What a packing session that was! The back of the plane was loaded down with all kinds of emergency equipment such as an extra propeller, tires, tubes, wheels, fabric, putty, hydrogen tank, blow torch, weather balloons and other necessities, ad infinitum—for Harbor Grace, Newfoundland, then possessed no aircraft servicing or facilities of any sort. I had already learned that if anything should go wrong in Harbor Grace, I might need any or all of these things. And it would take too long to get them by steamer, as I would miss the good weather season.

When I climbed up into the cockpit at last, I noticed that the tail skid was sinking pretty far down into the sandy field, but I believed the powerful engine would give the ship enough momentum for the field's short takeoff area. What I didn't count on, however, was the deadness of the air on that hot day.

After rolling more than half-way down the runway, I realized that the ship was not picking up speed fast enough. With only three hundred feet of runway left before *Akita* plunged into the bay, I was faced with catastrophe. It was too late to stop now. There was only one chance—super-throttle. I pushed the lever beyond the safety stop, and just before the end of the runway the stick lightened in my hand, *Akita* staggered off the ground and I managed to pull her up to clear the bulkhead by a bare foot. With a minimum flying speed, she immediately sank below the retaining wall toward the water. But again I concentrated every faculty on the "feel" of the stick, which, in split seconds, informed me by its "sloppy" control of the imminence of a fatal stall. *Very, very* gently, I exerted back pressure on the stick. . . . She started inch . . . by inch . . . to climb. But we were headed directly for the Bayonne Bridge, still without sufficient altitude, or speed for a sharp bank to avoid it. . . . Again, almost a stall . . . with a necessary flat turn. There . . . we had passed the bridge. I could now stop the rudder and aileron turn, so dangerous in a heavy-laden climb, and give *Akita* the proper angle of attack for a safe straight ascent in order to get adequate altitude over the surrounding city buildings.

Whew! I wiped off the perspiration that was dripping from my face. This was something I had not even considered —the possibility of cracking up at the start of a short ferry flight from Jersey to Long Island. It had been a close shave, and with it came the sobering realization that many other unknown conditions could develop, as the flight progressed. So it was in a somewhat grave mood that I flew over Jersey City, Manhattan and Brooklyn, with an occasional picture flashing through my mind of Renée Foncke's and other fairly recent, long-distance, heavy-laden, under-powered takeoffs, which had ended in death.

It was fortunate, I reflected, that I had this opportunity to test the plane's handling with a heavy load. I had not realized what a difference it would make. The weight in the back of the ship had shifted the center of gravity, so that it was unstable in both directions, and an easy prey to a flat spin. As I approached Floyd Bennett Field, I made a complete circle of the field, to ascertain exact wind direction. Cautiously I prepared for a landing, and all went well until *Akita* was only three feet off the ground, when one wing dipped in the dead "thin" air and she dropped, accordingly, on one wheel. I heard something crack, but the plane seemed to be rolling along the runway all right, and it was not until I had pulled up in front of the Administration Building that

I realized the impact on one wheel of our light, newly designed landing gear had broken the main bulkhead. As I clambered out to inspect the damage I saw that the tail skid also was damaged, having caught on the edge of the concrete runway as I taxied to a stop.

Within ten minutes Clarence arrived in his Crescent, took one look at *Akita* and said:

"Tough luck, Ruth. We'll have to take out all the fuel tanks and get new supports made to repair that bulkhead."

This was disaster. Such a major operation would take time and money, and I was running out of both. Chamberlin and his engineer, who had come along, were shaking their heads over the damage when a tall young Navy officer in immaculate white uniform joined the consultation, looked at my stricken face and said:

"Roll the Lockheed into our hangar. We'll see if we can't give you some help."

Though he did not wear a suit of shining armor or ride a white charger that young officer was Sir Galahad to me.

In the next few days I had an opportunity to observe the courtesy and efficiency of our Navy at work. Repairs on the plane were started at once with both high morale and good will. Three shifts of mechanics, directed by our engineer and Chamberlin, worked around the clock. They had to remove all the fuel tanks and then design, manufacture and reset welded fittings in the damaged bulkhead, to make it three times as strong as it was originally. In the steamy heat of those days, without factory conveniences, the men worked under constant pressure yet managed to maintain enthusiasm and good humor. Since then I have been helped by the Army, the Air Force and the Coast Guard, and after such experiences anyone who criticizes the courtesy of our armed forces will find me in open opposition.

After seeing the work started that first night, expressing my gratitude to officers and men and dashing out for cold drinks and sandwiches for the mechanics, I dragged myself wearily off to a room at nearby Far Rockaway, to snatch a few hours of sleep.

My first thought on waking was of *Akita*, and I rushed off to the field to see how the repairs were coming on, to encourage the men who were working so ably and generously, and to lend whatever assistance I could until long after midnight. This was a procedure that became routine during the next few days. I spent every waking hour in the Navy hangar, and with each step of progress on the repairs my heart lightened. *Akita* was almost her old self again—perhaps even better than she had been.

One morning when I was making up lost sleep after a late night at the field, I was wakened by the telephone. It was Clarence, who said excitedly:

"Doc Kimball [New York Weather Bureau chief] says two good days are shaping up over the North Atlantic. Better get up and get going. If you don't get out of New York this afternoon you'll be stuck here by bad weather coming in from the south and miss the Atlantic high."

I was only half awake, and at first couldn't take in the full meaning of this.

"How's the ship?" I asked automatically.

"She'll be ready," said Clarence. "All you have to do is check out and get over here."

So this was the way it happened! The biggest day of my life had arrived, and I wasn't even ready for it. I had expected to have at least twenty-four hours for preparation. But here it was. So much to do and so little time. Check all the last-minute details, make final telephone calls, pack, load the ship—could it be done? Hastily I flung things into my bags and ordered a taxi. As I dashed about the room I thought gratefully of Willda Chamberlin. This good friend had volunteered to take all my extra equipment, which had so overloaded the plane, by steamer to Newfoundland. She had started several days previously and by now must be almost there. How fortunate I was to have such loyal friends! How lucky to live in a country where the Navy came to my rescue and repaired my plane! How altogether born under a lucky star to have this wonderful day come at last, to find help always when I needed it, to be alive in a world full of such kind and generous people.

By the time I arrived at the field a small crowd had gathered, for the news had spread. Newpaper men, Navy officers, business representatives, mechanics, friends and curious bystanders were all milling around inside the hangar, despite the best efforts of airport officials to keep them out.

I was besieged with questions while I was trying to check off last-minute details in my little black notebook. I was kept busy writing checks to settle small bills with various tradesmen who had rushed out to the field to collect, feeling that I might land "plumb in the middle of the Big Pond." In order to raise some ready cash, I even sold my Stutz convertible for five hundred dollars. When the last creditor was paid off, I looked around for some place where I could get away from the crowd and collect my thoughts. Finally I found a spot behind one of the Navy planes which offered some degree of privacy. Here I began checking my list again to make sure I was not forgetting anything essential. I was grateful that increased engine power, better wing curve and aspect ratio, as compared to Chamberlin's and Lindbergh's planes, gave me plenty of leeway to carry extra items of safety on a still hazardous flight. This list of things to take along in the plane consisted of two pages of typed single-spaced items, including such things as: envelopes containing maps of the Eastern states, Atlantic Coast lighthouses and Newfoundland; government permits, customs papers and clearance for Newfoundland, code book, instructions for setting up the emergency radio, ocean charts, upper air charts, weather maps, a moon chart, a list of steamer sailings and routes, navigation equipment, including sextant and binoculars, charts of the European coastline, passport, insurance papers, customs and clearance for Europe, pencils, pad and two flashlights, my various pilot's licenses, medicine case; package of food containing three thermos bottles of coffee, soup and water, chocolate and malted milk tablets, crackers, gum, sandwiches; compact, comb and mirror; a box of silk stockings; letters to be delivered; emergency equipment including canteen of water, rubber boat, flashlight, rubber coat, life preserver, radio set, parachute flares, Very pistol and ammunition, parachute; and a Bible.

I must call my family. I managed to evade the crowd long enough to slip into an empty office near the hangar and use the phone. I called Rye, but none of the family was at home, so I left a message:

"Tell Mother and Dad I'm off for Europe. I'll cable when I land."

I dashed back to the hangar and slipped in through a side door. Clarence found me leaning against the wing of the Navy ship, scanning my coastal maps.

"How far d'you think you can make before dark?" he asked.

By now, we both realized, it was too late to hope to make Newfoundland tonight, because according to my insurance policy against crash and fire, I had to make at least one landing before Newfoundland, to refuel. Underwriters, like pilots, consider the takeoff with a heavy load the most dangerous part of a flight. A stop between New York and Newfoundland meant I would not have to carry full fuel capacity on the first takeoff. So Clarence and I agreed on two alternatives—Portland, Maine, or St. John's, New Brunswick.

Before we went back to *Akita* and the crowd, Clarence patted my shoulder and said:

"Take it easy, Ruth. It's easier than you think. Tomorrow you'll be in Paris."

Newsreel cameras were grinding, news photographers were calling for "just one more" and many voices were shouting good luck wishes as we walked across the ramp to the white-and-gold *Akita*. I climbed into the cockpit and began warming up the engine. There was one more delay while mechanics fixed a sticking stabilizer. Finally I called, "Okay!"

Clarence waved and called: "See you later!"

Then came the familiar call of "Clear! Let her roll!" The mechanics pulled the blocks from under the wheels and waved a comradely goodby. The Wasp roared deep and smooth as I taxied down the hangar apron. While passing the Administration Building to reach the runway and head into the wind, I was only dimly conscious of the cheers of the crowd and their waving handkerchiefs, being intent on the imminent takeoff and all its attendant problems.

I wheeled around into position on the runway, gunned the engine and riveted my eyes dead ahead, concentrating on keeping the plane perfectly straight. *Akita* thundered down the runway with such a burst of power that she practically flew herself off the ground.

As we gained altitude (*Akita* and I) and roared over New York harbor, I noted three Navy planes skimming ahead as an honor escort. Together we circled the Statue of Liberty. Then I headed northeast, alone with *Akita*.

It was a perfect day, June 22, 1931. There was not a cloud in the sky, and I looked down on the varied greens of trees and fields, the blue water along the coast, the tiny rooftops dotting the landscape like confetti. I felt like laughing aloud, like singing. The first big challenge had been met and conquered. I had made a perfect takeoff with a semi-load. I was confident that *Akita* would be equal to the full-load takeoff at Newfoundland. I was on my way. Ahead lay the broad Atlantic, then Paris.

All the years of my preoccupation with airplanes, all the months of preparation, all the weeks of day-and-night work in the hangar had been leading up to this moment.

In a few more minutes I was over Rye, and dipped *Akita*'s wings in salute as I flew over our house. I felt a pang of regret that I had not been able to reach any of the family to say goodby. Well, I would telephone again from wherever I stopped tonight. No doubt they would be under great tension until they learned I was safe in Paris. It's always hardest for those who stay at home, I realized, but Mother and Dad would not have long to worry—I'd be there almost before they had time to start worrying. Clarence would attend to cabling Captain Railey in Paris, and he in turn would notify Aunty that I was on my way at last. And I so hoped Don would be waiting for me; Spain wasn't very far away.

Anyway, we would have fun, Aunty and I, seeing the sights of Europe before starting back home. We'd celebrate my successful flight, and we would spend just a little of all the money I expected to collect, maybe hiring a car and driving through the back roads of France, or maybe even making a leisurely air tour of Europe. Already I had in hand a number of contracts for testimonials, endorsements, personal appearances, lectures, magazine and newspaper articles which would bring in a considerable sum, and I knew there would be other offers as soon as the flight was completed.

Lovely dreams! But before they could come true I must concern myself with the immediate tasks of watching the instruments, checking the maps, looking for landmarks. I was hitting off the towns on my Eastern Seaboard map with clocklike regularity, ahead of schedule because of a good tail wind. It seemed practically no time before I was over Portland, Maine, one of my two choices for the overnight stop. But it was still so early that there seemed no point in landing then, and besides the wind was blowing in strong gusts the short way of the small airport.

I decided to go on to St. Johns, N. B., figuring I had plenty of time to make it before dark, and so I held my compass course. North of Portland the coastline is rocky and forbidding, and I was glad that I would not have to attempt a landing in those boulder-strewn fields, but would find a good airport at St. Johns. I had been told by another trans-

Atlantic flyer that the field was large enough for *Akita*, although he had never actually landed there.

It was now about four hours since my takeoff from New York, and I began looking for the St. Johns field. Soon I spotted it a few miles in from the coast, and started a gliding descent to get a better look at it.

As I peered down at a tiny airport set like a bowl in the midst of surrounding wooded hills and cliffs, I thought at first I must be off course—this couldn't be the St. Johns field. But I checked the map again, determined my position and realized with a sinking heart that there was no mistake— this was it.

Twice I circled, studying the small, rock-enclosed field from every angle. How on earth could the heavy, fast Lockheed land there? Those crossed runways would be safe only for small or lightly-loaded planes. Furthermore the surrounding woods and steep cliffs would require a radical slipping approach in order to avoid them and still be low enough to touch and stop rolling within that tiny bowl. Moreover, the hard Floyd Bennett landing had shown that this redesigned gear would not take a slow heavy stall. I had had much experience in pinpoint landings during the Aviation Country Clubs tour, but this ship was far different from those light planes. I didn't know whether I could make it, but one thing was sure—I would have to try, because already the sun was setting and it was too late to fly back to the longer runway at Boston Municipal Airport, even if I had enough fuel, which was doubtful.

Because of the wind direction, I would have to use the shorter of the two runways—and even the longer one was inadequate. I flew back over the town, then headed back toward the airport while cutting the throttle to minimum flying speed.

I slid in over the trees and edged through a narrow ravine. So far so good. Maybe my luck was holding. Dead ahead was the runway. I made an S turn for the proper approach and headed straight into the blinding rays of the setting sun. I couldn't look ahead to gauge the length of the runway, because ahead was a fiery glare. Only by staring straight down through the cockpit window could I see even the edge of the runway. This was indeed coming in on a wing and a prayer.

In that split second, I realized if I could touch the wheels on the ground before the intersection of the two runways, then I could clamp down on the brakes to stop the plane in time. I couldn't risk a short dropped stall with the fragile landing gear, which required a feather-light landing. Cautiously, I eased back on the stick and kept my eyes glued to the edge of the runway. Now we were skimming the ground. Now the wheels must be about to touch.

Suddenly the dazzling blaze of the sun was doused by the shadow of a cliff and I saw to my horror that I had passed the intersection and still had flying speed. *Akita* was tearing straight toward an approaching cliff at eighty miles an hour. There wasn't a chance of stopping her in time to avoid destruction. Only one thing to do. I gave her the gun, pinning my last desperate hope on the chance that the speed of the ship at full throttle would pull her up and over the wooded crag.

You are not conscious of thought processes or even of fear at a time like this. There is only the awareness of stark necessity for lightning action. You act by conditioned reflex.

Akita shrieked at the suddenness of the climb, roaring toward the onrushing rocks. She lurched upward and I eased up on the stick to avoid dropping her into a power stall. The jagged edge of the cliff rushed at us. Here it was. I got set for the crash and it didn't come. By some miracle we had cleared the top of the crag by a hair. Even as I breathed a prayer of thanks, I saw another ridge ahead. Come on, *Akita*! Good girl, *Akita*.

She struggled, quavered, made one last desperate effort— then came a splintering crack as the tail broke through the treetops. More rocks ahead—a deafening shuddering C-R-A-S-H—then paralyzing silence. From seventy miles an hour minimum climbing speed with a load the motor impacted to a dead stop. The whole back end of the ship must be coming over on top of me, relentlessly bearing down, pushing my head and shoulders down between my knees.

Splintering pain, and the silence of catastrophe.

My breath came in long, shuddering gasps. Automatically I moved my hand toward the instrument board, and noted with detachment that all the fingers worked. What should I have them do? Oh, yes! Cut the switch. Always cut the switch when you crash. Harry Rogers taught me that. Good old Harry. Queer, we aren't on fire. Gas pouring down the sides from a broken fuel line. Boiling oil oozing out of the tank under my seat. What else was it Harry said? Get out— that must be it. Get out before fire starts. Hot engine. Hot gas. Hot oil. Bound to be an explosion. Get out. . . .

Safety belt. Undo buckle. Hatch overhead. Push it open. Dear God, how it hurts to move. But must . . . Must get out. Climb out hatch, get on top of wing. Then can fall off if explosion comes.

As I managed to push back the hatch and fresh air poured into the cockpit my head cleared. Painfully I dragged myself up. Every movement was torture, but I could move. I had to get out before red-hot manifolds explode the gas fumes . . . Must get out because I had to fly the Atlantic. Must get out.

Inch by inch I pulled myself up through the hatch, slid along on top of the wing toward its tip. A red-hot poker was stabbing my back, but I was alive. I could move.

Exhausted by the effort and the pain, I slumped on the wing, caught my breath and then wilted under the self-questioning that always hit me when things went wrong.

Suddenly I became aware that I was not alone. Popping out of the bushes was a news photographer, busily snapping pictures. No offer to help. No interest in whether I was hurt. This character was intent on getting a picture scoop.

A group of half-a-dozen men burst through the bushes, armed with pick-axes and fire-extinguishers. They stopped short and stared at me in embarrassed silence. There was no fire and I seemed to be alive and kicking. They weren't quite sure what to do.

For a long moment we gazed at each other in speechless uncertainty. I felt a sudden impulse to laugh. But the pain in my back was intense, so I only grinned and said to the men nearest the wing:

"I-I'm awfully sorry, but I'm afraid I'm not going to be able to walk. Do you suppose a couple of you could make a seat with your hands and help me get back to the field?"

They gazed at me curiously, but no one made a move. Then running up the hill, I saw an old friend, Frank Ambrose, who had given me one of my early tests in the Curtiss plane I had used in the Aviation Country Clubs tour.

"Frank!" I called shakily. "Oh, Frank, am I glad to see you!"

He rushed forward and put a steadying arm around my ankles, which were all he could reach from the ground, since the wing on which I was seated was about level with the heads of the men below.

"Just take it easy, Ruth," he said, "until I can get up there with you and we'll get you down. Don't move, now, until I come up. You'll be okay. Main thing is, you're alive!"

He scrambled into the cockpit and out through the hatch, bringing with him my handbag, which was lying on the seat, and my parachute, to preserve them from souvenir hunters. Sliding down on the wing beside me, he put his arm around my shoulders and I winced.

"Where does it hurt, kid?" he asked in quick concern.

"I think it's my back," I said softly, so the men below could not hear. "Frank, please don't let me pass out. I don't want to be carried back to the field horizontally. Show them how to make a pack seat with their hands, won't you? I'm sure I can make it that way, sitting up."

"Sure thing, kid," said Frank. "Just take it easy, now."

He stretched out on the wing, leaned over and gave instructions. A second man came up on the wing, and between them they eased me down to the waiting arms below. I don't know why it was so important to me to go back to the field sitting up, but it was. Once they understood what I wanted them to do, the men were wonderfully kind and gentle. So I sat on a seat made by their crossed hands, with an arm around the neck of a man on each side, and our little procession moved slowly back to the airport. It was an agonizing trek over the rocky ground, around stumps and hillocks, but I clenched my teeth and held onto their shoulders.

"We've ordered an ambulance," volunteered one of the men.

"Oh, I won't need that!" I said scornfully. "If you'll just put me in a taxi I'll go to a hotel and rest for the night, and by morning I'll be fine."

When we came at last into the cleared area of the air field, it seemed as if hundreds of people pressed forward to get a look at the victim. I knew they were kind and wanted to help, though curiosity was perhaps their primary reason for being there, but all I wanted at that moment was to get away—but quick.

A taxi was waiting at the edge of the field; slowly and carefully my rescuers eased me into it. Frank and another man climbed in beside me. But before we could go I had to give the airport manager instructions about stationing a guard around *Akita* and salvaging certain articles of value. That took a long five minutes, and then we were off.

The two men tried to ease me over the worst bumps of the corduroy road as the slow-moving taxi jounced along toward town. About half way there we met the ambulance on its run to the field, and my companions ordered the driver to pull up and hail it.

"But I don't want to go to a hospital!" I insisted. "I'll see a doctor at the hotel."

"You'll be better off at the hospital," said Frank. "You need some real care, Ruth. They'll be able to fix you up quick, I'm sure."

"Besides, just look at your knee!" said the other man. "It's cut open to the bone!"

I hadn't even realized until then that my leg was cut. So at last I agreed wearily to go to the hospital for one night anyway. Then began the struggle to get me into the ambulance. The pain in my back was excruciating as Frank and his companion eased me gently off the taxi seat and onto the waiting stretcher. Blood from my cut knee was dripping down my leg, and I remember some woman screamed. It was a nightmare in which my principal feeling was humiliation at making a public spectacle of myself. But at last we reached the hospital and what I hoped would be privacy to lick my wounds.

But here another ordeal awaited. Reporters and photographers were standing by and, as I was wheeled down the hospital corridor, they clustered around my stretcher. I told them my story as briefly as possible, and then dictated two telegrams. One was to Powel Crosley expressing my deep regret over cracking up his plane and my hope to repair it with the insurance money and make another try at the Atlantic flight as soon as possible. The other wire was to Mother, and read:

"All I did was wrench my back and wreck the ship. Everything under control. Awfully sorry about crack-up. Will do it next time. Love. Ruth."

At last I was pushed into the quiet haven of a private room and the blessed comfort of a bed, smooth sheets—and solitude. When doctors, nurses and interns finally left me alone I simply lay completely still, drained of both thought and feeling for a while, savoring the quiet. The respite was brief. All too soon the crushing weight of my disappointment

Clarence Chamberlin inspecting Ruth's monoplane at St. John, New Brunswick, following her nearly fatal crackup, June 23, 1931.

descended upon me, the full realization of disaster. My beautiful white and gold *Akita* lay broken on a rocky hillside,
along with my hopes. Tomorrow I was to have been flying
across the Atlantic. Even now beloved Aunty was waiting
for me in Paris. Why did it have to happen this way? Why
couldn't fate have given me just a few more inches to clear
that last rocky ledge? That was all we had needed—just
inches—then *Akita* and I would have been safe. Once on our
way we could have made the ocean flight—I knew we could!
But look at us now. Here I was stretched out on a hospital
bed with a bad back; there was *Akita* crumpled against a
cliff. Where did we go from here? Where *could* we go from
here?

My despair did not last very long, however. I was already
plotting ways and means of rebuilding the ship and making
a new start by the time another doctor appeared with another stretcher to wheel me into the X-ray room.

There waited more doctors and technicians. They took a
long time. And each time I was shifted to another position
for another X-ray picture, the pain was so hideous that all I
longed for was oblivion. After what seemed hours I was
wheeled back to my room. More than anything else I wanted
to know the verdict. Was my back broken? How long would
I have to stay in the hospital? When could I fly again? The
questions crowded to my lips, but before I could frame them
a nurse had given me a swift hypodermic. I was overtaken
by an overpowering drowsiness and slipped into drugged
sleep.

When I opened my eyes sunlight was streaming into the
room and Clarence Chamberlin was standing beside my bed.
He was studiously casual. "Hi-ya!" he grinned as I rubbed
my eyes.

"Hi-Bud!" I replied, not to be outdone.

"What happened?"

I told him. It took quite a while. Then we summed up the
situation. He already had seen *Akita*, he told me, and had

made further arrangements for its protection. He pointed out how lucky I had been. First I should thank a kindly Providence that the ship had not burst into flames with me tangled in the wreckage. Next, I could count myself favored by fate that the cockpit had broken right through the middle like a bursting pocketbook and had pulled the instrument board away from my face; otherwise, when my head and shoulders were pushed forward and down by that sudden crashing stop, I would have smashed my face into the steel and glass. If the cockpit had not been split in two, the boiling oil from the tank beneath my seat would have scalded me instead of pouring harmlessly down the hill. Gas from the broken fuel lines would have exploded. And if I had to crack up, Clarence finished, I had picked a wonderful place in which to do it, because St. Johns had one of the finest hospitals in the country. Then he told me the news I was waiting to hear:

"Looks like your insurance will just about cover repairs to the plane. If you can raise some extra funds for expenses, you can still try the Atlantic flight in the early fall."

"Thank you," I said from the bottom of my heart. "You and Willda I guess are about the best friends I've ever had. I wish I didn't have to give you so much trouble! But we'll do it yet. I'll be out of here right away, and we'll get busy on the ship. Clarence, I'm going to fly that ocean, no matter what!"

But the doctors had other ideas. The specialist in charge of my case came in soon after this, bent over my bed and said:

"My dear young lady, I hope you know how lucky you are to be alive. You're going to be all right, but it will take time. You might just as well plan to be with us for a while."

"Just how bad is it, doctor?" I asked.

He hesitated, cleared his throat, fiddled with his stethoscope and said:

"Oh, it's not too bad. We'll patch you up as good as new.

There are no injuries that won't heal, with time. You'll be walking, playing golf, even maybe flying again—in about a year."

"A YEAR! Doctor, what do you mean?" I stared at him in horror. "I've got to get out of here right away. I've got to fly the Atlantic!"

"I have just been examining your X-rays," replied the doctor. "They show you have five broken vertebrae."

10

GROUNDED

Through many years of highs and lows I, like most people with varied experience, have gleaned certain insights and made a few discoveries for myself. Among these, is that the will-to-continue after a major emotional impact is due to a great love, to a strong religious belief, or to a psychological compulsive drive for life and certain goals in that life. Whatever the motivating mechanism, the impelling urge must be obeyed.

In my case, each one of these motivations had been uppermost at various times in my life. At this particular period, I not only *had* to fly but I also felt an emotional need to meet the challenge of exploring new air frontiers, a need which was increased by the conviction that my responsibility to my parents could only be discharged through success in my career as a flyer. Yet here I was flat on my back in a strange hospital with specialists, nurses and interns ruling my life and telling me I would be grounded for a year. It was literally impossible for me to accept their verdict.

I don't know why the orthopedic surgeon waited so long to immobilize the spine in a cast, unless he wanted me to be consciously able to hold myself in a certain position while it was being applied. The pain of splintered bones grating against torn ligaments was so intense that it required four nurses merely to change a sheet. Sometimes the muscle spasms were so agonizing only chloroform knocked me out.

While waiting for this acute condition to subside, I tried to plan the next steps. Of one thing I was sure—I was not going to remain laid up in a hospital bed one minute longer than was absolutely necessary. And my job was to convince the doctors that it wasn't necessary.

Therefore I decided to maintain a determined cheerfulness. This was not too hard, because I was surrounded by good friends, who spoke my language. Willda Chamberlin arrived soon after Clarence, and the two of them devoted themselves to minimizing my injuries and keeping my thoughts turned toward the future instead of the recent disastrous past. Having deposited my gear in Newfoundland, Willda had managed to get a ride back and breezed into my room full of cheer.

Frank Ambrose also dropped in, and explained how he had happened to be in the group of men who came to my rescue after the crash. He had been surveying the Bay of Fundy from the air, and had landed at St. Johns shortly before my spectacular arrival.

"As I came in for a landing, Ruth," he said, "I had one devil of a time getting in against the sun and a huge boulder at the end of the runway. When I learned you were coming in, I remarked to one of the guys that landing against the sun on a runway too short for heavy planes, you were in for bad trouble.

"Then I saw your white ship heading for the field and held my breath while you eased it down. When the plane touched ground toward the middle of the runway, I thought maybe you'd made it. But when I saw how fast you were heading for those cliffs, I said, 'She's got just one chance in a thousand if she'll take it!' And you did."

All this was balm to my wounded ego, and my spirits rose. I ignored the pain and concentrated on outwitting the doctors. Twenty-four hours after I was safely encased in a plaster cast, I started putting my plans into action. The Chamberlins had to leave next day, and this would be my only chance to get home by plane. When the doctor came in I gave him what was intended to be a dazzling smile and said:

"Doctor, I can't thank you enough for all you've done for me. Everybody here has been wonderful, but I have to go now."

"You—what!" He stared at me with professional concern, obviously convinced that the shock and pain finally had been too much for me, and I had gone out of my mind.

"I must go home," I repeated patiently. "What I now have to do requires a great deal of telephoning, and if I stayed up here my phone bills would break the Bank of England."

"Nonsense!" said the doctor. "You just relax now, and the nurse will bring you a sedative."

"Doctor!" I said, taking care to speak slowly and distinctly. "I am not crazy and I am not delirious. Except for this cast, I never felt better in my life. The Chamberlins are flying back tomorrow, and I must go with them. It's my only chance to get home without being bounced on a rocking steamer or jolted on a bumpy train. I do appreciate the excellent care I've had here, but I'm determined to get home by plane."

"By plane!" exclaimed the doctor, with a horrified look in his eyes. "Absolutely out of the question! What would the New York doctors think if I allowed you to be moved within a week with five cracked vertebrae, to say nothing of letting you go back in a plane?"

"You can tell the New York doctors that I left without your consent," I said, "because, I'm sorry, but that's what I'm going to do. I have the greatest respect for your knowledge of surgery, but I also have a specialized knowledge of air travel, and I know it's the easiest, safest and best way for me to get home. And I'm going!"

"I've had many patients," said the doctor grimly, "but never one as incorrigible as you. If you insist on this insane move, I shall wash my hands of your case."

With this he stalked out of the room, and Clarence and Willda dashed gleefully in. We made excited plans for a takeoff the next morning, and prevailed upon my day nurse to accompany me on the flight, just to be on the safe side.

The rough ambulance ride out to the airport next day gave me some twinges of doubt as to just how smart I had been in overriding the doctor's orders, but it was too late to turn back now and so I gritted my teeth and resolved to go through with the trip if it killed me.

At the airport I was amazed and somewhat disconcerted to see the doctor waiting for us. I thought at first he had come to see that I was taken forcibly back to the hospital. But he explained that he had come to supervise my shift from ambulance to plane, and I felt a surge of gratitude. Despite his annoyance at my stubborn determination and his complete professional disapproval of the trip, he nevertheless was fulfilling what he considered his duty to a patient —even a bull-headed one. In return I knew I must not let him see any sign of weakness or pain on my part.

Getting me into the small passenger compartment of Clarence's Crescent turned out to be quite a trick. Since it was impossible to jockey the stretcher through the cabin door, I had to be bent into an S-turn, cast and all, and slid through the door. Once inside, however, I was installed on bags of hay, which Clarence, bless his heart, had got hold of and with my feet elevated, I was quite comfortable. Then the nurse climbed in beside me, Clarence and Willda took their places in front and the doctor bade me bon voyage.

Clarence taxied the plane into position on the runway, gunned the motor and we were off. As soon as we were airborne I felt a dizzy sense of elation and a certainty that all would be well. In the smooth air there were no bumpy roads to jolt on, and I relaxed with a warm sense of well-being. Over his shoulder Clarence tossed occasional bits of news on our progress:

"We're passing Bar Harbor now. Fog's rolling in off the ocean. Sky's blue as indigo."

The only one in the plane who was not at ease was the nurse. Miss Jones had brought along an impressive kit of stimulants and hypodermics to revive the patient, but as we proceeded it seemed she needed them more than I did. Apparently it was her first plane trip, and her tense apprehension could not be concealed. I tried to ease her qualms by chatting companionably, explaining the various gadgets in the plane, pointing out how much smoother and faster it was to make the trip by air instead of on land or sea. She maintained her professional attentiveness, but her face was distinctly pale and her knuckles white from clenching her hands.

We had to land at Boston to refuel and to check through Immigration and Customs. This turned out to be a hectic half hour. Police had to hold back a crowd of the curious who had gathered at the field after learning by newspaper and radio that I was returning by plane. The inevitable reporters also were on hand. I told them I was doing fine and that my plane already was being shipped to Jersey City for repairs. Yes, I most certainly planned to make another try this fall for a solo flight across the Atlantic.

When we landed at Armonk, there was a similar reception committee of news cameras and movie equipment, curious bystanders and friends waiting to greet the prodigal. I was removed from the plane by reversing the S-turn, placed again on a stretcher and then in an ambulance and driven swiftly and fairly comfortably back home to Rye, though by now pretty tuckered out.

The family was waiting—all except Aunty, who was still in Paris—and they tried heroically to conceal their shock as I was carried up the steep staircase on the stretcher and deposited finally in my own bed in my own rose-pink room, which looked like a greenhouse full of flowers. There were stacks of telegrams and notes from friends, relatives and well-wishers, and a general air of festivity in my cheerful room, now crowded by stretcher-bearers, nurse and family.

It was good to be home. That was all I could think of as I stretched out one hand to Dad and the other to Mother, who was saying, "My darling, how *awful* this has all been!" and winked at my solemn sister and brothers. Dad, as he often did in emotional moments, lapsed into a T.R.ism; he cleared his throat and said, "It's bully to have you home."

And I repeated, a little shakily, I'm afraid, "It sure is bully to *be* home!"

When the ambulance men had left, the nurse went briefly off duty, and after the family had tiptoed out, I finally relaxed against the pillows. For a while I savored the heavenly quiet of my favorite room, gazed with a warm glow of gratitude at the banks of flowers sent by kind friends, sniffed the fragrance of roses, carnations and mixed bouquets and let peace flow through me. There was only one small flaw in all this sense of well-being, and that was the absence of Don. Although I had had his wires and although there were more ardent messages now beside me, I knew that he should have been here in person. And he was not.

If the situation had been reversed, and he was lying somewhere, *anywhere,* with a broken back, I knew that wild horses could not have kept me away. Certainly not a mere business trip, such as he had explained in what I considered too much detail in one of his telegrams. But even this disappointment could not mar my content for long, and as I sank off into drowsiness I told myself with a sense of discovery that men might be unpredictable but home was always the same.

My first visitor next morning was Ethel Tilson, friend and secretary whom I had nicknamed "Tillie," and who was to help me navigate the difficult course through convalescence during the weeks ahead—a course I found much more difficult than any I had encountered in the air. Together we worked every day toward the goal of another Atlantic try in the fall. She took dictation and typed out the hundreds of letters of thanks to people who had sent flowers and wires after my crackup. I held conferences with engineers, insurance men and lawyers over my bedside telephone. I got daily reports on repairs to *Akita* and Captain Railey's business arrangements. I chatted with friends who came to visit— fellow flyers such as Harry and Ruth Rogers and M. K. Lee, as well as kind-hearted Rye neighbors and casual acquaintances from the air field. I was interviewed and photographed in a swinging lounge on our veranda, and was quoted in headlines:

"I'LL FLY AGAIN SAYS RUTH."

Four weeks sped by, *Akita* was nearly back in shape again, and I knew it was up to me to match her progress. If I were going to fly the ocean in another few weeks, I'd better start getting in condition, and I wasn't going to build up strength by lying in bed. For the last week I had been able to spend some time each day in a perpendicular position, and I figured it was time now to get out of the bedroom. Tillie entered enthusiastically into my plans.

I reasoned that if I could sit up I should be able to drive a car, and if I could drive a car I should be able to pilot a plane. The Atlantic solo flight would not call for acrobatics, but chiefly for endurance. So it was to test my endurance that we planned an all-day automobile trip, a month after my return from New Brunswick.

Tillie helped me hobble down the stairs and into the driver's seat of the family car at nine o'clock one morning, and climbed in beside me. We started off and drove aimlessly along country roads. I was pleased but not surprised to find that my feet were able to manipulate accelerator and brakes and my hands were steady on the steering wheel. We stopped for lunch, which we ate in the car, looking out over a majestic vista of wooded hills with the Sound in the distance, and then continued the drive. I drove all day and when we finally returned home, I had not left the driver's seat for thirteen hours and I still felt fine. Of the two, Tillie appeared the more tired. I was jubilant, because the hours at the wheel of the car had approximated the longest unbroken stretch of flying time required for an Atlantic hop, and the actual handling of a plane required less physical exertion than driving a car, except at takeoffs and landings or during emergencies or blind flying.

As Tillie climbed stiffly out of the car and came around to help me out, I looked at her sympathetically and said:

"Poor lamb, I'm afraid I've tired you out and I guess you've been worried, too. But actually I feel equal to driving right on for hours."

That night I was more confident than in any of the weeks since the crash, and when Harry Rogers dropped in for a visit next day I demonstrated how well I could get around with the use of a cane, and entered into an enthusiastic discussion of plans for the flight.

Harry told me he was mighty pleased over the records I'd made with the Lockheed, allowed as how he took a little credit for having given me my first wings, but mostly he grinned and listened. As he left he patted my shoulder and said:

"You're a lucky babe. Just be careful I don't have to send lilies next time."

I was lucky indeed, I told myself. And nobody was going to have to send me lilies for a long time yet. Through the efforts of Captain Railey and Colonel Chamberlin, we had sufficient financial backing (in addition to the insurance money) to put *Akita* back in the air. Paramount News, Columbia Broadcasting System and the American Oil Company had been generous with their advances. Chamberlin's daily bulletins assured me that *Akita* would be better than ever when he was through with her. I knew I would never be able to express fully the depth of my gratitude to Clarence for his able direction of the disassembly of the plane at St. Johns, transportation back to Jersey City, followed by locating a then scarce fuselage to replace the one broken in half, the subsequent rebuilding and testing, and—even more—his constant encouragement and optimism. Such friends as Clarence and Willda didn't come down the pike very often, and anyone fortunate enough to have such friendship couldn't fail.

And besides all this, I had Aunty. Since her return from France she had been with me almost constantly.

"I guess it was just not meant for thee to make that flight," she said one day. "But it's clear that there are greater things to look forward to, dear, for thee *was* miraculously spared."

But when I confided to her that in another week I figured I would be limber enough to fly again, Aunty gave way to shocked protest.

"I have to, Angel," I said. "Remember how Dad always told me to get right back on the horse after I took a spill? It's the same idea."

Early in August Clarence flew over to Armonk, where I met him in the car, and he flew me to Teterboro Airport for a reunion with *Akita*. When I saw her, spruce and ready, shining in a new coat of paint, all white and gold, it was like meeting a long-absent lover. Leaning on my cane, I hobbled around her, stroking her smooth fuselage and patting her golden striped cowlings.

"She's more beautiful than ever, Clarence!" I exclaimed. "I can't wait to try her. How about now?"

"Well," said Clarence, "let's have a warm-up flight in my Crescent first, and I'll go along until you get your air legs."

In the dual-controlled Crescent, Clarence was leaning back in his seat. He grinned and said, "She's all yours." But the moment I gave her the gun and pulled her off the runway I realized the effects of a month in bed on a pilot's coordination and timing. I made a clumsy takeoff, and my feet reached the rudder pedals with difficulty, due to the confines of the cast.

Maybe I shouldn't have rushed things quite so much. Probably the officials of the Bureau of Aeronautics would not

have cleared me to fly if they had known (I carefully had
avoided telling them) that I was supposed to wear my cast
for another month, and then graduate to a steel corset for
two more months.

As we lumbered about the sky, Clarence snapped out his
opinion of my flying with his usual frankness, pulling no
punches. I countered with the remark that his plane didn't
handle as well as the Vega anyway.

"Well, why don't you fly your own plane?"

"That's just what I intend to do," I retorted.

I landed the Crescent with unnecessary speed, and hobbled as fast as I could toward *Akita,* which was waiting.
With a Herculean effort I clambered up a steep ladder onto
the wing and was eased into the cockpit with the assistance
of Clarence and a mechanic. Everything was new and
shining, the Wasp engine barked reassuringly, and I knew
I was back home where I belonged. While the engine
warmed up I noted that the cockpit layout and gadgets were
as they had been before. Quickly I headed for the takeoff
and *Akita* streaked down the runway. Then my heart lifted
along with the plane as we were in the air again together.
She was powerful, she was mine, and we knew each other.

Up and up we climbed, just *Akita* and I. I took great
breaths of the winey air, which reacted on my spirits like
champagne. Now I could forget the weeks in bed and the
dull pain of convalescence. Now I was alive again!

I put *Akita* and myself through our paces with increasing
confidence, feeling my hand steady on the stick and my re-
flexes regaining their timing. Gloriously we zoomed and
banked about the sky and then came down for a landing.
Here I experienced a moment of anxiety, as I realized that my
depth perception and speed sense were not acute. I was
indeed out of practice, and found it difficult to get good coordination of stick and rudder in a slight cross-wind. So my
landing was ragged, but safe. And as I clambered clumsily
out of the cockpit, with ample assistance, I was beaming.

"Not too hot on that landing, Ruth," remarked Clarence, helping me back toward the Crescent for the return flight to Armonk.

"I know," I admitted happily, "but it's all right, Bud. In fact it's wonderful. All I need is a little practice to get back in shape. Don't worry, I'll be ready to fly the Atlantic!"

11

POURING ON THE COAL

During the autumn of 1931 I found that the body followed the dictates of the mind. Still in a plaster cast, I went almost every day to the Jersey City field to make test flights in *Akita*, getting acquainted with my beautiful plane again, forcing aching muscles to perform the functions required.

The family protested daily when I set out from Rye, but Clarence backed me up. We agreed that it would be perfectly possible for me to make another try at the solo Atlantic flight—if the weather was right. After all, once I was seated in the plane all I had to do was sit there and manipulate the controls until I reached Paris, I pointed out. And there would be plenty of people to help me into *Akita* at the takeoff and out of her on arrival. Dr. Ogilvy, my orthopedic specialist, supervised the posture-angle of my cockpit seat and while at the airport worked out an installation of armpit hangars to relieve back pain if it became severe. He also said that on arrival in Europe I should remain in bed for a week. *That*, I said to myself, would be impossible!

So once more I worked over charts and check lists, studied weather maps and held business conferences, while Clarence tuned up the Wasp engine and made daily calls to Dr. Kimball at the New York Weather Bureau.

Early in September Paris newspapers reported a new record of twenty-five consecutive days of rain. With each day of bad weather reports my chances of making the hop grew slimmer, for flyers agreed that by the first of October it would be too late to make a try that year.

Then one day Clarence took my arm and steered me toward a corner of the hangar where we sat on a bench and he said:

"It's tough luck, but it looks like the Atlantic flight will have to wait for spring. I wouldn't like to see you try it this late in the year—no telling what sudden storms might come up. But I've been listening to some of the boys, and it seems they think you've been stalling—lost your nerve after your crackup."

I stared at him incredulously.

"How could anyone say that?" I gasped. "They've seen me making test flights every day. They know I've been ready to go for weeks, and they've had the same weather reports that we have."

"People can be darn cruel sometimes," Clarence replied soothingly.

It took a while for these words to sink in. I was dazed and hurt; why, oh why, I thought, can't people inquire what goes on under such circumstances? What could I do?

He brought me out of this self-questioning quickly.

"Why not break the women's long distance record on another transcontinental flight? It's more miles than the Atlantic hop, and it'll prove to everyone that you're up to endurance flying."

All of a sudden I had a bright idea.

"Clarence," I said, "how about this? Just this morning I got an invitation to take part in an air meet at Charlotte, North Carolina, to open the new airport there. With an honorarium, even. Why don't I do that, and then fly the southern route to California? It will be right on the way."

"Good idea," said Clarence. "Why not take it by easy stages to the coast, and then go out for a record on the flight back east. It'll be duck soup with the Lockheed's extra fuel capacity."

"I'll leave Friday, in plenty of time for the air meet," I

told Clarence. "It will be good to get into action again, and I'll keep in training."

It was good to be back at the field early Friday, savoring the bustle of departure and looking forward to action. In honor of the occasion I had changed from my plaster cast to an enormous, vise-like steel corset prescribed by my doctor, and found it much easier to climb into the plane.

The flight to Charlotte was smooth and beautiful, and I couldn't help wondering if I shouldn't have been headed east, across the Atlantic. But I knew that the good weather was strictly local, and that storms and ice-forming clouds were building over the ocean. With still no two-way radios for weather reporting available, nor the ice-breaking mechanisms which modern air transports possess, might as well make the most of what was possible. Lucky to be able to take part in the North Carolina air meet before heading for California.

Almost before I realized it I was approaching Charlotte, and the first glimpse of the new airport gave me a start. The runway looked short and too closely surrounded by trees, but as I glided down for a closer look I saw that there was ample space for a safe landing, even in a heavy plane like *Akita*. There would be no repetition of the nightmare at St. Johns.

Serene and confident I circled for wind direction and made a smooth landing. Waiting were many old friends, among them Wiley Post, with his warm grin and his twinkling one eye, Frank Hawks, Dorothy Hester, Al Williams. It was like Old Home Week that evening, as pilots got together and tried to outdo each other in "hangar flying," like fishermen swapping fish stories. I know of no other group in which such warmth and camaraderie prevailed as in that early bunch of record breakers and air racers.

Because of my recent crackup and the fact that I was still wearing a steel corset, I was accorded some special attention. There was a lot of kidding, but always the underlying congeniality of people who speak the same language and fly the same sky. It's difficult to explain, but impossible to ignore—this strange fraternity of flyers. And I wouldn't have missed being a part of it for all the tea in China.

Next day the air meet opened, with a side-splitting speech by Frank Hawks on how he got lost on a flight from nearby Richmond. Then we all put on our special acts; since the Lockheed Vega was not designed for acrobatics my exhibition consisted merely of chandelles, power dives, and wingovers.

We all cheered when Dorothy Hester, of Oregon, set a new record for outside loops. And I watched as breathlessly as any landlubber as Al Williams, famous stunt flyer, began his spine-chilling routine.

He was flying upside down barely one hundred feet above the runway when his motor quit. The crowd didn't realize what had happened, but every pilot there froze in horror. He didn't have enough altitude to roll out and make an airport landing. Surrounding the field was a crowd of fifteen thousand people and behind them a solid mass of cars packed for half a mile in all directions. Al was faced with the alternative of crashing on the runway or hurtling through the crowd, undoubtedly killing hundreds of people as well as himself. As we watched we saw a miracle. In the split second he had for a decision, Al spotted the one open space around the field—a spot about ninety feet wide and too steep for parking cars—rolled over and headed straight for it. Without enough space to squash, he slipped the plane into the ground on one wing to absorb the shock, then cartwheeled over and over up the incline. A wave of hysterical screams burst from the crowd, and I found my knees shaking violently. Al had chosen to sacrifice his own life and had taken the one chance to avoid crashing into the spectators, we realized, as the plane disappeared behind the hangar.

"The show must go on"—in an effort to stave off public hysteria Wiley Post and I were asked to put on another exhibition. To my delight, I set *Akita* down in a space several hundred feet less than that used up by Wiley's Winnie Mae. This small triumph was particularly gratifying since it bolstered my returning confidence in my flying skill. Afterwards I learned that, incredibly, Al was not only alive but almost unscathed. His uninsured plane was a total loss, but his only injury was a sore stomach from the tight seat strap.

I had often given thanks to God for saving me; now I murmured the old phrase, for Al's sake . . .

Suddenly I had an inspiration. I knew what the loss of his plane meant to Al, since it had been newly remodeled and was not insured. So I made my way over to Swanee Taylor, the delightful and gifted radio announcer who was emceeing the show and suggested that we ask the spectators for contributions to help Williams get a new plane. "Swell idea!" he said and instantly grabbed the mike for a stirring appeal. We literally passed hats among the crowd, collecting something like three thousand dollars.

On the next to the last day of the meet I had a wire from my brother Snowden that he was returning from leave and wanted me to fly him back to San Antonio, where he was stationed with the Army Air Corps.

Snowden—Nick to his family and friends—had just started on a career in military aviation, in which he was to achieve steady progress and solid distinction, emerging eventually with the rank of Colonel. Though I suppose I did pass along to him some of my own feeling for the freedom and the exhilaration of speed and height, he was to surpass me by far in his knowledge of the most advanced types of military aircraft.

Now, however, I had some qualms. I felt a strong responsibility for his safety, and I hated to have to stow him in the cubby hole behind the gas tanks in *Akita*'s cabin, but that was the only possible passenger space in this single-seater experimental Lockheed Vega.

When Nick arrived, however, he had such a bad cold that he didn't much care where he sat. I was determined to take all precautions, gave him an extra parachute and rigged up a pulley whereby we could trolley notes back and forth.

"If you hear the engine quit," I warned him, "and feel the wings waggle, that means you're to jump, and fast, because if that engine conks out over mountains or wooded country, that's what *I'm* going to do and I won't be able to see what's happening to *you*."

Nick grinned good-naturedly and replied:

"Aw, come on, Sis! You've never had to bail out up to now, have you? Quit worrying!"

Our course to Texas lay through Atlanta, New Orleans and Houston, and on the way we hung up some new inter-city speed records. Nick's cold was no better, but he seemed to enjoy the trip, including the parties given us at overnight stops.

I enjoyed it, too, and established a closer companionship and understanding with this brother who shared my urge to fly. During the last couple of hours of our trip no notes came over the trolley, and I concluded that Nick was catching up on "sack time" after the festivities of the previous night.

Just as I was coming in for a landing at San Antonio, a small open Army ship above me cut off my approach in a most irregular manner. I was definitely annoyed, so I cocked *Akita* on her ear and slid her down vertically three hundred feet to land alongside the other plane and tell its pilot what I thought of Army manners.

Nick in the windowless cabin, being rudely awakened by the vertical slip, said to himself, "Holy Mackerel—this is it!" and clutched wildly for my lap chute, which he had wedged between the gas tank and fuselage as a pillow. Still half asleep, he snapped it on his chest harness, pulled the rip-cord in pushing against the door, and as we came to a stop, out of the plane lurched my military brother enshrouded in parachute silk, right in front of the Post Commander's private plane, which turned out to be the one which had cut me off. . . .

My wrath dissolved in a burst of laughter as Nick gasped, "Ye gods! The Commander's plane!" and frantically scrambled behind *Akita* to try to disentangle himself from the yards of floating silk.

Instead of delivering the dressing-down I'd intended I summoned my best smile and paid my respects to the Commanding Officer, as Nick disappeared in a girl friend's car. Next morning, I felt particularly energetic after an evening of dancing and thought how doctors sometimes don't know the speed with which humans can recover. What was it the New Brunswick surgeon had said—that I wouldn't be able to fly again for at least a year? Well, it was only three months since the crackup, and here I was, after a strenuous week of flying feeling fit as a fiddle.

I made an early takeoff from Brooks Field for a proposed thirteen hundred-mile non-stop flight to Los Angeles. I noted that the field was very rough and that the plane, with its heavy fuel load, took the bumps hard, but I didn't think about it until six hours later.

I had put some eight hundred miles behind me, flying over Texas badlands and into southern Arizona, when the Wasp engine gave warning coughs that it was running out of gas. This was routine, and I switched on the last hundred-gallon tank—but she kept on gasping. I tried vigorous priming with the wobble pump, but nothing happened. Since I had only about two thousand feet altitude over rugged terrain, I couldn't afford to let the engine quit, so I hastily switched on the emergency gravity reserve tank, and she caught. However, this tank held only fifty gallons, and I had already used some for safety on the takeoff, so I figured I had about a half hour's flying time left. Anxiously I scanned the horizon and with relief spotted Phoenix airport ahead. This was a break, but I was disappointed at having to land when I'd been making such good time on a long hop. Clambering stiffly out of the cockpit I went aft to check on how much gas was left in the tanks, which might indicate feed-line trouble. I noticed that one of the dump valves was hanging open. Evidently the rough takeoff in Texas had jarred it loose, and I'd lost a whole hundred gallons of gas—no small item on my limited budget. I watched the men refill the tanks, and jiggle the dump valve to see if it held. It did, and I gave the matter no more thought until a week later, when I had reason to wish that I had insisted on a mechanic actually tightening up further on the valve screw. On such apparently small details may hinge a flyer's fate.

Next day I ran into foul weather, which forced me into three emergency landings on the last leg to the coast. The first was at Yuma, a small, sandy Arizona airport which I remembered from the Aviation Country Clubs tour and where Amelia Earhart's plane had nosed over during the first Women's Air Derby. I had to wait two hours for the clouds to lift, at least enough for the mountain passes to be clear, and then had to walk to a nearby wireless station to find a man to pull the prop against the engine's stiff compression and the terrific wallop of its back kick, as I had no self-starter.

Off again, I crossed the California border and climbed through San Gorgonio Pass when I ran into more heavy black rain clouds hanging over the mountains and the coast. Slipping under them, I tried to sneak up to Los Angeles parallel to the mountains, but I soon found myself in a box canyon with barely room enough to make a sharp wing-over turn to keep from smacking into the hillside. The clouds behind me were down to about two hundred feet and as an open field showed up ahead, I quickly decided to set the plane down. Hoping the clouds would lift, I kept the engine running and at the first break I took off again, climbed three hundred feet and spied March Field ahead. This was a large military airport even back in 1931.

Luck was with me. Rather than risk tangling with Los

Angeles skyscrapers I decided to land there and check the ceiling at Burbank. When I rolled gratefully to a stop on the long cement apron, nobody paid any attention to me, although officers, privates and mechanics were all around, busy at their own chores. Then a brisk top Sergeant strode up to the plane and demanded:

"May I ask, Miss, why you're landing here? This is a military post and civilian flying from here isn't permitted."

Often before I had landed at military fields and always received a courteous and cordial welcome. I was dismayed.

"But Sergeant, look at that sky!" I protested. "I don't want to plow into that soup without checking the weather ahead. But if I can't stay here, why, I can't. I'll take right off at once. Thanks so much!"

"Oh, no, you won't!" rasped the sergeant. "Now that you're here you'll have to get permission from the C.O. to leave. Regulations."

I was fuming, but regulations were regulations, and I trekked across the field to the C.O.'s office. Then I waited in line for half an hour; finally I was cleared to take off. It seemed a recent spy scare had caused a tightening up of security measures.

The weather check I received was not encouraging, but all I wanted was to escape from exposure to any more "regulations," so I gave *Akita* the gun and slid into Burbank some thirty minutes later, just as the airport lights went on.

As soon as I landed I telephoned Margaret Cooper, who was living with her husband in Beverly Hills, and had invited me to stay with her. Since our first meeting during the Aviation Country Clubs tour, Margaret had become one of my closest friends.

Margie argued that I should stay with them for a rest ("Trying for records with a broken back!" she protested. "It's plain crazy"). But I was adamant, so in the end the Coopers decided to drive up to Oakland where they would keep me company while I waited for favorable weather.

On my arrival at Oakland I left word with Operations that I was to be called twenty-four hours in advance if a good transcontinental weather map began shaping up. Soon afterward I set off with the Coopers for a charming inn on the eastern slope of the coastal range.

"What you need is a good rest," Margie kept saying. "And I'm going to see that you get it."

That evening we went over my various flight arrangements and speculated on how long a wait I would have before favorable weather developed most of the way across the continent. At that season, October, the Nautical Almanac showed about eleven hours of darkness, with dawn beginning a little before five and twilight ending about five-thirty. A pilot flying east meets the sun more quickly, and can subtract about an hour and a half of darkness. But no matter how much ceiling I might have, an overcast sky meant flying almost blind over the western mountains and deserts, where there are no city lights or highways below, and the horizon line disappears. Since there were no radio beams in those days, distance pilots who went out for records had to gamble on the weather much of the time.

"Ten hours of instrument flying is more than I want to plan on," I told Margie. "Even the airmail pilots, who have to fly in all kinds of weather, seldom have more than two or three hours of soupy flying."

"There'll be a moon," said Margie helpfully. "That should give you a horizon line."

"Sure. But heavy overcasts blot out the moon. It's too much to expect clear weather clear across the country with a full moon thrown in. I'm not *that* lucky!"

"Well, let's forget the weather and relax," said Margie. "You'll have three or four days at least before this soup clears up. Let's have fun, and catch up on our gossip."

We sat up late talking. Margie thought it was time I gave up competitive flying, got married and settled down.

"It's no life for a woman, Rufus," she said, "risking your

neck every few minutes. Look at you now—running around in a steel corset, fretting over how to get back east without banging into a mountain, waiting on weather, getting circles under your eyes. You've had enough adventure to last anybody else a lifetime. Why not take it easy, rest on your laurels and enjoy life?"

"I don't quite know why," I said slowly. "The right setup for marriage hasn't come my way and without that I'm not happy unless I'm flying. Besides"—I hesitated—"when I get married I have a certain man in mind, and I don't think he's ready yet."

I told her then about Don. She exclaimed over his picture, which I kept in my wallet, and said:

"Well, for Heaven's sake, if he's that wonderful, don't let this one get away! He must be crazy about you or he wouldn't be around so much. You go right back and marry him!"

"It's not as simple as that," I laughed.

I was still sleeping blissfully very early the next morning when the telephone rang. Oakland "weather" was calling:

"Looks as if you ought to start tonight, Miss Nichols. Clear weather is suddenly developing from California as far east as Ohio. From there on are storms, but chances are they'll diminish."

So much for my anticipated three or four days of rest. In less than two hours we were on the way back to Oakland. At the airport I worked frantically. No matter how carefully a long-distance flight is planned, there are always myriad last-minute details. Airport officials decided an incline should be built to give my heavily loaded plane enough initial momentum for a takeoff on the turf field.

Without runways for guidance, it is difficult to keep a heavily loaded plane rolling exactly straight, and this is imperative, since the slightest swerve may cause a disastrous ground loop. In addition it was necessary to maintain a direct line toward the longest point of the field windward, as this field had no objects on which to focus one's eye since it ran off into the bay. So as a further aid to my takeoff, flags were placed as markers over the longest smooth stretch of turf. About four in the afternoon the airport manager said:

"Now, look! You'd better get some rest before starting. We've got a room in the Administration Building with a bed reserved for you."

I knew I would have no further chance to sleep for many long and perhaps bad hours, but as I stretched out on the bed and tried to make my mind a blank, last-minute details of the flight kept churning around in my head. After an hour of this I got up, put on my flying suit and went out to *Akita*. She was ready. Her load of five hundred gallons of gas and forty gallons of oil was aboard, her engine was tuned up, everything had been checked.

It was not yet five o'clock and I hadn't intended to start before six. But as I looked at the sky I saw the evening fog bank beginning to roll in from the ocean earlier than usual, and I knew it was time to go—but quick. I turned to the mechanic in charge and said:

"Warm her up, please. I'm taking off now."

Last-minute interviews with news reporters, last-minute checks on items in the cockpit, a last-minute wave to the Coopers, loyally waiting to see me off. Then I opened the throttle, tested both magnetos as well as top r.p.m., and gave the familiar signal:

"Okay! Pull the chocks!"

My watch showed 5:17 p.m. Pacific Time on October 23 as I let *Akita* start her slow roll down the incline. With eyes glued to a point dead ahead of the line of flags I steadied stick and rudder. She picked up speed with the prop in low pitch and the throttle pushed to supermanifold pressure. A glance showed me 135 m.p.h. on the airspeed indicator, which was very fast ground speed for commercial planes of that day. The stick was lightening and much sooner than I expected we were airborne. The powerful Wasp engine had lifted a ton and a half of fuel off the ground in a little over fifteen hundred feet. I kept her nose down, however, to gain added momentum and headed out over San Francisco Bay only fifty feet above the water until I could pull the throttle back from emergency to full standard r.p.m., switch the prop into high pitch position, then slowly gain enough altitude to turn inland. In less than two minutes we were headed east, climbing at three-quarter throttle to eight thousand feet. Then I leveled off at the cruising air speed of one hundred sixty miles per hour, without regard to the wind velocity, upon which we had determined as the most efficient for the heavily-loaded plane. It seemed no time before Sacramento came into view and I saw that the city's lights already were on. So the long night had begun. From here on there would be few airports offering a possible landing for a heavily laden plane in trouble. And since I had cut every possible corner in plotting the course, contacting even these few landing fields was unlikely.

I was on my way to break the world distance record for women, now held by the French flyer, Mlle. Maryse Bastie, who had flown eighteen hundred and ten miles non-stop. I took a deep breath and settled into the rhythm of flight. As darkness fell, it was comforting to see an occasional lighted beacon flash, generally pointing an eastward path. The moon was up and almost full. It looked as if unusual luck were with me again. But even in the moonlight the horizon line was hazy and, to be sure I would clear the mountains, I climbed to ten thousand feet. There I knew there would be a strong tail wind and I had unlimited visibility. The beacons were now curving away from the more direct course I had charted. From then on this trail of intermittent lights swayed sometimes near, sometimes far, throughout the night.

After Sacramento my first check point for several hundred miles was Lake Tahoe, and I could see its great silvery expanse shining in the moonlight for half an hour before actually passing over it. As I did, it shone like a huge oval dia-

mond in the blackness of the surrounding mountains. Tiny
Reno, off to the left, was passed at 7:55 Mountain Time.
This meant that with my seventy-mile tail wind I had been
making a speed of three hundred miles an hour—sensational
for that era. I grinned with elation as I whispered, "Keep
blowing, Wind!" Again I was filled with the familiar ecstasy
of space and flight which were wings for my heart. I was
soaring on top of the world, with the sky ... the moon ... and
the stars as celestial company. Who would trade all this for
—*anything*?

The engine sputtered. I snapped back to the reality of the
smaller universe as I switched on another tank of gas, figuring the fuel consumption at thirty-five gallons per hour. Too
high for my estimated average of twenty-seven gallons, but
still all right for the first part of the flight, with so much
climbing at full throttle. Peering down at the pine-timbered
peaks below I thought of the pack trips I had enjoyed in
country such as this, from the Canadian Rockies to the lofty
Himalayas. Suppose my motor quit right now. I'd have to
jump, steel corset, fractured back and all. And then there
would be a long, difficult trek to a railroad. But I had my
compass and my knapsack—I'd make it. Then I jerked my
wandering thoughts up short. What nonsense! This good old
Wasp engine wasn't going to let me down. I was sailing
along through the glory of a star-studded sky in silvery
moonlight, high above the world. What more did I want?

Whenever a hundred miles stretched out without towns,
I'd check my course by the color of the beacons. They
flashed a code signal which made locations definite. Although
I didn't have the code book with me, I knew the green flash
meant an emergency field. These fields were illuminated
only by boundary lights, and were too small for safe landing
of a fast ship, but then I didn't figure I'd be needing to land.

About once an hour I saw the pinpoints of lights that
meant a town, and between these twinkling landmarks rose
snow-capped mountains incandescent in the moonlight.

When leaving Nevada I realized I was hungry. Although the need for constant alertness on a long flight makes it impossible to eat much, the average pilot *has* to take some nourishment about every six hours to maintain energy and sure reactions. I remember Amelia Earhart once said her stomach was so contracted during a flight that she could swallow only liquids, and she liked tomato juice best. As for me, I preferred caviar sandwiches, and I washed one down now with coffee. A couple of malted milk tablets served as dessert.

The food and coffee, which I never drink except on long flights and pack trips, renewed my energy immediately, so that I could feel the stimulation almost like an electric charge. But there was one mishap. During my snack a small thermos bottle rolled off the ledge beside me and wedged back of one rudder pedal. This was serious. To correct an air bump or possible emergency stall required full rudder, so I must dislodge the bottle. Leaning down to reach it was impossible, in my high steel corset—and besides leaning forward pushed the stick forward, inclining the ship toward a dive. I'd have to find another way. I tried to roll the bottle out with my toe, but it wouldn't budge. What a thing to happen! Just one of those stupid little accidents which could mean the difference between life and death. Finally I tipped the plane in a steep bank and the thermos rolled far enough so I could grab it.

That crisis kept me wide awake for a while, but now I began to feel drowsy. Everything was CAVU. I had plenty of altitude, unlimited visibility and in those days and at that late hour there was practically no possibility of meeting another plane. So I decided to rest my eyes for a few minutes by closing them. I knew I could remain alert even with my eyes shut for a brief time. It's part of the same subconscious discipline which has always enabled me to set a mental alarm clock guaranteed to awake me at any specified hour. My ears were attuned to each throb of the engine, I'd know

nstantly if there were any change. After five minutes relaxa-
ion I was refreshed, and flew on for two more hours with-
ut incident.

But over northern Utah fatigue overtook me again. I had
een flying about six hours at an altitude of fifteen thousand
eet. It was irritating to feel so tired. Maybe the frantic haste
of the previous day was catching up with me, or maybe my
fractured vertebrae cut down my usual endurance. Maybe I
needed some oxygen.

Turning on the oxygen tank, I sucked in a big breath
through a rubber tube. Suddenly I felt that I was floating
right out of the ship like an inflated balloon. I was exerting
too much back pressure on the stick as my senses reeled, and
Akita's nose went almost straight up, while she settled rapidly, wobbling on the edge of a power spin. Instinctively, I
pushed the stick forward in a dive, pulling back the throttle
for less strain on the still high wing-loading. We had dropped
six thousand feet, and were now at an altitude where the
normal oxygen content of the air restored my reeling senses.

I saw with relief that we had levelled off over flat desert,
in a valley *between* the mountains, and once more I was
clear-headed. I knew that for a moment I had been near a
blackout, and that unconsciousness, or a few miles difference
in course, would have meant death.

"Thank you, God," I whispered. "That was close, Angel!"

Flying at nine thousand feet, I soon passed over Salt Lake
City at exactly midnight, Mountain Time. Once more I
pulled up to sixteen thousand to clear the Continental Divide. After I crossed this great backbone of the nation, I felt
I was gliding down to the eastern seaboard and home. The
night was still brilliantly clear, with the engine's roar deafening in the surrounding quiet.

The majesty of the night engulfed me. There was resplendent Orion, shining alike on China and Utah. There
was the dazzling path of the Milky Way—countless millions
of whirling celestial bodies, each traveling through space at

speeds unimaginably greater than mine. Yet all were held in order as part of the infinite universe, disciplined by an Almighty Power. Far as I was above earth, I was still held by its gravity, whirling with it through the infinity of space even as I sped forward at the puny speed of three hundred miles an hour. What would it be like to break through the atmospheric barrier and swing free into limitless space, at one with the whirling spheres? Maybe someday man would find out. Maybe I would—someday.

Meanwhile I was dependent on the six hundred horsepower of a trustworthy engine, on the discipline of my own mind and body, on the benevolence of an all-supporting Power that granted me this rendezvous with stars and sky.

As the hours flowed by, my eyes grew so-o-o heavy. It took maximum will power . . . to force them open. All long-distance pilots have known the terrifying feeling of drowsing off and the tremendous effort it takes just to stay awake.

Then the horizon seemed to disappear completely, and I realized the truth of that old saying, "The darkest hour is just before the dawn." . . . But what was that? A streak of red across the darkness! At last the long, long night was over and I was witnessing the dawn of October 25. I had come safely through a night of indescribable splendor, *Akita* was still purring smooth and steady, and ahead was Des Moines, Iowa.

As swift as this was the transition from the sublime to the practical. Far ahead I could pick up the beacons of airlines converging on Chicago. As I drew nearer, the many flashing points radiated like the spokes of a great wheel. It was difficult to tell which line of lights were directed to Chicago, now sleeping and unlighted in the gray haze of dawn. There was a strong wind from the north causing such a wide correction angle on drift that I pointed the plane in an entirely different direction than that specified on the chart. After twenty minutes it was apparent that my compass compensation to offset the heavy cross wind had not been correct. I had missed Chicago entirely.

For the next two hours my attempts to make a position check were unsuccessful. Remembering the Oakland weatherman's report on the storm-bound Alleghenies, and having missed Cleveland, my one pre-arranged check point for ground-code weather signals, I decided that it would be the better part of valor to put down at the next airport. It seemed strange that I had not passed over a railroad. Could I be over Canada? At last I found a river, followed it to a large town, and to my amazement saw a sign that read—Louisville, Kentucky!

How in the world did I get there? I figured I had been flying for some time over wooded stretches of Michigan, in the section between Lake Michigan and Lake Huron. Then, without going far enough east to sight either Lake Huron or Lake Erie, and thinking the country looked like Canada, I had turned south. But I must have been much further south in the haze of dawn than I had believed. Anyway, here I was.

Swiftly I computed the night's flying. At 9:40 a.m. Central Time I had covered nearly two thousand miles on a great circle course, discounting extra mileage for my final detours. Of approximately fourteen hours in the air, ten had been flown in darkness at an altitude of more than fifteen thousand feet. I was fairly certain I had broken the women's distance record, and I knew also that my time and distance in the air were more than those required for a flight between Newfoundland and Ireland.

"Okay, Ruth," I said, "you can come down now."

12

SOME FLYERS NEVER DIE

Sometimes the solid earth looks mighty good, even to a flyer in love with the sky. It felt wonderful to me on the morning of October 25, 1931, when *Akita*'s wheels touched the runway at Louisville and rolled to a stop after two thousand miles in the air. What matter that at the end I had been lost, and had nearly blacked out over the mountains? I was here, wasn't I?

I sat for a minute in the cockpit, too weary to unfasten my seat belt. Then as mechanics and airport officials came running up to the plane I grinned, rubbed my eyes and called:

"Hi! Could somebody please give me a hand?"

Willing hands helped me clamber awkwardly out of the plane, stiff in my steel corset. Somebody said:

"How'd you ever see to get down, with that windshield covered with grease like that?"

It had in fact almost blotted out downward vision, but I had managed to peer through one relatively clear corner of the glass, with barely enough radius of sight to avoid wires and obstructions around the airport. I had known my depth perception probably was out of focus from fatigue, too. But somehow I'd managed a respectable landing.

Sitting on the sofa in the airport drinking hot coffee, I suddenly was overcome by waves of weakness and nausea.

The strain had been greater than I had realized. Gratefully I accepted the invitation of my friends, Captain and Mrs. Albert Woody, to get some rest at their home.

But even after I was stretched out in a soft bed between cool sheets, I found it impossible to relax. My nerves were still wound up tight, my cracked vertebrae were protesting, I ached in every bone and sleep was only a far-off dream. Even a hot bath did no good. It wasn't until a masseuse came to work on my muscles and put hot towels on my spine that I was able to let go. Relaxed and drowsy at last I sank into the blessed relief of sound sleep.

That long overdue rest lasted only four hours, because news of the flight and my new distance record had reached New York, the newspapers were out with headlines and I had to make a national radio broadcast, originally scheduled for New York and now rearranged in Louisville.

Sleepy as I was, I felt a glow of satisfaction when I saw the headlines: "RUTH NICHOLS BREAKS WOMEN'S DISTANCE RECORD—FLIES WITH BROKEN BACK" . . . "RUTH DOES IT AGAIN" . . . "AVIATRIX SETS NEW RECORD DESPITE INJURIES."

After the broadcast, during which I described high spots of the flight and skipped lightly over the matter of why I happened to land in Kentucky instead of New York, I went back to the airport to arrange for servicing of the plane before my departure the next day. Then I returned to the Woody home for more relaxation, good conversation and a long, wonderful night's sleep.

I woke next morning feeling jubilant, to open a stack of congratulatory telegrams from family, friends and fans. Officials had computed my flight at nineteen hundred fifty miles—five hundred better than Mlle. Bastie's record. *Akita* had proved her air-worthiness for long distance flights, and so had I. A few cracked vertebrae weren't going to stop me. By cinching this record I had become the first pilot in history to establish marks in three different maximum international categories—altitude, speed and distance—while flying the same Lockheed plane.

After being told by doctors only a few months before that I couldn't fly for a year, if ever, this was a great feeling. Looking back, on that bright morning in Louisville I realized it was one of my life's high points. I arrived at the airport walking on air, to find everything ready for the takeoff. *Akita* had been cleaned, was tuned up and waiting, looking beautiful with her white and gold paint shining in the morning sun.

A mechanic helped stow my gear, and I climbed into the cockpit and started slowly warming up the engine, when he climbed up beside my open cockpit and said with a worried look:

"Miss Nichols, I wish you wouldn't fasten your safety belt until you're ready to go. Just a month ago another girl's plane was here, and it backfired while warming up. The whole ship burst into flames so fast we barely got her out in time."

I smiled at him reassuringly and replied:

"This Wasp always behaves like a lady, so don't worry."

After the oil temperature gauge indicated sufficient heat, I opened the throttle to its maximum standard r.p.m. on the ground and was pleased to note that the Wasp responded beautifully. The slight miss I had noticed just before landing was gone, and she was hitting on all cylinders in smooth, powerful rhythm. With a wave to my friends, I released the brakes and let *Akita* start rolling down the field, to get in position for takeoff.

Suddenly the stick was jerked out of my hand.

"That's queer," I thought, and pulled back the throttle. Again I felt a jerk, and opened up the hatch to look back. Instantly the cockpit was filled with smoke, and I saw flames licking the fuselage. My friend, the lugubrious mechanic, was frantically tugging at the elevators to attract my attention. Seeing a spurt of flame, he had run after the plane and grabbed at the tail to tell me something was wrong.

Sliding down into the thick smoke, I made a pass at the ignition switch, which I couldn't see. As I struggled to stand up on the seat, I found that I was wedged in by my parachute.

Through the open hatch I heard the mechanic's frantic yell:

"Get out! GET OUT QUICK! She'll EXPLODE!"

A mass scream rose from the crowd watching the takeoff, and I tried desperately to get one foot on the seat for an upward push. But the steel corset and my heavy flying suit, plus the wedged parachute, held me in a vise. With fumbling fingers I tried to unfasten the stiff 'chute buckles on my legs. Was I to die now, held by this tight harness?

Flames were shooting up both sides of the cockpit, and I knew it was now or never. A last desperate wrench at the buckles and straps, and they gave. Ignoring the pain of movement in my steel corset I lunged up, out and onto the wing. It was no longer possible to get down the side of the ship. Flames ten feet high leaped around the fuselage. Scrambling to the wing tip, I jumped—and landed squarely on top of two mechanics. At that split second the gas tank behind the pilot seat in the cockpit exploded.

Dragged into the yelling crowd by the mechanics, I looked back at the burning ship and saw with amazement that the propeller was still turning. Blinded by the smoke, I had missed the right magneto stop on the switch, and I realized with a numbing awe that this small accident had saved my life. The turning propeller, acting like a fan, had created a draft which kept the flames back from the cockpit just long enough for me to escape. Shakily I whispered:

"Aunty! God did it again!"

Airport mechanics were aiming fire extinguishers at the blazing plane when three fire engines clanged up and joined the fight. But nothing could stop the gasoline-fed inferno, as other gas tanks exploded. Firemen fought to get a hose into the cockpit, and while I watched, horrified, one climbed astraddle the plane's nose with his back to the propeller. At any second another explosion within the cockpit from alcohol in the compass might detonate him into those whirling blades. How could we halt that slicing prop? It was impossible to get inside the cockpit to turn off the ignition and shut off the gas. I saw there was only one way.

Thrusting aside restraining hands I dashed out to the plane, and with arms shielding my face from the searing heat, screamed at the fireman:

"Point the hose at the air intake! It'll cut off half the mixture! That's the only way to stop the propeller! The intake! Look! Point it at the intake!"

He didn't hear me, and continued to play the stream of water on the motor. But Clarence and I had taken every precaution against any onslaught of water over the north Atlantic, and I knew you couldn't drown that good old Wasp engine. I spotted the fire chief, and repeated my frantic instructions to him. He didn't seem to understand. Other firemen clustered around, and finally one got what I was talking about. He aimed his hose at the air intake, and at last the Wasp coughed and died.

Two firemen were taken to the hospital to be treated for burns, and the blackened carcass of my beloved *Akita* still smoldered on the runway. The pain in my heart as I looked at her was for a loyal friend, not just a machine of aluminum and steel. We had been through a lot together, *Akita* and I, and she had never failed me. Who had failed her? My mind went back to that airport in Phoenix, where I had made a forced landing because of a leaking dump valve. That was it! Why, oh why hadn't I insisted that the hinge be tightened, instead of just charging it all off to a bumpy takeoff in Texas? Leaking gas had ignited from the exhaust, of course. And my beautiful *Akita* was a charred wreck, no longer proudly white and gold, but black and twisted.

Only a few minutes ago I had been shaking hands with Lady Luck. Now I was sunk in a self-accusing low. One thing was sure. I would not let *Akita* die. I would save what was left of her. But how?

My mind flew to Chamberlin. He had performed miracles already in building and rebuilding the Lockheed. After my long-planned ocean flight I was going to reimburse him in dollars and cents, as well as with the publicity his company had been receiving for remodelling *Akita* for record flights. Would he help again? I headed for a telephone and put through a call to New York. Willda answered. I swallowed my pride, got a tight grip on my shaky voice and said:

"Willda! The plane burned up on takeoff! Yes, I'm all right but *Akita* is a wreck. Willda, I can't just leave her here for junk. I'm sure there's enough to save. Will you *please* tell Clarence I'll never ask help like this again, if he'll only come down to Louisville now and help me get her to New York. I'll call Powel Crosley. I'll convince him that we can crate the plane back to New York and rebuild it. I'll make him see that he must help us. Oh, please!"

Willda hesitated, and then Clarence got on the phone. I knew he was acting against his better judgment, but both he and Willda were warm, generous people, and they were my friends. Within a few hours he was in Louisville, and never have I been so glad to see anybody in my life. His casual grin and easy voice made anything seem possible.

Already I had been on the phone with Crosley, and his first reaction when he heard of the disaster was businesslike and chilling. Ship the remains back to Cincinnati, he said. It sounded like a funeral. Tears streamed down my cheeks as I argued.

"Oh, please no!" I begged. "Please, Mr. Crosley, let me get her rebuilt once more. I'll raise the money somehow. It won't cost you a cent. I've got to make it up to her, don't you see? She's a great plane, and she's seen me through a lot of things. I can't just leave her like this. I know *Akita* is your plane, but if you'll just let me keep her a while longer I'll have her good as new again. I think the engine is still all right. It was still running after the fuselage was almost gone. Oh, won't you please give me just this one more chance? Anyway, talk to Clarence before you decide . . ."

The conversation terminated on a discouraging doubtful note. However, during a second call both Clarence and I combined our arguments to such good effect that, however reluctantly, Powel Crosley agreed that I could have another chance, and once more I found words inadequate to thank him.

Clarence looked over the charred remains of *Akita* and shook his head but admitted that she could be salvaged—*if* I could raise the money. This time there was not adequate insurance for the repairs that must be made. But I was determined that somehow, somewhere, I would raise the necessary cash. Clarence superintended the crating of the plane, and finally we made the trip back to New York in his plane, leaving *Akita* to follow by freight. It was a strangely silent flight. I tried to express my gratitude to Clarence, tried to tell him how much this meant to me, stammered over promises to repay him for all his time and effort on my behalf, but I knew before I started that this was the sort of thing that could never be fully repaid. I realized then what a very precious thing friendship is. For the first time I really began to think about that old question: what is a friend?

Well, perhaps it is someone who is there to come to your aid when times are really tough. To stand by and lend strength when you are down. To restore your hope and faith when your spirits have touched bottom. In all the many and desperate lows of my life, there have been good friends to help see me through. Willda. Clarence. Crosley. Harry Rogers. Margie. Aunty . . . With such friends, nobody could afford to give up.

Ironically, I was greeted on my return to New York with

the kind of reception that awaits a champion—interviews, newsreels, broadcasts, tons of fan mail.

I gave interviews and interviews, and did broadcasts and broadcasts, and spent many days answering my mail. I couldn't ignore these letters from people all over the country, people I had never seen, who wrote to offer me their congratulations or their sympathy. I couldn't just send out a form letter; in simple human gratitude I had to answer each one myself. Anyone who would take the time and trouble to stretch out a hand to a stranger deserved an expression in kind.

Back home in Rye, Aunty helped bolster my sagging spirit. Standing on tiptoe to kiss my cheek, bright blue eyes boring into me, she patted my shoulder and said briskly:

"Cheer up, dear. Remember that God helps those who help themselves."

I was faced with the fact that already I had raised a sum of approximatcly $100,000 in terms of airplanes and equipment borrowed, contracts, loans and insurance—all this before the disastrous fire in Louisville. Only a small part of the sums advanced for the ocean flight were due to be returned, but there was a heavy obligation to make good for the sake of those who believed in me in addition to raising additional funds for *Akita*'s rebuilding and another Atlantic attempt.

So I took advantage of every offer for lecture engagements, endorsements, public appearances and first-person stories to add to the fund needed to restore *Akita*. The Fédération Aéronautique Internationale gave me official recognition for the new long-distance record for women, and this helped. Every public accolade made the fund-raising a little easier, and so I accepted them all, including an invitation from the Aero Club to join some four hundred other pilots and air enthusiasts at a gala ball in Washington. There certificates of achievement were to be awarded to those who had set air records during the last year. Among the group were Jimmy Doolittle, Wiley Post, Harold Gatty and six women, of whom I was one, who had piled up more than half the seventeen records cited for 1931.

It was a festive gathering of people who spoke the same language and had faced the same hazards, men and women all bitten by the same aviation bug. A series of cocktail parties preceded the formal banquet, the guest list including trans-Atlantic pilots, record flyers and military officials, all in formal evening clothes. On the way from one cocktail party to another in the same hotel, a group of us were packed like sardines into one small elevator when suddenly it plunged five floors, with sickening impetus. This was more frightening than any airplane dive. We were all pale and shaken when the elevator bounced to a stop halfway between the ground floor and the basement, and we were hoisted by our arms to the lobby floor. Next day the following headline appeared in the *New York Sun* of January 5, 1932:

15 FLYERS CRASH; BUT IN ELEVATOR

There were more bright spots during that winter, the high point of which was a citation from the Ligue International des Aviateurs as "American Champion Woman Flyer for 1931"—the first such citation awarded to a woman in this country.

In between times I wrote magazine articles to swell the *Akita* fund and to give me something to live on, made new contacts with backers and enjoyed some concerts, plays and dances for which I had had little time during the past few years. Now that I was at last out of my steel corset, dancing was fun. Between writing bouts I joined other flyers in the shows put on for the unemployed, whose numbers were growing in that depression year. And I made a speech at Wellesley College, where I discovered considerable interest in flying among the students—so much, in fact, that I decided someday to start a course of lectures on aeronautics in women's colleges.

Through these various activities I had almost reached the financial quota needed to complete repairs on *Akita* and new plans for an Atlantic flight in the spring, when I received a flattering offer from the National Council of Women, which included both the General Federation of Women's Clubs and the National Federation of Business and Professional Women. They were all cooperating in plans for the 1933 International Congress of Women to be held in Chicago, and they invited me to make a good will tour as "Air Ambassadress for Five Million Women." My assignment was to secure a hundred thousand signatures to a petition to be sent to governments around the globe, asking them to send delegates to the Congress. I accepted delightedly, since this presented an opportunity not only to keep flying and earn money but to enter actively into work for the betterment of international relations, a subject which had interested me, intermittently, since my world cruise as a girl just out of college.

A preliminary for the tour was a dramatically staged farewell to Dr. Mary E. Woolley, president of Mt. Holyoke College, on her departure as one of the American delegates to the International Peace Conference at Geneva. My part in her sendoff was described in the January 21, 1932, issue of the New York *Times*:

"An innovation almost without precedent in the harbor, the anchoring of a trans-Atlantic liner at Quarantine on her way out to sea, marked the first stage of the delegation's journey. When the *President Harding* was passing the Statue of Liberty, Ruth Nichols, the flyer, soared by in a silver amphibian. With Captain Harry Rogers as co-pilot, she zoomed about the ship all the way down the upper bay and at Quarantine, came to rest on the water as the *President Harding* dropped her anchor. Tying up to a tug which made fast to the liner, Miss Nichols came aboard and presented two bouquets of flowers to Dr. Woolley.

"After posing for camera men with Dr. Woolley, Miss Nichols, who wore a purple dress under a purple leather flying suit, the same that she had on when she attempted her Atlantic flight last summer, climbed back into her plane. As the liner weighed anchor and steamed past Sandy Hook, she again circled about the ship in final greeting to the delegates."

Often in the years since I have looked back on this gay excursion with mixed feelings, because this was the last time I was to see my old friend and flying instructor, the man who started me on my adventurous flying career— tough and gentle Harry Rogers. A month later, as I sat in a formal conference with representatives of the National Council of Women, the news was brought to me that Harry Rogers had been killed in a plane crash. He was taking off from North Beach Airport, a routine operation which he could have done in his sleep, when his engine quit. Why he had not fastened his seat belt and had turned back at low altitude nobody knew. Other great pilots have taken similar chances. My first and greatest teacher was gone, and his passing left me with an empty feeling.

As I prepared to start on the National Council tour, work on *Akita* was going ahead steadily. Life Savers, Inc., the famous candy company of Port Chester, New York, and my brother Nick, had made generous donations, and we needed only another thousand dollars to have her back in condition, as good as new. It was about this time that Clarence met Powel Crosley at a get-together of flyers and aviation enthusiasts and suggested off-handedly that he might ante up the balance. Both were in a jovial mood, and Chamberlin's proposal was a casual, "Oh, give the little girl another thousand, Crosley!" To which my long-suffering benefactor good-naturedly agreed.

So it was in high spirits that I set off in mid-April on the tour. I knew that when I returned *Akita* would be reconditioned and ready for the long-planned Atlantic hop. And I was feeling in top shape, my backbone as good as new.

A notable group of women, including novelist Fannie Hurst and Lena Madesin Phillips, president of the Council, gave me a rousing sendoff at Floyd Bennett Field. Mother and brother Nick, handsome in uniform, also were on hand.

While *Akita* was receiving her finishing touches, I was flying Chamberlin's diesel-powered Lockheed, in which a month before I had made an official altitude record for both men and women in aircraft powered by an engine of that type. The record, I believe, still holds. It was a rugged, dependable plane whose experimental oil-burning engine nevertheless had a number of bugs. For one thing, it was constantly blowing out glow-plugs used for warming the fuel mixture, and when that happened long white plumes of smoke would stream out, giving spectators the impression that the ship was on fire. For another, the vibration was so bad that out of ten standard instruments on the plane, seven were broken from the jarring before my return. The diesel fuel also produced a strong odor in the cockpit, the fumes so permeating my luggage and clothes that my public appearances during the tour always were highly and not very agreeably aromatic. Having a strong stomach, I soon became accustomed to the fumes, but another pilot who ferried the plane between cities for me on one occasion when weather had forced me to take a night train in order to keep a public appearance engagement, was almost overcome. On arrival he said:

"I wouldn't fly that oil-burner another mile!"

The tour only lasted two weeks, and covered three thousand miles. So tight was the schedule that my previous tour for Aviation Country Clubs seemed like a leisurely holiday. The itinerary included visits to eleven cities, as far west as Omaha, and hitting each exactly on schedule, which meant flying to a different city nearly every day, with no allowance for weather or unforeseen delays.

This was probably the busiest fortnight of my career. Since most airport mechanics knew nothing about servicing a diesel engine, I had to supervise most of the work myself at each stop. Then, stepping out of the roles of pilot and mechanic, I would spend the rest of the day as speaker, business woman and social representative of the National Council, with a constant round of luncheons, teas, dinners and press interviews. The signature campaign demanded a speedy tour, and this suited my plans, for I was itching to get back to New York and start test hops for the new trans-Atlantic try.

The weatherman did nothing to aid me. A low-pressure area over the middle west refused to budge, so most of my flying in that region consisted of hedge-hopping and landing in pea-soup fog. One particularly hair-raising emergency landing was just across the river from St. Louis. As I reached the middle of the Mississippi I realized that if I tried to burrow under the lowering clouds I would wind up in the river, so I turned back toward a nearby pasture on the Illinois side, and as I made a ninety-degree turn to land, one wing was in the clouds while the other barely missed the telephone wires. It was comforting to learn that Jimmy Doolittle had also been forced to "sit down" nearby because of fog that same day.

As always, some of the most jarring experiences of the tour were the motorcycle escorts sent to speed me from airport to city, careening with open sirens through red lights and across busy intersections as I shut my eyes and held my breath. My terror of these shrieking trips was shared by Amelia Earhart, who used to say:

"If you want to travel faster than forty-five miles an hour, do it in the air!"

It was at Chicago's Municipal Airport, however, that I received the most startling welcome of the trip. I was just ready to set the plane down when I saw a closed white car that looked like an ambulance dash directly across the runway.

Why should they send an ambulance to meet me? Maybe I had lost a wheel. Maybe the plane was on fire and I didn't know it. It must be a warning of some kind. I gunned the motor and pulled up for another circle of the big airport, hovering uncertainly over the opposite end of the field. Maybe, I thought, they were trying to warn me that I was landing on the wrong runway. But again the white car dashed across my path.

This must be something serious. I peered over the side, but it was impossible to see the landing gear from the cockpit. I checked the plane for smoke, but couldn't detect anything wrong. I circled again and tried to decide what to do. At last I said to myself:

"Well, here goes! I'll just have to make as light a landing as possible and see what happens. Can't circle around like this all day."

I brought the plane down for a beautiful landing, and before the wheels came to a stop the white car was alongside. As I climbed out of the cockpit to see what was the trouble, out stepped the mayor's aide. This was not an ambulance, but an official city car sent to welcome me. Later, in thanking the mayor, I suggested that if this car were used to greet any other flyers, it be painted another color; moreover, the driver should avoid crossing the runway in the path of a landing plane.

Chicago was the last stop on my itinerary, and I headed for home. Checking the cost of the trip I was amazed to find that I had flown three thousand miles on fifteen dollars' worth of diesel fuel. I had arrived at every city on schedule (always by plane, with one exception) had collected the required hundred thousand signatures, and had told the story of the International Congress of Women all over the country. Definitely, the tour had been a success.

Now I was free to concentrate on the project nearest my heart—preparations for an ocean flight. As I landed at Floyd Bennett Field I was greeted by the Council president with a massive bouquet of roses, and handed over to her the rolls of signatures while newsreel cameras ground. On the edge of the crowd I glimpsed Clarence Chamberlin, and so escaped from the feminine furore as fast as possible to join him in the airport restaurant for a coke and news of *Akita*.

"How's it going?" I asked eagerly. "How does *Akita* look?"

"Well, she looks fine," grinned Clarence. "Had to make a few changes in the original plans, but she's rarin' to go."

"What changes?" I asked quickly. Before I left we had agreed that for the sake of greater safety, the cockpit should be rearranged so that the pilot's seat would be behind the gas tanks.

"Well, it turned out to be too expensive to do that rear cockpit job," he drawled, "so we've used the sunken-wing construction after all."

This was the alternative we had discussed, whereby the wing would be dropped fourteen inches down into the fuselage, permitting a wider opening at the top of the cockpit and greater visibility for the pilot, whose head would now be above the wing. We figured the dropped-wing placement also would make for more efficient performance, since the wing would be nearer the line of thrust.

At first I felt a quick flash of annoyance that my decision in favor of a greater safety factor had not been followed, but then I realized that Clarence was, after all, my technical adviser, that he was doing me a priceless service, and that I certainly should be able to trust his judgment, so I thanked him profoundly and said:

"You're the doctor. If you say it's okay, that's good enough for me."

We made two more additions to the rebuilt Lockheed. I suggested the general idea for a streamlined windshield which would open more easily and give good visibility. Clarence worked out a belly-skid by which for the first time a high or mid-wing monoplane could land after detaching its landing gear, by pulling a cable handle in the cockpit, thereby gaining thirty miles per hour in speed plus the added factor of a safer emergency landing if over rough terrain or water.

Remodeling always is time consuming and the weeks sped by. Toward the middle of May news stories about my contemplated Atlantic hop began to appear, although I had not sought publicity this time. I already had the required financial backing, and I was growing superstitious about too much advance ballyhoo, in view of the disastrous end to my previous attempt.

One day about this time Amelia Earhart had lunch with me at our home in Rye, and we discussed the various problems of ocean flying. I knew that she also was planning a flight, but I didn't know whether it was to be over the north or south Atlantic; anyway, whoever was ready first would start, regardless of anyone else. I described to Amelia the work that had been done in rebuilding my plane, and of the safety factors that had been added. But she said:

"You know, Ruth, I always feel that you have to take some chances on long-distance flights, so I don't bother to go into all the possible accidents that might happen. I just don't think about crackups."

Amelia, like many flyers, was a fatalist, who believed that you would go when your number was up and not before, and meantime there was no use worrying about it.

Two mornings later, while awaiting word from the factory that *Akita*'s last remodeling installations had been completed, I opened the paper to be greeted by screaming headlines: "AMELIA EARHART OFF ON OCEAN FLIGHT."

Bernt Balchen, noted pilot, had flown Amelia to Harbor Grace, Newfoundland, where she would take off alone for a flight across the North Atlantic.

Amelia hopped off next day, in the early evening of May 20, 1932, and landed on "a long, sloping meadow" in Ireland. Amelia, not I, was the first woman to fly solo across the Atlantic.

13

PULL CHOCKS!

At first news that Amelia had beaten me to the title of first woman to fly the Atlantic alone, I felt pretty low. If I hadn't cracked up last year on the first leg of my flight . . . If I hadn't taken so much time trying for perfection in the rebuilding of my plane . . . If I hadn't had to work so hard to get financial backing . . . If . . . If . . . If. . . .

I was leaning forlornly against *Akita*, when Clarence breezed into the hangar. While I was brooding, he was doing his best to cheer me up.

Suddenly he asked me why I didn't try a non-stop flight from New York to Paris. There would be no fiddling around between Newfoundland and Ireland—just a hop off at Floyd Bennett Field, no danger of unknown airport landings and a straight flight to Paris. *That* would make people sit up and take notice!

It certainly would, I realized. But what a terrific number of hours in the air and most of it over the ocean!

I pondered this new idea. After all, hadn't I always had faith that any worthy goal could be accomplished? Amelia had beaten me to a solo hop, so why not set my sights on breaking another frontier? Dwelling on a lost opportunity wasn't going to get me anywhere. There *were* other flights to make which would put aviation that much ahead. I knew

that I had a great ship, had had excellent and varied experience and there was the whole blamed sky to fly in. I sure
better snap out of it.

After these reflections I felt a great weight float away and
once again my heart had wings. What a way to have acted!
I felt thoroughly ashamed of myself and better than I had
since I'd sent off my congratulatory cable to Amelia.

Clarence and I promptly settled down for serious discussion about the feasibility of a non-stop New York-Paris
flight. That would mean thirty-six hundred miles of flying
without a stop. Could I do it? Could I keep my brain focusing
well enough for twenty-four solid hours in the air?

We spread out the maps and charts and talked over all
the angles. It was possible, all right. After all, Lindbergh
had done it, five years earlier, in a small single-motor plane
not nearly as fast or as modern as the Vega. *Akita* had all
the latest improvements, and we had worked long and lovingly to make her the best of her class in the air. Clarence
figured she could carry another fifty gallons of fuel for the
flight, making a total of about six hundred and twenty gallons. But would my endurance be adequate?

I recalled that on my West-East record flight last fall,
which was just short of two thousand miles, I had made an
error in navigation judgment during the last hours. But of
course I was still wearing that steel corset then, and my
broken back had not entirely healed. Now I was in better
physical shape. But the strenuous flight as "Air Ambassadress" for the women's clubs, plus my frantic efforts at
financing, unable to retain again a business manager, seemed
to have left me pretty exhausted.

I went home to Rye to think things out, and dropped the
Paris idea into Aunty's ears to see what reaction I would get.

"It's a much longer flight than I first planned, Angel," I
pointed out. "It means I'll have to stay in the air and alert

for twenty-four hours and thirty-six hundred miles. Does thee think I can do it?"

"Well, I won't allow myself to worry about thee, because I know thee can do anything thee wants to," said Aunty decisively. "That is a thing I have noted since thee was small, dear; so make up thy own mind to the best of thy present knowledge, profit even emotionally from setbacks and trust in the rightness of any outcome."

With faith and love to urge me on, how could I fail? I felt a wild desire to laugh and cry all at once, and with it the purely feminine need for a strong shoulder to cry on— Don's shoulder, to be specific. Why did he have to be away whenever I needed him? If we ever did get married, what kind of a life would it be to have a husband who was never at home?

I hugged Aunty, murmured, "Thee *is* an angel," and fled to my room. There I went over and over again all the pros and cons of the prospective flight. And before I fell asleep I had reached a decision.

"O.K., Clarence," I said to him early next morning at the field. "I'll make that New York-Paris hop. But first I want to take a quick trip to Europe, so I can fly around the coastlines of France, England and Ireland and get acquainted with some landmarks. If I'm to hit Paris on the nose after twenty-four hours of flying, I want all the guide-posts I can get. And besides, the trip by ship not only will give me a chance to rest and build up some reserve strength, but also to brush up on celestial navigation."

So it was arranged. I booked passage on the next boat for Paris, and checked in at a hotel owned by the French aviator Lotti, one of the crew of the *Yellow Bird*, which had made a splendid trans-Atlantic flight a few years before, by way of the Azores. As soon as I had deposited my bags, I sought out Lotti and asked him if he could dig up a plane for me to fly early next morning—a dependable one that would not cost a fortune. After the usual Gallic amenities, Lotti stared, shrugged and said:

"Mais, Mademoiselle! You are now in France, and here we do not accomplish things so quickly as you in America."

I turned on what I hoped was a disarming smile, and pleaded:

"Oh, please, dear M'sieu Lotti. I know for most people this would be impossible, but not for *you*. You understand the urgency of these things, as other men could not. Won't you try?"

Thus challenged, Lotti got busy on the telephone, and by dint of threats and imprecations in machine-gun French, all accompanied by lavish gestures, he located a plane within the hour. Next morning, accompanied by a cheerful and talkative French pilot, I took off for a delightful day's flight —not too enlightening, since the plane was too slow to cover the northern coast of France—but fun.

Both time and money were short, so next day I hopped a trans-channel plane for England, figuring the coastline of the British Isles would be more important in my plans than the coast of France. Once I had spotted England or Ireland, I certainly would be able to get to France. Almost immediately I located a Puss Moth plane, with the help of Colonel and Mrs. Warwick Wright, old friends from my world cruise days. Next day I took off from Heston Aerodrome, accompanied by Pilot Philip Weedon.

The plan was to make a survey flight along the coasts of Devonshire, Wales and Ireland, after which I would sail for home from Cork, and Weedon would fly the plane back to London. I was well supplied with maps and charts, on which I made ample notes of the coastlines of the British Isles. The reconnaissance flight was most valuable, except for one near mishap, on a hop from Holy Head, Wales, across the Irish Sea. Visibility was low, the little Moth was not equipped for blind flying, and the situation was precarious, to say the least, before we finally landed on the beautiful buttercup-starred airport of lush green at Baldonnel, Ireland. A mechanic came to look over the motor, gave one glance and exclaimed:

"Saints be praised, Ma'am, in another five minutes y'r motor would've quit for lack of oil!"

I felt a chill between my shoulder blades. Baldonnel was right on the coast, the first point of land on the flight from Wales, so any slight delay, such as headwinds, would have meant coming down in the open sea, where the flimsy fabric-covered structure of the Puss Moth could not have floated for more than a few minutes.

Next day we flew north to Londonderry, scene of Amelia's landing, made a swing over Belfast and then headed down the west coast of Eire. That hectic last day included a tangle with sheep in Galway, where we set the plane down in a pasture to have lunch. Previous arrangements had been made to refuel here, but it was Sunday, and we spent a frenzied two hours trying to find someone to open a warehouse and dispatch a fuel truck. A storm was coming up, and I had to get to Cork that evening in time to catch the steamer for home. Finally we gassed up, took off and skirted thunderstorms all the way down the coast, and I made the ship with minutes to spare.

The trip home aboard the H.M.S. *Britannic* was relaxing and gay. I had daily sessions of deck tennis with an interesting and attentive young doctor, and was beaten in the finals of a ping-pong tournament by the amusing, debonair actor, Clifton Webb. Also, I made use of the further opportunity to check up on marine navigation in preparation for my forthcoming Atlantic flight.

I arrived home rested and ready for adventure. But some more work had to be done on *Akita*, and before it was completed new storms built up over the Atlantic. September was drawing to a close with no break in the weather. With October came the hard facts that ice hazards and storms would be routine from then on through the winter. My long-planned Atlantic flight once more would have to be postponed until spring.

After all the preparations and all the careful planning, this was another frustration! I simply couldn't afford to sit idly and wait for spring. The ship was ready for a long-distance flight. Where could I go, where snow and ice would not present a hazard? Suddenly an idea took shape. Why not fly the Pacific? Of course, that was the answer. It was agreed I would do a West-East flight from Honolulu to San Francisco, with the Japanese current insuring temperate weather.

I would have loved to hop off that minute. But once again I was faced with the problem of more expenses for the transcontinental crossing, as well as shipping *Akita* and myself to Hawaii. I would also have to figure added travel cost and salary for a mechanic.

This was 1932, when Herbert Hoover was running for re-election against the new Democratic candidate, Franklin D. Roosevelt. The campaign was entering the home stretch, and excitement was high. An emissary from the Republican National Committee heard of my efforts to finance a transcontinental flight, and proposed that I make it a campaign flight, and drop Hoover leaflets along the way.

This was manna from Heaven. I was delighted, not only with the practical solution to my problems of how to get across the country, but also with the opportunity to aid the campaign of President Hoover. As a Quaker, I had long been an admirer of the President's integrity, courage and statesmanship. If I could help him in such a way, I was eager to do so.

So it was arranged that I would attempt a non-stop record from New York to Los Angeles, dropping campaign literature along the way. And the Republicans would underwrite the costs of the flight. This was a last-minute idea, and I was scheduled to take off from Floyd Bennett field early in the morning of November third, only a few days before the election. Chamberlin and I went out to the field the night before, and he supervised the final details of checking the plane and superintending the loading of six hundred gallons of gas and forty gallons of oil. Meanwhile I went off to take a four-hour nap on a cot in the Navy hangar.

I awoke in that blackest hour before dawn, when the hangar, the field and the world looked dark, cold and forbidding. My fingers fumbled with the zippers on my flying suit, and I stumbled out to the hangar ramp, where *Akita* was waiting, and with her my faithful friend and secretary Ethel Tilson. Laughing at my sleepy approach, Tillie said:

"Anyway, I have a thermos of coffee and some caviar sandwiches for you!"

Final checks. Last directions. I taxied to the far end of the cement apron, where I was to line up on the shortest runway because of the wind direction.

Since a takeoff on the short runway was a somewhat ticklish operation with a heavily loaded plane, I gave the Wasp full throttle with the brakes still on, to use maximum power right at the start. As I released the brakes, *Akita* rolled slowly forward, but did not seem to be picking up momentum fast enough. Then I felt her turn toward the right. I pushed hard left rudder to correct the course, but she continued to swerve. I tried left brake and continued rudder pressure with engine still open to correct the swing, but the ship was now careening violently. Death was seconds away. I yanked the throttle closed and slammed on both brakes.

But the runway was wet in the pre-dawn mist, and the brakes wouldn't hold. *Akita*, with her heavy load, skidded sideways, caught a wheel in the mud and lurched as though about to turn over on her back. Crack! One side of the landing gear let go and I felt a wing dig into the ground. When she finally slid to a stop, gasoline was gushing out in a torrent. I had already cut the switch, and the engine wasn't hot enough to ignite the fuel which formed a spreading pool on the ground.

As I clambered out on the wing, the first man to reach me was Fred Fetterman, one of the best early Lockheed mechanics in the country. He helped drag me to safety, and just as we were well clear of the ship we saw an excited bystander about to toss a lighted cigarette into the pool of gasoline. I yelled and Fred grabbed him, barely in time.

What had caused this disastrous ground loop? We walked around the plane to try to find out. In order to lessen resistance we had removed the shoe, and during the original turn from the concrete hangar apron onto the runway this must have shoved the remaining stem over to one side, and then it had not swiveled back to its position in line with the fuselage because of the overload on the tail. Thus the tail stem was prevented from revolving freely in its universal joint, and instead it pulled the plane to the right. From such small experimental changes can stem disaster.

"Holy cow!" That was Clarence standing beside me, hands in pockets, eyes fixed on the wreckage. On the other side Tillie pressed my arm in sympathetic and discreet silence. As for me, I could only stare in utter anguish at the once proud *Akita*, crumpled in the middle of a gasoline lake, with a broken wing, burst fuel tanks, crushed main bulkhead, and mangled landing gear. I felt a little like a mother gazing at a beloved child who had been nursed through measles, whooping cough and chicken pox only to fall out of a tree and break its neck.

So ended any thoughts of a flight this year. The repairs needed now to get the plane back in shape would cost money—and money was what I didn't have. It would take months to raise the necessary cash, and already I had exhausted every possibility for backing. This was the finish.

Now came the reporters. I had to summon my last remnants of will power to answer their questions. Somehow I managed to grin as I said:

"Injured? Not a bit. Nothing can hurt an old hand like me."
But to myself I said, "I've had it! I've finally hit bottom!"

Silently Tillie and I trudged over to my car. Silently I drove through the dark, deserted outskirts of Brooklyn. Over the Williamsburg Bridge, on to Rye. I knew the house was deserted except for a caretaker, as the family had taken an apartment in town for the winter. I didn't want to face them just then, and there was no place else to go. I was so flat broke that I had barely five dollars in my purse, and nothing in the bank. Saying she'd see me later, Tillie dropped me off at our bleak home.

My key rattled in the lock, and I tiptoed into a dark, cold house. I was hungry, but I knew there was nothing to eat at home. With leaden feet I climbed the stairs and crawled shivering into bed. The first streaks of dawn were just stealing through the drawn shades as I closed my eyes, but there was darkness in my heart.

14

BLIND FLYING

On a chilly November day in 1932, sitting among the dust-covers in the empty house at Rye, I took stock of my achievements, prospects and hopes after ten years of flying. The balance sheet was not encouraging.

However I tried to explain and justify, I came back to the grim fact that I had had three major aircraft failures in one year, and that I seemed to be hopelessly grounded, as far as a professional pilot's career was concerned. I had to face the fact that this was about all any financial backer would take. Furthermore the public was no longer greatly interested in "first flights," there had been so many of them.

At this point a reasonable human being would have said: "Okay, so this is *it*. From now on I must keep my feet on the ground and find an orthodox earthbound job."

But pioneer flyers were not exactly average humans. This is a fact I have discovered through long observation of what makes a certain type of frontier-breaking pilot tick. You could take away his job, his money, his security and the shirt off his back; you can take away his backers and his plane, but you can't clip the wings off his heart.

He may be broke, down and out, but he knows that somehow, by hook or crook, he'll get up in the air again. In my apparently hopeless situation the question with which I wrestled was not whether I should fly again, but merely *how*. Fly I must and fly I would. Something would turn up, I assured myself—and of course it did.

Its first evidence was in the arrival of Aunty, who had been staying with my parents in New York. She came tearing up the driveway in a taxi, deposited her bags in the front hall, kissed me briskly and announced:

"I've come to keep thee company, my young'un. I packed up as soon as I heard thee was here. And I've brought some tea."

When we had a small blaze crackling in the fireplace and sat in front of it sipping hot tea and eating sandwiches, life all at once seemed brighter.

"Aunty dear, what would I do without thee?" I asked. "Always when I hit a low point, thee comes along to boost me out of it. Why, Angel? . . . I should think thee would be completely sick of me by now. Actually, I'm pretty sick of myself."

"Stuff and nonsense!" replied Aunty, a twinkling eye belying her stern expression. "Have patience and gratitude for all the blessings that thee and life possess. Thy message will eventually come!"

Though my frustration and not too well controlled patience erupted with occasional snappy remarks or unsociable conversation at the family table, a bright star did appear in the form of an invitation to unveil the majestic granite memorial beacon honoring the Wright brothers and man's first flight, at Kitty Hawk, North Carolina.

"See?" said Aunty jubilantly. "What greater honor could come to thee? Of course thee'll go, and make a good speech —not too long."

On November 19 I was flown by Roger Q. Williams to Washington in the famous record-holding Bellanca, *Miss Columbia*. From the capital our official party took an overnight sail down the Potomac to Norfolk and then proceeded to the North Carolina town where modern aviation was born.

As we gathered on Kill Devil Hill at Kitty Hawk, where the Wright brothers first proved that man could fly, a drenching sou'wester blew in, dampening somewhat both the spirits

International News Photos

Ruth Nichols at unveiling of memorial to Wright Brothers at Kitty Hawk, North Carolina. Among the governmental, diplomatic and Army officials present were, left to right, Rear Admiral W. A. Moffett, Chief, Naval Bureau of Aeronautics, Representative Lindsay Warren of North Carolina, Secretary of War Patrick J. Hurley, the author, Orville Wright and ex-Secretary of the Navy Josephus Daniels. November, 1932.

and the gold braid of the high-ranking Army, Navy, Marine Corps and diplomatic officials present. But nothing could rob the ceremony of its solemn splendor, or the great memorial of its impressiveness. I was deeply moved and my speech was reported by the Raleigh *News and Observer* in a story that both embarrassed and secretly delighted me— obviously the reporter was influenced by my obedience to Aunty's orders about the length of the speech:

> The best speech and the shortest (it often happens that way) was by Miss Ruth Nichols, whose few well-chosen words showed true appreciation of the magnificence of the historic occasion. She was thrilled and showed it. No other speaker had her backgound or knowledge and experience in flying, and she seemed to convey to the audience the high emprise of the achievement. . . . She herself is a modern Joan of Arc, if I may compare her to a maid who was as fine a horsewoman as Ruth Nichols is mistress of the central blue. She said she "felt honored" to be chosen for an event which all here understood would one day be transferred to canvas and would live in bronze, to let future generations know the contribution the Wrights in this secluded place made to science and the conquest of the air.

An even greater inspiration than the unveiling of the monument was the opportunity to meet and talk with Orville Wright, a small, white-haired gentleman with a quick step and a gentle manner, whose spirit of adventure was revealed only in his sparkling eyes.

Among those present at the banquet following the ceremonies were: Secretary of War Patrick Hurley, Josephus Daniels, former Secretary of the Navy, Admiral Moffett of the Naval Bureau of Aeronautics, assorted Congressmen, military officials, diplomats, aviators and both the sculptor and the architect of the memorial. At dinner I had a lively conversation with Admiral Moffett, who was deeply disappointed that the weather had prevented the appearance of the great Navy dirigible *Akron* to give a salute from the sky during the day's ceremonies. It was in this same dirigible that the admiral was to lose his life some years later, when she broke in half over the Atlantic during a storm.

Other honors came my way that winter, among them an invitation to attend the brilliant annual diplomatic reception given by President and Mrs. Hoover at the White House. As an added thrill, Air Corps Headquarters detailed my brother, Snowden, to fly me down to Washington in an Army plane. This was my first experience in being piloted by my military brother, handsome in his lieutenant's uniform, a full-fledged pilot now. As protection against December winds in the open plane, we bundled up in Army leather flying suits, enormous fur gloves and, of course, parachutes. As I settled meekly in the rear cockpit I was surprised to see a news cameraman, as this flight had been quietly and informally arranged. Next day the picture appeared with the caption, "Taking back seat for once, Ruth Nichols was piloted to Washington by her brother."

This, however, was not strictly accurate, for we were hardly over New York Bay when Nick pulled back the throttle, turned around with an impish grin and yelled: "You fly it, Ruth!"

So, I said to myself, Lieutenant Erikson Snowden Nichols thinks he is going to put one over on his big sister, does he? Well, we'll just show him. The rear cockpit was awkward, I could hardly reach the rudder pedals and I had neither compass nor maps. Nick obviously was enjoying himself hugely, so I decided to show him a thing or two. Taking over the controls, I figured the angle of the sun slanting across the struts, spotted a few landmarks to check direction and wind drift and took the controls. Flying by the seat of my flying suit, I headed for Washington—I hoped.

As we sighted the Washington Monument dead ahead on the horizon, Nick turned around grinning, and gave me a surprised salute. When we landed, he helped me out of the cockpit with marked respect and said:

"This is your round, Sis! Nice goin'!"

It's funny, but this approval from my younger brother, whom I had helped start in his flying career, was as important to me as any public honors I ever received. After having been pretty severely battered from time to time in my own flying career, this was balm to a pretty bushed spirit. If you can win respect from a kid brother, especially a brother wearing the wings of the Air Corps, you've got to be good. In the years since I have experienced deep personal pride in Nick's Air Force progress. He is now Air Attaché at the U.S. Embassy in Havana, Cuba.

The gay whirl at the capital, escorted by my congenial brother, made a welcome break in the frustrating routine of a flyer without wings, and when I came back, a wonderful surprise was waiting. Again it was Clarence Chamberlin who supplied a boost to my morale by offering me a job as Sales Promotion Manager and reserve pilot in a brand new enterprise—his own New York and New England Airways, which was to carry passengers between Holmes Airport in Jackson Heights, Long Island, and Hartford, Connecticut. On the airline's first day of business I piloted the inaugural flight to Hartford, and thus became the first official woman nonscheduled airline pilot. December 29, 1932 was the date of this run—it seems that many turning points in my life have occurred around New Year's Day.

I was enthusiastic over my new job and threw myself into it heart and soul, even though financial remuneration was small.

So 1933 dawned, with its financial tensions, its foreboding and its drama, ushering in a new president who spoke brave and hopeful words against a threatening sky.

Because of the impoverished state of the nation, Chamberlin's airline folded without a requiem, and I took to barnstorming tactics, flying passengers on sightseeing trips from Floyd Bennett Field on occasional weekends, the only time a sufficient crowd turned up at the airport.

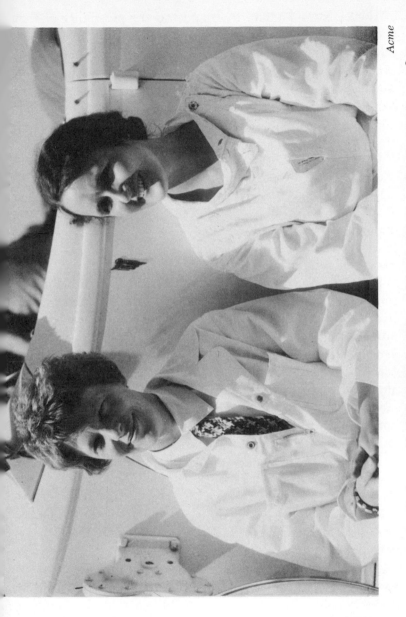

Amelia Earhart and Ruth Nichols at Santa Monica Airport after competing as first women entrants in the Bendix Transcontinental Trophy Race. Summer, 1933.

Always in the back of my mind was the possibility of that Pacific flight, but backers were few and far between in those days, I had no resources of my own, and before I could even marshal my forces into any kind of workable plan, Amelia Earhart with her promotion-minded, energetic husband's wide publishing contacts, once more beat me to the goal. In the spring of 1933 she made a triumphant flight from Honolulu to San Francisco.

This sort of thing was now becoming routine, and so I wasted no time brooding on the cruelty of fate when flash of Amelia's new victory came through, but merely plugged along, taking up sightseeing passengers, and shifting my objective to a world flight, since by now technical advances in aviation and my own experience seemed to make such a project more feasible.

Late in June a unique opportunity opened up. For the first time women flyers were invited to compete in the famous Bendix transcontinental air race, and both Amelia and I were invited to enter. Cliff Henderson, an old friend and the manager of the National Air Races, added to the main prize of $10,000 a special award of $2,000 to the winning woman pilot and a consolation prize of $1,000 to the other. This inducement was offered to offset the fact that, although men pilots had been working for months to prepare for the race, Amelia and I were given only two weeks' notice.

Amelia at least had her own aircraft and I had not even been able to raise sufficient funds to rebuild *Akita*. It took me half the time to finagle the loan of a plane—a sumptuous, speedy, low-wing Lockheed Orion with retractable landing gear, on which I had had my eye for some time. Even an expensive high-powered plane needed special attention to be fit for a long-distance race, however, and once again Clarence Chamberlin was good enough to agree to help. Together we flew the Orion over to Holmes airport, where we telephoned Fred Fetterman, the recognized best mechanic to install extra gas tanks and tune up the engine.

"Ruth," said Fred, "Wiley Post is about to start his solo round-the-world flight on Sunday. Wait until I get him off and I'll work day and night to have your plane ready Wednesday for the race."

It was cutting time short, but we knew no other mechanic would do the job so quickly or effectively, so we waited. I borrowed five hundred dollars for expenses, and obtained free gas and oil from the Raciche Co. But I was jolted to learn on Monday that Fred had flown to Alaska to rescue Jimmy Mattern, another famous flyer who had been forced down in the wilds of Siberia. Good sport that he was, Clarence rolled up his sleeves, commandeered the assistance of the airport mechanics and went to work on the plane himself. The day before the start of the race we tried to fly the plane over to Floyd Bennett Field, but the fog was too thick, and so I had to wait until the day of the race before I had a chance even to pilot this ship.

Time and money, money and time. I never seem to have had enough of either at the start of any major undertaking, and once again I was stymied by these twin bogies. I wired Cliff Henderson for permission to start a day late, and we worked frantically to get the ship ready for the flight. Even so, there was time to check the two magnetic compasses only on a westerly course—if I had to detour on account of weather or mountains at any point, it would have to be by very general compass headings and by maps.

Finally, exhausted by the last-minute scramble, I climbed into the unfamiliar plane at four in the morning of July 2, roared down the runway and in a few minutes was headed west at two hundred miles an hour over the Jersey hills. No ground loop, no takeoff mishaps this time.

As the first streaks of dawn lightened the sky and the big Orion roared smoothly west, my tiredness vanished and once again my heart had wings. Here I was in a powerful, sleek plane headed for new adventures in the skies. Even the gray ghost-rivers of mist which clung to the valleys ahead stirred no foreboding. I felt fully alive for the first time in months, back to my natural element—the limitless four-dimensional challenge of the skies.

What if I was a day behind the other contestants? This was a lapsed time race and I was on my way. It was not, however, to be a lucky trip. First, the suction of the propeller's slipstream yanked out my map while I was trying to adjust the cockpit hatch-cover to overcome the excessive heat in my face from the engine and oil tank. Then I ran into a solid wall of fog at six thousand feet over Johnstown, Pa., and had to set a course by my uncertain compasses over the top of a limitless cotton sea of clouds, whose bordered horizon and high vaulted dome above were clear blue. For two hours I did not see the ground. But when suddenly the opaque froth of what looked like white cake icing began to break up, I saw by my map that I was only thirty miles off course. I landed at Lambert Field in St. Louis six hours after takeoff time.

After refuelling, dashing cold water on my face and grabbing a bottle of soda, I was on my way again in fifteen minutes flat. Hardly was I at cruising altitude, however, when the retractable landing gear started to slip down, causing severe loss of airspeed. I kept pumping it up by hand until I wore a large, angry blister in my palm, but the wheels would not stay up.

Because of the added resistance of the landing gear, plus a stiff headwind, my speed had dropped to one hundred thirty miles an hour, and I knew I would never be able to make my next destination, Amarillo, Texas, before dark and so I headed disgustedly for Wichita. Over the hot Kansas plains in the late afternoon, the cockpit was stifling with oil fumes and I began to feel both nauseous and light-headed after ten hours of flying preceded by only four hours' sleep. When I reached the Wichita airport I slapped the Orion down on the nearest runway, taxied across the airport and said to the first mechanic I saw, "Take her! She's all yours!"

While mechanics repaired the landing gear mechanism and corrected a sticking cylinder valve, I headed for an air-conditioned hotel room, fell into bed and slept until the telephone shrilled at dawn. At the field I learned that although Amelia Earhart had left a day before I did, she too had met with a series of bad breaks, including losing the hatch cover of her Vega, and was still delayed for engine repairs in the southwest. Maybe I had a chance.

Borne along by a helpful tailwind, the Orion was really making knots that morning, the engine was purring perfectly, the landing gear stayed in place and I, refreshed by a night's sleep, was feeling very chipper when far ahead I glimpsed a towering, funnnel-shaped black cloud mushrooming a wide platform above it, which must mean a Kansas tornado. Figuring fast, I decided I could beat the twister, which should move counter-clockwise, from southwest to northeast. Nearing the inky mass, I noted that it seemed stationary, and that the sky was clear all around it. Then the reality dawned—it wasn't a cyclonic cloud, but smoke from a burning oil well! I laughed until I nearly burst.

My wheels touched at Albuquerque in excellent time, only to learn that Amelia had just landed in Santa Monica, site of the National Air Races. So for me, the race was over, and there was no need for further hurry. But I had no premonitions of the series of mishaps which were to plague my flight from then on. Only a short way out of Albuquerque the landing gear slipped again, the engine dropped revs and the ceiling closed in with black thunderclouds on all sides, so that I was barely able to make it back to the Albuquerque field. There, none of the mechanics could find the answer to the engine trouble, and so it was not until the next morning that I limped the Orion into Santa Monica, taking five hours for the trip instead of the normal three, and dove over the line at the air races.

It was an ignominious arrival. I expected a razzing from my friends of the flying fraternity and I got it. But when I walked into Cliff Henderson's office and asked for my consolation prize, I did not expect his reaction. He guffawed:

"What! Three days from New York— You call that a race?"

I knew he was partly right. Even so, technically I had met the requirements and I was determined to stand my ground. I had borrowed money to make the trip, and I couldn't even get back home without some cash. So I grinned brashly and said:

"Ah, come on, Cliff! After all, Amelia took two days to get here, and it's a wonder either one of us made it at all, with so little time to get ready. You wanted women in the race for publicity, and I've given you three days' worth instead of one."

After some additional good-natured sputtering, Cliff offered a compromise which I accepted happily. Amelia and I watched the end of the National Air Races in high spirits, despite our misfortunes. As we sat together on the running board of a car, a news photographer snapped our picture, which was printed next day with the caption: "They tried but failed."

To all such quips, which were frequent, we replied that if women flyers were given an equal break with men in time to prepare for the Bendix, we'd show 'em. This prophecy since has been amply fulfilled by such flyers as Louise Thaden, Laura Ingalls and Jacqueline Cochran.

The entire sequence of that Bendix Air Race and its aftermath were a comedy of errors. Two days after the races I was scheduled to make a speech in Chicago at a meeting of the National Federation of Business and Professional Women's Clubs, on the results of a survey I had made on the status of the more than five hundred licensed women pilots in this country. I had intended to fly the Orion to Chicago on the way back to New York, but mechanics at Burbank airport told me it would be impossible to make the necessary repairs in time. I couldn't afford the round-trip airline fare of nearly three hundred dollars, so I scurried around and promoted a ride on a plane being ferried to Salt Lake City, where I caught a regular passenger plane for Chicago.

After the speech, I wangled an airline pass back to Los Angeles, a customary procedure in those early days of air transport, before the CAA tightened up rules on "free-loading." In return, I was expected to give interviews at the various stops enroute.

That return trip followed the bizarre pattern of all the rest of the incidents surrounding the Bendix race. A fellow passenger on the plane was Tallulah Bankhead, clad in black satin slacks and traveling "strictly incognito." At each stop waiting reporters spotted her as their idea of what a woman flyer should look like and swarmed around with such queries as "Hi, Miss Nichols! Do you think women pilots can compete with men?"

After several such skirmishes I was shaking with suppressed mirth, but Tallulah was distinctly annoyed. If she was going to be recognized, she naturally felt that it should be as herself. Then the weather took a hand to complicate our lives still further. I had been invited by the pilot to fly the twin-engine Boeing transport for a while, a courtesy no longer permitted by CAA regulations, and was having a wonderful time when we ran into a thunderstorm front. The regular pilots took over and tried to find a way around the storms, but finally had to make an emergency landing at North Platte, Nebraska. It was midnight, the rain was coming down in sheets and the hangar where we took cover was cold and cheerless.

Tallulah, still in her black satin slacks, took one look around and drawled:

"Oh, for crying out loud, da-a-a-ahling! There's nothing else to do in this dismal dump, let's play bridge."

So the only four women on the plane—Tallulah, her secretary, the stewardess and I—squatted on the cold cement floor and played several rubbers of contract. Tallulah's lively wit and broad comments on the world in general, the weather, the hangar and air travel in particular kept us all in gales of laughter until the storm passed over and we took off again at dawn. Here was a great trouper doing her stuff for the benefit of a huddled group of dreary fellow passengers.

Back in Los Angeles I was faced with the old familiar dilemma of how to get my borrowed plane back to New York. I was staying with Margaret and Larry Cooper while repairs to the Orion went on, and we all agreed that the best solution was for me to try for another west-east women's speed record with a sponsor to underwrite expenses.

All the necessary preliminaries of finding a sponsor and getting permission from the Orion's owner for the flight took time, but I didn't mind, as it was always fun to be with Margaret and her husband. During my time on the coast, I had also an opportunity to meet Amy Mollison, who had just arrived in Los Angeles after flying the Atlantic with her husband, Captain Jim, and to take her on a tour of local airplane factories.

At last everything was set for my flight east. I had a contract from a film company to advertise their new aviation picture, "Night Flight," starring Helen Hayes. The nicest part of the assignment was getting acquainted with this great and charming actress and learning how warm, genuine and unaffected she really was.

I took off from Burbank Airport an hour and a half after midnight, into a sky bright with stars. But even with perfect weather bad luck still rode my rudder, the engine began to miss, and after crossing San Gorgonio Pass, I realized I should return. After limping back to Burbank—the nearest commercial airport large enough on which to land a heavily gas-filled plane with no dump valves—I found the fog rolling in off the ocean. This made an immediate perilous landing imperative with an ailing motor, an inherently unstable, as well as still overloaded plane and a rheostat that wouldn't function. Next morning came the climax of this whole ill-starred adventure— a wire from the plane's owner saying he had sold the Orion to a man in Los Angeles, and ordering me to turn it over at once to its new owner.

I was angry, because I had spent a great deal of money on repairs to the plane. It took considerable time and argument to secure even partial reimbursement for these expenses. I still didn't have enough money for a plane ticket East, so I managed to secure a pass and at length arrived in New York, home again and broke.

15

ADVENTURES OF A BARNSTORMER

1933 and '34 comprised a period in my life of marking time, of aviation lectures at eastern women's colleges and even a few men's engineering classes, of volunteer activities in club and community work, of continued efforts to arouse political interest and obtain engineering facts regarding a Westchester airport—and of pursuing every possible angle to promote funds for a round-the-world flight. People were amazingly kind. During this period, even the famous fund raiser, Mr. John Price Jones, cooperated by donating ideas, contacts, a desk and a brochure advocating the flight . . .

My flying, however, was confined to piloting light aircraft to a lecture, to a dinner meeting of the 99's in some other state, or similar minor jaunts. Occasionally, I'd give my brother Bill (William Bowne Nichols) some flying instruction. He became so enamored with aviation that he too made it his career. During World War II, he was with Grumman Aircraft Corporation. Then, he became one of the founders and managers of the Hicksville Air Park on Long Island. When it was closed, because of zoning pressures, Bill affiliated himself with Republic Aircraft Corporation, also on Long Island, with which he has been associated ever since. He has made his home in Hicksville with his vivacious wife Charlotte and their two sons, Norman (who recently took his two years of military training with the Air Force) and young Chester.

But all that was a long way in the future. Meantime, there was ever the flyer's delight of "hangar flying," where I seized every opportunity to talk with pilots such as Wiley Post, Harold Gatty, Jimmy Mattern, Harry Lyons and others, always on the topic of world flights. To keep my hopes up, I kept a file of pertinent data on distances, weather conditions, size and terrain of airports abroad, availability of fuel, difficulties of language differences, comparative performance of various planes, itemized costs and so on.

It was not until the summer of 1935 that I got sturdy wings again, and once more it was Clarence Chamberlin who supplied them.

He too was fed up with trying to conduct big-time aviation business during the depression, and had already embarked on a widespread barnstorming tour. It sounded like a wonderful idea to me. He had bought three big Condor planes from Eastern Airlines, which was putting in new and more modern equipment, and outlined his plan to spend the summer touring around New England, taking passengers up for brief rides at a dollar a head, perhaps helping to educate the public to the comfort and safety of travel aboard large transport planes.

During the course of the tour he asked me to sign on as a co-pilot, and he didn't have to ask twice. This was manna from Heaven. I would have taken the job for nothing, just to get up in the air again. After my long grounding, this seemed too good to be true.

The Condors were a far cry from the rickety canvas-and-bailing-wire planes of the early barnstormers. These were big, twin-engined transports carrying over fifteen passengers plus crew composed of pilot, co-pilot and sometimes a stewardess. Each plane also had a mechanic, and a ticket seller who sometimes subbed as an advance publicity man. This was living!

The big planes were easy to handle, and I learned a lot about twin-engined planes from Captain Harry Hublitz, the fine pilot to whose plane I was finally assigned. Early in the tour we picked up an eager young would-be pilot, Jane Hyde, of Cumberland Mills, Maine, who was fascinated by everything connected with aviation, and who practically shanghaied me one evening to her family's beautiful Sebago Lake home, where she convinced me that she should join our flying troupe. She offered to act as flight hostess without pay and on her own expense account, in return for the experience and whatever flying lessons I could find time to give her.

This turned out to be one of my most fortunate encounters, since Jane proved a delightful companion, an eager pupil and a loyal friend.

It was a glorious summer of new experiences, new friends and constant flying. Sometimes one plane took up as many as a thousand passengers in one day of a fine weekend. I was surprised and naturally delighted to find how many people were eager to fly, and to see their excitement and pleasure during a first flight. It proved also that organized barnstorming could be a financial success.

We were all jubilant over the success of the tour. Our itinerary took us through Massachusetts, New Hampshire, Vermont, Maine and upper New York State as we hopped from town to town; Skowhegan, Augusta, Waterville, Sanford, Ogunquit Beach; Portsmouth, Nashua, Whitefield; Fitchburg, Worcester, Quincy, Springfield, Northampton, Great Barrington, Pittsfield.

At beach stops, passengers piled aboard in bathing suits and slacks, sunsuits and shorts, barefooted or in sandals, excited and happy. Men passengers would observe me, sitting at the controls in a summer dress, and remark, "If that girl can fly, I ought to be able to do it too!" Their wives would giggle, "Just imagine flying in an airplane in a bathing suit—isn't it thrilling?"

Jane always was a member of my crew, and her job was to stand in the doorway of the Condor, tearing off one end of the tickets and returning a souvenir stub, which most passengers prized. After everybody was seated, she would fasten their seat belts, and on special occasions go up and down the aisle serving refreshments. She learned to deal smoothly and competently with all kinds of passengers.

One night after a takeoff from Lawrence, Mass., there were few passengers aboard and I noted a red-faced, exuberant man who had been sitting toward the front now standing and looking over my shoulder at the controls. I asked him to sit down.

"How high up are we, sister?" he asked.

"About fifteen hundred feet," I replied.

"Fifteen hundred *miles!*" he gasped, and subsided into his seat, staggered by his own thoughts. At intervals during the flight he repeated his query, and each time sank back muttering, "Fifteen hundred miles!" He was still shaking his head and muttering when the plane landed.

One day the aerial caravan took a side jaunt to Armonk Airport, near my old home in Rye. While there, I gave Jane her first flying lesson. Here is her account of it:

" 'Feet off, hands off.' I remained motionless while Ruth took the plane off the ground and climbed to a reasonable altitude. 'All right, now. The nose is pointed toward North Beach. Put your feet lightly on the rudder pedals and take hold of the stick.' I surrounded the joy stick with both hands. One hand too many, so I relinquished my left hand, leaving the right clasped around the stick. The smooth flight stopped abruptly. The wings began to wag. The plane began to wave, at no one in particular. But bumping along as we were, I was fervently happy. 'Your right wing is low.' A gentle movement of the stick. 'Your right wing is still low.' The plane looked straight to me. A glance over the side at the wing. Well, maybe it was sort of slanting downward. We neared North Beach. 'Make a turn to the left and be sure that your rudder and stick coordinate.' Around we went rather suddenly. 'Do it again, and not so much pressure on your rudder pedal this time.' Ah, this was swell! 'Now turn to the right.' We completed the turn. I relaxed while Ruth landed the open sport plane. My part in the flying was ended, but I was still feeling the controls of the ship under my touch as we walked through the hangars. I wanted to be in the air again . . ."

Toward the end of the summer the three Condors had a reunion, at the races in Springfield, Mass. Each day the trio of planes flew in formation to the field beside the Agawam race track, settled down until the races were over, then took up the crowds of eager spectators. On the last day of the races, we decided to put on a flight that would be remembered—an aerial bridge party.

We invited eight presidents of leading women's organizations in Springfield, set up two bridge tables in the back of the plane, and turned the seats around. Most of the women invited had never flown before, and there was great excitement about the special flight. One asked if her insurance policy would cover her while in the air. Another said she must telephone her husband to get his permission, called back a little later to say, "My husband says I can go if he can come too!" This club president arrived bringing not only her husband but also her little boy.

When the bridge party finally got under way, it was a definite success. The clubwomen chattered like magpies, the several husbands who came along for the ride grinned benignly from their front seats, and after the takeoff, as I held the plane on an even course at cruising altitude, there were repeated shrieks of glee from the players. It seems there is no thrill quite like making a grand slam, doubled and redoubled, at two thousand feet.

Jane was aboard in her capacity as hostess-stewardess, with the job of serving sandwiches, coffee and ice cream to the guests. She told me later that she was praying throughout the trip that I would hold the plane steady and that the Condor would behave like a lady. I did, the Condor did, and Jane served the refreshments triumphantly, without a single mishap. We stayed up long enough to allow the ladies to play two rubbers at leisure, and landed to the tune of enthusiastic thanks and declarations that this was a bridge party nobody would forget.

After Springfield we moved on to Pittsfield, Mass. and Mother joined me there for a brief visit and made one of the few flights of her life, when she flew with me from Pittsfield to Troy, N. Y.

One Sunday in Troy we flew from ten in the morning until eleven at night, carrying more than a thousand passengers. On one of the last flights that night, over the city's pinpoint lights and the Hudson shimmering like quicksilver, I detected a stutter in one of the motors. I asked Harry if he thought it was safe to fly at night with an ailing engine and so many passengers aboard. He replied reassuringly that the second engine would hold her up if one conked out.

Next morning we squared accounts with the airport officials and the boys who had helped sell tickets, then said good-by to Troy. Aboard the Condor were only Hublitz and I, our two mechanics, R. "Bill" Holt and Roy Hanes, and their girl friends. Both young couples planned to be married as soon as we reached Newark. Hublitz took the plane off after a short run, and we gained altitude rapidly, pushed along by a thirty-five-mile tail wind. It was a beautiful clear morning —blue sky with white fluffy clouds, and all of us felt a sense of keen enjoyment, over a summer of successful accomplishment behind and a happy homecoming ahead.

Shortly after the takeoff one of the mechanics came forward and stood behind the pilot's seat. Leaning over Hublitz, he said:

"I think perhaps we'd better stop off at Poughkeepsie to take on some more water. That left motor is running pretty hot."

He had barely finished speaking when an explosion shook the ship and the left motor quit. The two girls screamed, their fiancés tried to reassure them and I looked anxiously at Harry. He appeared unperturbed.

"I think we'd better go back to the airport at Troy, since it is so near," he said.

I nodded, and he swung the plane around to the left so abruptly that my head cracked against the side of the ship.

The air was very bumpy and despite full power applied to the one remaining engine, the plane was losing altitude. Hublitz told the mechanic, who was still leaning over his shoulder, to go back and sit down and said to me:

"I think we'd better land downwind right now."

I understood that he felt it would be better to land *with* the wind than to take a chance on circling the field to land against it. We were just approaching the edge of the airport, the plane was still settling rapidly, and I agreed wholeheart- edly with his decision. At the last minute Hublitz made an- other left turn, apparently to counteract a quartering tail wind drifting us away from the field. Immediately the left wing dropped and the right engine pulled us around in a flat spin. Dead ahead was a grove of eighty-foot elm trees. Staring at onrushing doom, Harry remarked as casually as if he were commenting on the weather:

"We're not going to make it."

I had one instant of horrified realization that death faced us, when I remember praying, "Oh, please, God, not yet . . ." Then came oblivion.

I don't remember the tearing sound of the great crippled Condor plunging through the trees the rending crash as the front end of the plane was torn open and one wing hit the ground.

I have no recollection of being torn out of the plane, still strapped to my seat and hurled on my face from a height of about twenty feet.

I don't remember the thunder of the final crash or the inferno of flames when the four-hundred-gallon gas tanks exploded.

When I woke up later at Samaritan Hospital, witnesses told me the story of the death throes of the Condor.

Charred skeleton of Condor transport biplane in which Ruth Nichols as co-pilot was severely injured and the pilot killed, October 21, 1937.

The two mechanics and the two girls, all in the rear of the plane, were not badly hurt when the great plane finally ground to earth and burst into flames. The two men dragged the hysterical girls out of the plane, having to climb over the inert Hublitz, slumped in the pilot's seat. The main door and emergency exits were jammed and the only escape was through the jagged open front of the plane.

After the girls were pulled to safety, one of the mechanics (I am not to this day sure which since they left Troy and my life next day) rushed back to get me. I was sprawled on the ground alongside the plane, still strapped to my seat, directly under a flaming wing. Were it not for his heroic action in dragging me clear of the blazing inferno, this story would not have been written.

Meanwhile Hublitz was struggling to free himself from the flaming furnace of the plane. He had remained conscious, suffering only a broken leg in the crash. But his clothing and hair were on fire when he finally broke loose and crawled out of the roaring flames, inching along by digging his fingers into the ground and crying:

"My God, I can't see!"

Two C.C.C. construction trucks engaged in work at the airport came tearing up (so I was told) and rushed Hublitz and me to the hospital. The surgeon on duty took one look at us, made his professional decision and said to the still-conscious Hublitz:

"The girl is hurt the worst. She's unconscious, and hemorrhaging, a lot of fractures . . . I'm the only surgeon on duty, so I think I'd better attend to her first."

"Of course!"

This was the same man who once had said to me, when refusing to take a chance on flying through fog, "I don't want to be a hero."

Apparently, he remained aware of all the things that happened—the things that had to be told to me later. Both of us were wheeled into the operating room. All available interns and nurses were commandeered to cut off our clothes and apply first aid. Then the surgeon set to work to set my innumerable broken bones, while Hublitz waited his turn. Whether he realized that he was blind, I never knew, for he died some tragic hours later. I think he would have preferred it that way, for blindness to a pilot would have been hell on earth.

16

ZERO-ZERO

My first memory of events following the disaster at Troy is of waking up in a hospital bed late the next afternoon to see two of my family bending over me—cheery, chirpy Aunty and grave, concerned Nick. I managed to smile lopsidedly beneath the bandages and Aunty turned to the doctor hovering in the background to say with decision:

"There! Now I *know* she'll be all right."

Nick had been spending the weekend with me in Troy and had flown his Army plane back to New York to be greeted with the news of my crash when he landed. Aunty had been waiting to greet me at Armonk Airport when she received the news. With her customary decision, she at once chartered a plane and flew to Troy.

Both Nick and Aunty had arrived at the hospital within a couple of hours after the crash, while I was still in the operating room, to be greeted by doctors who held out little hope for my recovery. Aunty refused to accept this gloomy outlook, however, and shook her finger under the head surgeon's nose, saying:

"Nonsense! It's not time for Ruth to go. She won't give up, and you mustn't either!"

A tally of the damage to my personal chassis revealed the following: one leg broken in nine places including knee, ankle and heel; a broken right wrist; a severely burned left hand; a fractured cheekbone and jaw, and a nose completely flattened.

Little by little I learned of the drama in Troy that night, of Harry Hublitz' death which saddened me terribly, and the happier events involving the two young couples who had been in the plane. They decided to be married then and there, in a hotel suit, and my brother Nick served as best man for each bridegroom. Reporters trooped in and out of the hospital and telephone and telegraph wires were kept humming.

Although I have no memory of the events of the night, apparently I was semi-conscious at times, and lived up to my family's opinion that "Ruth has an innate sense of managing things." I was told that when I came to briefly in the operating room I gave explicit orders to the doctors and nurses!

Clarence Chamberlin arrived in Troy the next afternoon and walked into my room with his usual casual air, to get the details of the crash. Still a little hazy, I told him what I could, but by the second day was able to dictate a thousand-word statement for the press describing the Condor's finish.

My naturally sturdy constitution stood me in good stead during these days, enabling me to recuperate faster than the doctors had thought possible. Broken bones had become routine for me by this time, and I knew that it required only time to make them good as new. So I was able to reply with easy banter when Clarence assured me that I had used up only a few of my nine lives, and to wish him better luck when he left at length to go south with his other planes, and resume his barnstorming operations. These he continued for the next two years, making a sufficient financial success to see him safely through the worst of the depression.

Nick had to return to his post, after assuring himself that his sister was still indestructible, and Aunty rushed home to stay with my mother who she thought needed help more than I did.

Then, one day a letter came from Don. There I lay, wrapped in bandages like a mummy, suffering from multiple fractures, lacerations and contusions of both body and spirit, thinking that everything had happened to me that could happen. But there was one more thing. Don wrote to say that he had fallen in love with someone else, and was going to be married.

This was the end. Coming with the inspired timing of Greek tragedy, this agonizing blow was infinitely more pulverizing than my broken body. There are some things too intense or too painful or sometimes too big to be put into words, and this was one of them.

The human spirit is tough, however, I have found. So is the human body. As my bones slowly knit, I began to piece together the broken threads of my philosophy. It was evident that I had reached a crossroads, and that I'd better decide which way I was going from here. I could either descend into cynical bitterness, without hope for the future, or I could try to put my life back together again and find a goal worth working for.

I had plenty of time to review my life and search my soul. I had read that some people were "accident prone" because of their own inner conflicts and guilt complexes. As honestly as I could I reviewed each of my aeronautical disasters, asking myself if any had been caused by my own failure—if an unrealized psychological conflict had been responsible. And in each case, as I marshalled the facts, I decided there had been specific, scientific and mechanical causes for each, such as would be recognized by any qualified objective aviation authority. Some had been due to the limited technical knowledge of the day, some had resulted from mechanical failure of the plane, but of one thing I was sure. They had not been emotionally induced by any personal guilt complexes.

Having come this far, I felt better. I began to feel that life might be worth living after all. Sometimes you have to hit bottom before you can start back up. I had certainly hit bottom again—but this time devastatingly. If I was going to move at all, there was no other way but up.

Even though I still felt a deep open gash where my heart

was supposed to be, I decided I might as well *act* happy, no matter how I felt. So I made an effort to smile and talk cheerfully with Aunty and the nurses, and thereby at times found that I actually felt better.

Through the days after Aunty and Nick left, my greatest comfort came from the almost constant presence of Jane Hyde. Fortunately she had not been on the Condor at the time of the crash, and had been preparing to go back home after the summer's barnstorming adventures.

Jane proved her staunch and loyal friendship by refusing to leave Troy after the crash. She took a room in a boarding house and spent every day at the hospital, coming laden with books and delicacies to sit beside my bed and read aloud, to bring gossip of the exploits of other flyers, to keep me entertained and cheered up by any means at hand.

For when the sedatives wore off and I gradually realized the full extent of my latest disaster, I needed cheering. Even my natural recuperative powers were not quite equal to the complicated multiple fractures of my bones, and I had to undergo three more sessions in the operating room before the surgeons were satisfied that they had done all they could. The most stubborn problem was my leg, with its nine breaks, the most troublesome of which was the kneecap. For a time, the doctors doubted that I would ever be able to use the leg again, while I wondered if I would ever even sit up again. But they gave me the benefit of all their skill and hope, and in the end told me I had been lucky—I would walk with a slight limp, but I would walk again. After what seemed an eternity, I could spend short periods in a wheelchair.

My face had taken the full force of the fall when I was blasted out of the plane, and because of puffiness lasting for months and a nose which is still slightly crooked my features were then a mess. In the end I came out with a shorter and what I thought was a better-looking nose than before, and no obvious facial scars. God was kind.

It took all this time in the hospital to complete the necessary repairs to my battered frame before I could actually start convalescence, and though weak as a rabbit I was anxious to go home. I was not strong enough for an all-day ambulance ride, and so, through my brother, arrangements were finally worked out for him to fly me home in an Army plane. After a period in a New York apartment, the family was once again back in Rye, though operating the household on a curtailed scale. This meant that I could land at Armonk, and have only a short ambulance ride home. At that time there was only one ambulance plane in the entire United States Army, which was out of commission after a crackup in Texas; my flight home, if it could be managed at all, would have to be in a regular plane with no special equipment. But even that was far preferable to a long trip over bumpy roads on the ground.

The complicated details involved in getting me home by air, made me think seriously about the urgent need for more ambulance planes, especially in the event of another war. Already war clouds were gathering in Europe, and I had a feeling that before many years aviation would have to develop in many ways to cope with events of the times.

Before I could leave the hospital I had to submit to a coroner's inquest held in my room. This had been postponed until I was able to sit up in a wheelchair, as I had flatly refused to have an official crowd, plus reporters and photographers, view me in a horizontal position, swathed in bandages. News pictures of a bandaged pilot were bad publicity for aviation; anyway, I had my own personal pride.

When I learned at last that a date had been set for my removal by Army plane, I knew that the time had come to face the inquest. While I sent word to the coroner to bring on his party, Jane scurried around to procure a sweater and skirt in a hyacinth shade which I liked. Dressed in real clothes for the first time in months, and lifted into a chair, I steeled myself for the ordeal which turned out to be a little more than I had bargained for. The coroner, district attorney, public stenographer, reporters and photographers crowded into the room. The demands of the camera men took almost as long as the inquest itself. Sitting upright for an hour trying to give helpful, accurate answers required all the will power I possessed, and at the end I didn't much care whether school kept or not.

It was December 6 when Nick arrived in an Army Fairchild monoplane, accompanied by Major M. C. Grow, a flight surgeon. I was put on a stretcher and carted out to the air field in an ambulance, where my brother and the doctor supervised my transfer to the cockpit of the plane. When I was finally installed, Major Grow said:

"You don't mind if I put you in a parachute harness, do you? Army orders."

I was amazed and amused.

"How on earth do you expect me to pull a ripcord with both arms and hands bandaged?" I giggled.

"Just leave that to me," replied the surgeon soothingly. "If we have to bail out, I'll slide you out the door and pull the ripcord myself."

I was entranced with the mental picture of myself, in splints and bandages, floating rigidly through the air to crumple in a final landing. But orders were orders, so I submitted. Swathed in blankets and parachute straps, I was reasonably comfortable despite the zero weather. Just before the takeoff Jane thrust a thermos bottle of hot coffee into the plane, patted my shoulder, said "Happy landings, Ruth! I'll see you soon," and darted hastily out of the plane. With a jaunty wave, she yelled above the roar of the engine:

"Don't do anything I wouldn't do!"

It was an hour's flight from Troy to Armonk, and after the takeoff I amused myself by mentally visualizing the familiar countryside over which we were passing, since I couldn't see out. Nick was at the controls and Major Grow was beside me.

Once again the prodigal daughter was coming home, once again in an ambulance. No wonder Mother had such a horror of everything concerned with flying. The real wonder was, I reflected, that she had not expressed herself even more violently on the subject. For all my efforts and hopes, I seemed to have succeeded in bringing little but distress to my family. I was always being dragged home to lick my wounds, it appeared, before taking off on another disastrous adventure.

As we neared Armonk, I pictured the small airport, surrounded by hills, and wondered if Nick, still a comparatively green pilot, would be able to make it. I knew he had never flown this type of plane before, and I realized the problems facing him. If he made a short landing, he would have to drop the plane in, and he would worry about the resulting jolt to my still painful fractures. If he came in for a smooth, fast landing he might overshoot the field and tangle with telephone wires at the far end. A bumpy safe landing was better than taking a chance, I decided, and so I asked Major Grow to tell Nick that I was feeling wonderful and not to worry about me, but to be sure to slap the ship down close to the trees. Soon I felt the motor idling as we began the descent, and I waited for the bumps. Now! I held my breath. But the plane landed smoothly without the slightest jolt, and Nick had used only half the runway. I beamed with pride. My young brother had become a finished pilot.

Much to my annoyance more photographers jumped out to snap pictures as I was eased out of the plane. Then we were on the way home, with the Army flight surgeon still in attendance. And at last I was back in my own room again, with Dad, Mother, Aunty and my sister all on hand to welcome me.

It was good to have a home to come back to, a blessed comfort to have a family to fuss over you, I thought gratefully as I sank into exhausted sleep. The excitement of the trip had been more of a strain than I realized. All I wanted now was rest.

Days stretched into weeks and weeks dragged into months

as I waited in forced idleness for stubborn bones to knit with little ambition or strength for serious reading. I had nothing to do but think. And thinking at this point was more painful than my bodily fractures.

For a time I simply refused to face the multiple mess in which I found myself. I used any and every means to avoid looking at the facts. I read western adventure stories, on doctor's orders I did some knitting; I started writing in order to exercise the fingers of my right hand, and sometimes I just sat and read the labels on the medicine bottles that crowded my bedside table.

After a while, as the physical anguish subsided a little, I began to be able to think things out. It was natural that I should first review Aunty's simple faith and the difficulties, discipline and dedication of my Quaker ancestors. They certainly had the great merits of courage and direction, but they did not seem to offer answers to many of the complicated problems, arising from modern activities and new types of relationships. I realized that only I, myself, would be able to discover satisfactory answers—if I could—from the advantages which I had had in a college education, and in later reading and considerations, which I had given to scientific, philosophical and religious schools of thought. With so many months in bed, followed by a long period of restricted activity, there was plenty of time to reconsider my ideas on such questions as Einstein's early discoveries which led to Heisenberg's Principle of Uncertainty as applied to freedom of will and to re-evaluate the Vedanta-Sankya philosophy of the East. From them I distilled certain concepts through which I believed I would be able to live with greater spiritual emphasis than I had before. But it was a long, slow, often discouraging process, and only much later did I understand the strides I made in those dark days towards a new maturity and, even, a certain degree of wisdom.

Aunty had said that the way would be revealed to me in due time. But at the moment practical matters were pretty

desperate. I still was able to move only with the greatest diffi
culty and with considerable pain.

One bright spot in that long winter confined to my room
was a visit from Jane Hyde, who came to stay with me for
several weeks. For the most part I was able to assume a non
chalant air before the family and the friends who frequently
dropped in. But with Jane I talked earnestly, and I think only
she and Aunty realized the depths of my despair.

This grim winter of 1936 seemed endless. Life had closed
in, and it seemed totally impossible to make a move in any
direction. Yet I *must* move—though I didn't yet know where—
and the first step must be to condition my protesting body
once more, to force painful bones and flabby muscles into
action. So one raw day in March I was carried down the steep
stairs and eased into the family car for a ride. The trip was
such agony that I lapsed into semi-consciousness before we
got back home.

A little more time, a little more strength. The second try
was better. In the middle of April, six months after the Troy
crash, I took my third drive—to Armonk airport. I had telephoned in advance to the airport manager to arrange to go
up for a hop. I hobbled out of the car, leaning on my crutches,
and was helped into the waiting four-place cabin Stinson
plane. The pilot was an understanding friend, "Spinney"
Leech. When we were up he turned over the controls to me.
I couldn't bend my knee, so it was impossible for me to take
off or land, but once we were in the air I could handle the
control wheel, and even this small achievement marked the
first crack in the cocoon of helplessness which bound me. I
felt the first faint surge of returning life and hope as I guided
the Stinson through the clear, free sky, and when we landed
I thanked Spinney with tears in my eyes.

After that I sought every opportunity to go to the airport
and practice. After a month my knee seemed to be limbering
up a little, it was less painful, and at last I was able to negotiate both takeoff and landing in a lighter Fairchild land plane.

"Nice going, Ruth!" said Spinney, as he helped me climb laboriously out of the cockpit. "Why don't you apply for a renewal of your license now?"

So I visited the officials of the Bureau of Aeronautics at Roosevelt Field, still walking with crutches, my face gaunt and hollow-eyed. They shook their heads. I'd better take more time to regain strength, they told me, and get in at least ten more hours in the air before I could safely renew my pilot's license.

During this recuperative period I picked up some of my early years of piano and singing practice. But soon came a providential invitation from Jane Hyde's family to visit them at Lake Sebago, Maine. Jane drove us up and there I rested, almost lived out of doors, put in a lot of flying time out of the Portland airport and even rode horseback. I had to be hoisted off my crutches and into the saddle, but the joy of riding again was almost as good as flying.

While I was in Maine I was invited to speak at the International Rotary Convention in Augusta. During the address I explained some of the international aspects of aviation, and pleased the Maine residents by pointing out the possible future of Portland as the United States' most easterly airport, and as a great circle point on flights to the Orient. When I received a fee for speaking, I looked lovingly at the check. It was the first money I had earned in nine months.

"What are you going to do with all that loot?" asked Jane.

"Make a down payment on a car!" I decided on the spur of the moment.

I had to hock the jewelry I had with me to eke out the necessary amount, but in the end I acquired a little green Ford, and felt a new sense of freedom as I drove it back to Jane's home. Early in August I drove alone the nearly four hundred miles back to Rye, making it in nine hours. I felt wonderful. This had been an endurance test, and I had passed it.

To complete payments on the car I sold some family silver that had been given me for my "hope chest," an item for which I felt I would have little use now that Don had gone out of my life. Then I set out to look for a job. I had now graduated from crutches to cane, but I still found it almost impossible to get in and out of public conveyances when both knee and ankle were piercingly stiff, and even more difficult to walk more than a block or so. So job-hunting, dreary enough in itself in the fall of 1936, presented obstacles. Nevertheless I hobbled from office to office, renewing old contacts, trying to present new ideas. Each night I returned home exhausted mentally and physically. With Aunty's guidance, I prayed for vision to see the path I should take, and for the will and strength to take it.

Through another fall and winter I seemed only to be marking time. Occasionally I was asked to speak at aviation meetings or to write an article on the subject closest to my heart. In the spring of 1937 I regained my commercial pilot's license, and the first use I made of it was to give Jane Hyde some concentrated flying lessons.

That summer marked great gains in aviation for women—other women. Lady Markham made her historic westward crossing of the Atlantic, flying against the prevailing winds through mists and fog to land safely in Newfoundland. I thought it was the greatest flight a woman had ever made.

Then I was asked to be an official for the start of the Bendix Transcontinental Race, in which three of the six planes entered were piloted by women. Though I longed to enter the race myself, this time I was consigned to the sidelines. But even that opportunity to savor the excitement and thrills of the famous race made me feel alive again.

Race regulations urged all entrants to have their planes at Floyd Bennett Field forty-eight hours before the start. Amelia Earhart with her beautiful twin-engine Electra, her husband, her co-pilot, Helen Ritchey, and her mechanic were assembled punctually. Louise Thaden and her co-pilot, Blanche Noyes, did not get there until the afternoon before the take-off. Blanche is still flying today in her directing of the ex-

remely important government air marking program. And the
hird woman pilot, Laura Ingalls, was still somewhere be-
ween St. Louis and New York, delayed by forced landings
ind other problems.

Contestants and officials had a gala dinner at the Half
Moon Hotel in Coney Island. Everybody was there but Laura,
and all the contestants retired early, to be fresh for the next
morning's takeoff. After I had seen Louise and Blanche to
their rooms about nine o'clock, I went back to the airport for
news. There I learned that Laura Ingalls had landed a short
time before and immediately rushed off by car to Roosevelt
Field for spark plugs, then to her apartment in Great Neck
and was probably by now on her way back to the field. The
other officials were concerned.

"Look, Ruth," said one, "as the only woman on the committee, don't you think we'd better rule Laura out of the race?
She's flown all day, she's had emergency landings, now she's
dashing around all over the place, with no time to rest. She's
bound to run into trouble in the race, and it'll be bad for aviation and maybe curtains for Laura."

I remembered my own struggles in the Bendix, fighting
weather, engine trouble and the whimsies of a borrowed
plane, and I couldn't agree. After all her struggles, this girl
should be given a break.

I suggested that the official doctor examine Laura, and if
she seemed all right, she should be permitted to start. In the
end the others accepted this decision. The doctor gave Laura
a clean bill, and suggested that she get a couple of hours
sleep in the hangar. But she said she'd already had some sleep,
and rushed back to her plane.

There I found the slight figure of this stalwart woman pilot
perched on a wing holding the hose from the gas pumps and
filling her tanks. Shouting up to her, I begged her to let one
of the mechanics take over and get some rest. But she shook
her head stubbornly. For three hours she held that hose, after

changing all her own spark plugs, and I knew exactly how she felt; if you want a thing well done, do it yourself, is not a bad slogan for a racing pilot, as I had discovered.

Amelia arrived at the field about midnight, with her efficient co-pilot, Helen, looking brisk and efficient with her maps under her arm. Next came Louise and Blanche, wise cracking and casual. Both had taken leaves of absence from their jobs with the Bureau of Air Commerce and had rushed up from Texas to enter the race. They climbed into their waiting Beechcraft, and Louise put her head out the window, giving us a carefree wave.

"Well, so long!" she called, "we're just going to California for the ride!"

It was not until six in the morning that Laura, last of all the contestants, made her getaway, gunning her plane around by locking one wheel and speeding down the runway and off into the wind before the officials had time to flag her.

The finish was a triumph for women flyers. Louise Thaden and Blanche Noyes crossed the finish line first. Second came the girl they had wanted to disqualify, Laura Ingalls, setting a record for endurance and grit. Amelia and Helen ran into difficulties and placed fourth—but still in the money. One man had dropped out. One had crashed. The other came in third.

It was the first time in history a woman had won the Bendix, and even though I had only watched from the sidelines I felt a thrill of triumph and renewed hope.

It was during the acclaim for "petticoat pilots" following the Bendix that I received my long-awaited signal as to the future path of my life.

Aunty and I were sitting in my "sky parlor" at Rye a night or so later, and I was describing enthusiastically to her the importance of Louise Thaden's victory to the future prestige of women flyers, when she looked at me with her head on one side and remarked, with a twinkle:

"Thee seems to have come back to life, child. Thee's like

thy old self tonight. Perhaps there will be some light on the path ahead now."

I stared at her, and an idea began to take form.

"I've been reading about the Emergency Peace Campaign," I said slowly. "Maybe I could work with them. Maybe I could even find a way to help the campaign by flying. I could cover a lot of territory in a plane. Aunty, I just may have something here, and I'm going to find out what it is."

17

FRIENDLY WINGS

To fly in the cause of world peace! All at once that seemed the goal toward which I had been working, the solution to my inner conflicts. I heard that the organizer and director of the Emergency Peace Campaign was in New York —Ray Newton, who had taken a two-year leave of absence from the American Friends Service Committee to lead this work. After pursuing him all over the city for an entire day, I finally caught up with him at the Pennsylvania Hotel, just before he was due to take a train to Philadelphia. I had only ten minutes to state my case—ten minutes that might be the turning point of my life.

In a torrent of words I poured out my hopes and dreams of a world flight, pointing out how this could focus attention on international peace. Aviation, I told him, was the means which inevitably would bring the nations of the world closer together, since the speed of flight would shrink distance. Why shouldn't I be the one to carry a message of peace and good will around the world?

When I stopped for breath, Mr. Newton smiled and said: "You should be working for us."

Much as I needed a job, I was reluctant to settle for this, while there was a remote possibility of fulfilling my cherished dream. I thanked him, took a deep breath and started in again on my arguments. He agreed with all my ideas, but said he saw no way to finance an around-the-world flight. He repeated his offer of a job. If I would help with fund-raising, he said, he thought the committee could meet my salary needs.

"All right," I said impulsively, "I'll be glad to help."

After he had gone I sank down on a lounge in the lobby and caught my breath. I hadn't attained backing for a world flight, but at least I had a job working for a cause in which I believed. It would be a privilege to work with the distinguished men who headed the committee of the Emergency Peace Campaign—Charles P. Taft, son of the former president, Rear Admiral Richard E. Byrd and Dr. Harry Emerson Fosdick.

So I went to work in the interests of peace, and found that this was exactly the psychological lift I needed. Most of the people in the Philadelphia headquarters of the committee were Quakers, and I found a warmth and satisfaction in associating with them. I learned a great deal, too, about the causes and conditions of war, the economy of our country, the psychological conflicts then dividing the world and the means by which they might be resolved by peaceful measures. "Might be"—how sad a phrase that is!

During the months of my work for the Emergency Peace Campaign I covered a wide circle throughout the midwest and northeast, and found in my work a satisfying sense of accomplishment. But I also was appalled by the lethargy of a great majority of the American people, who did not seem able to realize the threat of imminent world war. As I talked to groups and individuals in many cities, my conviction grew that aviation must play a large part in any future unification of the nations of the world. Most flyers have an outlook instinctively international, and no matter what their nationality, they speak the same language. They share the freedom of the skies, they are familiar with height and distance, and they know how close together the air lanes can bring the most widely separated lands and oceans.

As I worked I studied, becoming more and more certain that in this field of international relations I was traveling in the right direction.

In the spring of 1937 I was dashing back and forth organizing international relations committees, holding fund-raising conferences, and between speaking engagements, occasionally taking time out for a brief respite. Among the activities was the annual dinner of the Women's National Press Club in Washington, where I sat next to the noted hostess, Evalyn Walsh McLean, owner of the famous Hope diamond, who invited me to visit her spectacular home, "Friendship." On an overnight stay at this fabled mansion, I pushed the wrong button to ring for breakfast and inadvertently set off the shrieking siren of the burglar alarm, installed to protect the McLean jewels. The entire household was aroused, a frantic group of guests, family and servants rushed into my room, to find me sitting red-faced and appalled in bed, saying, "I only meant to ring for tea!"

This was the year that dual tragedy struck our family. My patient, courageous father had been steadily losing his gallant fight against his long illness, although he would never admit it. One Sunday afternoon in May I sat beside his hospital bed, postponing until the last possible moment my departure for Providence, R. I., where I was committed to give a lecture before a large audience on the bases for building stable world relations. It was too late to cancel the engagement, even though I had a foreboding premonition that I would not see him alive again. I wanted to stay, but I had to go. Bending over his bed I kissed his cheek and whispered, "Everything's going to be all right, Dad darling, believe me." He patted my shoulder, smiled with a spark of his old gaiety and murmured, "Beloved girl."

Those were the last words my father spoke to me, and I shall always remember them, because somehow he packed into them a reassurance that he understood all the compulsions that drove me, forgave my mistakes and shared my belief in the eventual rightness of life. There was love and comfort and a kinship of spirit in those two words.

When I returned to the hospital after midnight, Dad had slipped into a coma from which he never awoke. The end came next morning and with it release from long years of pain and frustration. Now once again he would be remembered as the dashing sportsman, the rider to hounds, the Viking adventurer of his youth.

The peace campaign was soon coming to an end, but I wanted to go on with this work which had stirred my imagination, and so in June I enrolled in the Institute of International Relations at Cheney College, West Chester, Pennsylvania, one of a number of such groups conducted throughout the country by the Peace Section of the American Friends Service Committee.

It was while attending this session that I read with shock and sorrow the news of the disappearance of Amelia Earhart and her navigator somewhere in the Pacific, near the end of her ambitious second attempt at an around-the-world flight near the equator. After a ground-looping takeoff in Honolulu, Amelia had been convinced that the plane was overloaded, and had thrown out everything that was not absolutely essential. As I recall my conversation with her husband soon after her disappearance, she had discarded two radios, keeping only one. When she left the Island of Lae, New Guinea, she was headed for tiny Howland Island, a minute speck in the vast stretches of the lonely Pacific. In order to reach it, her navigator had to pinpoint a landing either by dead reckoning, celestial navigation, or cross bearings. An Hawaiian radio station and a Coast Guard cutter off the shore of Howland were taking bearings on her flight, but apparently Amelia couldn't hear their radio reports.

A photostat of a newspaper article, given to me by her husband during a conference I had with him in California, quotes directly from the Coast Guard cutter *Itasca's* radio log. Almost her last recorded message was this:

"Gas running low, unable reach you by radio."

There was a request that the *Itasca* take a bearing on her; then the log states that her last message was hurried, frantic and apparently not complete.

After that there was silence.

There has been much speculation and long argument over Amelia's final fate. Some people held the theory that she had landed on some island and had been taken prisoner by the Japanese or by savages. For months and years her friends and family clung to the forlorn hope that somewhere, somehow, she might still be alive, that once again they would see that cropped golden head and that boyish grin, hear that gay voice and grasp that strong, slender hand. But after almost twenty years have passed, I feel now as I did then—that Amelia flew on across the trackless Pacific until her last drop of fuel was gone and then sank quickly and cleanly into the deep blue sea.

If it must come, this was a fitting end to a flyer's career—to disappear at the peak of fame, on a final glorious attempt to conquer new frontiers of the sky; never to know the erosions and disappointments of age; to live on in memory as young, golden and unafraid.

Poring over the accounts of her final flight and receiving additional information from official sources, I was struck again with the many strange parallels in the careers of Amelia and myself. Though our early backgrounds and environments were quite different, our later aims and activities were much the same. Each was a student of sociology, each had had the thought of becoming a doctor, and we had shared the same love of height, speed and the freedom of the skies. Time after time we had planned the same ocean flights at almost the same time, each unaware of the other's plans.

I thought of our last meeting, at lunch in New York a few months before, when Amelia had remarked that she had one more flight left in her. We had got around to the subject of religion, talking more seriously than we ever had before, and she had expressed her fatalistic philosophy:

"When your number's up, that's it."

After the end of the Institute session, I treated myself to my first real vacation in nine years, on a Wyoming ranch. The trip was made, of course, by air, with a stop in Colorado Springs to visit Evalyn Walsh McLean, who had become a good friend. The morning after my arrival at Pitchfork Ranch, the largest in Wyoming, Charles Belden, the owner, greeted me with news of a raging forest fire in the nearby Shoshone Range and invited me to go along on an inspection flight.

"Antelope Charlie," as he was known to sportsmen all over the country because of the huge antelope herd on his sagebrush hills, and Bill Monday his pilot, warmed up a ten-year-old Ryan cabin monoplane, similar to Lindbergh's famous *Spirit of St. Louis* and we took off over the mountains. Soon huge billowing clouds of black smoke signaled the location of the fire. For a stretch of five miles we circled over roaring flames and smoke clouds while Charlie took photographs to be used in defining the spread of the fire and working out means of controlling it. Returning to Cody, we went to the hospital to do what we could in helping to care for and cheer the badly-burned C.C.C. boys and state foresters who had been fighting the fire. A number had been killed in the roaring inferno. When we felt there was no more we could do, we returned to Pitchfork, some miles away.

A week of riding over the hills, more scenic flying and a hunting trek through the rolling sagebrush mesas was shockingly interrupted by a wire from Aunty that my young sister, Bets, was critically ill with pneumonia. It was a frantic trip back to Rye. After driving three hundred miles over the Big Horn to catch a plane, I had two long delays, at Cheyenne and Chicago, before I could get passage on an eastbound plane. I finally reached my sister's bedside at midnight, just two hours before her young life flickered out.

It was a cruel blow, following so closely the death of Dad,

and it seemed senseless and unnecessary that Bets should have had to die before she ever really lived. Mother was inconsolable. In order to divert her, I took her to the Cleveland Air Races and to see my brother, Nick. While viewing the Air show, Nick met Madeleine, a lovely and brilliant southern girl, who later became his wife.

During this period I was asked to be a member of the Honorary Committee of the Amelia Earhart Foundation at Thiel College, and made a side trip to Pittsburgh to discuss their plans.

One result of this was that, during Air Mail week, Webb Schmaling and I flew the first mail to be transported out of New York state by seaplane, carrying a special cachet of three thousand airmail letters from Rye in commemoration of Amelia.

During the summer of 1938 Doug Corrigan made his famous "wrong way" flight to Ireland in an antiquated airplane, while Europe's war cauldron seethed and subsided in turn. I gave a few flying lessons, had many talks with government officials in Washington, did some work for an aviation magazine and had an amazing windfall in an offer from Twentieth Century-Fox Film Corporation to go on an air tour to help publicize a new aviation picture. They offered three thousand dollars plus all expenses for myself and my secretary, paid half of it in advance and assured me that I would be doing a service to the cause of women in aviation, while at the same time having a whirl of banquets and public appearances.

This offered a welcome break in the monotony of job-hunting and pot-boiling. It also afforded me the opportunity to take along as secretary one who had become a most congenial friend, as well as a student pilot, Mercedes Ormston, who paid many times over for the widely interspersed flying lessons I gave her by helping me to organize the original material on which this book is based, by typing innumerable business letters and answering fan mail.

The picture was "Tailspin," starring Constance Bennett, and the trip to Hollywood was fun, since the other pilots invited on the tour were old friends—Betty Gillies, Teddy Kenyon and Margot Tanner. At our first conference with the producers, however, we came to an impasse. We were told that we were all to dress in flying togs like those worn by Miss Bennett, while the bevy of movie starlets who were to accompany us would wear replicas of the outfits of the two supporting actresses, Alice Faye and Nancy Kelly. This seemed all right—until we saw Connie Bennett's outfit. The reaction of four experienced women pilots at sight of a so-called flying costume consisting of a double-breasted, high-collared jacket of exaggerated cut, jodhpurs, boots, helmet and goggles was to hit the ceiling with a simultaneous bang. Betty Gillies led off:

"Imagine stepping out of a closed, heated airliner in helmets and goggles! Imagine walking through the streets of Chicago in jodhpurs! Why the pilots would laugh us off the map. Why not skirts and berets?"

We all agreed vigorously and I added a suggestion:

"It's going to be cold on most of the northern half of the tour. Why don't you let us wear nice big polo coats? That's what most old-time women pilots wear now."

We won our battle with the promotion men, but since the poor little starlets had no voice in the matter, they had to wear white coveralls, helmets and goggles, and were not provided with coats for deplaning at snow-covered airports. Instead they were told to wear long underwear. . . .

We were installed in luxurious suites at the Beverly-Wilshire Hotel, subjected to a whirl of hairdressing appointments, costume fittings and publicity pictures at the studios and, as a climax to the tour preparations, rented a car and drove out to spend a weekend at the ranch of a distinguished fellow flyer, Jacqueline Cochran, in private life Mrs. Floyd Odlum, at Indio, California. Already holder of many flying records, Jackie was to win new laurels during World War II training women pilots for the Women's Auxiliary Ferrying

Squadron and as director of the WASPS—the Women's Air Force Service Pilots, who flew over sixty million miles in wartime. She was awarded the Distinguished Service Medal for her work as head of the WASPS, has won countless awards and trophies and today is the outstanding woman flyer of America.

The weekend at Jackie's ranch was a refreshing change from the hectic whirl of Hollywood, giving us a chance to rest up and relax before the start of the next week's tour.

Betty and Teddy, with four starlets, were assigned to one airliner, to cover the southern part of the country. In another were Margot, Mercedes, four starlets and myself, with a northern itinerary. The whole trip was a lark, and we pilots got huge amusement out of the crowds at airports who clustered around the four little starlets, who had never flown before in their lives, beseeching: "Oh, do tell us your most exciting flying experience!" The actual women pilots remained fairly safe from such questions, thanks to the protective coloration of our polo coats.

It was a hilarious but strenuous trip, with a daily schedule of luncheons, broadcasts, public appearances and previews of the film. By the time we neared the end of the tour we all agreed with one of the starlets, Dorothy Deering, who remarked one gray dawn:

"I feel like a bad case of embalming!"

The tour, besides offering a respite from serious endeavors, also repaired my morale by providing a great deal of flattering masculine attention. About this time I had another serious romance, but again, it was not right. At Rye I still spent many happy hours with various entertaining escorts. I still hoped for marriage, a home and children, but I didn't feel ready to accept just any proposal.

At any rate, I came home this time with money in the bank.

18
RELIEF WINGS

When Germany marched on Poland in September, 1939, setting the match to the powder keg of Europe, many Americans still felt that our country would remain safe and neutral. I knew only that I must do something to help, and the thing I knew and loved best was aviation.

A government Civilian Pilot Training Program had been developed and I was asked to inaugurate the first such flying school to include women at Adelphi College in Long Island. As the group consisted of both boys and girls, I tried to tell them what future there was in aviation aside from a military career for I felt these young people should be alert to all fields of service.

Ever since my first crackup in St. Johns, N.B., and my painful trip home in an ordinary plane, the idea of an air ambulance service had been in the back of my mind. Even if, by some miracle, we managed to stay at peace, there was wide need for "mercy flying" right here at home. Air ambulances could do an inestimable service in disaster relief, at times of flood or hurricane and even in everyday civilian emergencies. It would also be of great value should our cities be laid waste by bombs.

I discussed my idea with Aunty, and she applauded it, her eyes sparkling with interest.

"That's a fine idea, child," she said enthusiastically. "Thee can help people and fly, too!"

"Well, I'll probably be doing more organizing and fund-raising than anything else at the start," I laughed. "But, Aunty dear, it may seem odd—actually I want to establish such an air rescue service as intensely as I've ever wanted to accomplish anything. Oh, I *do* hope I can put it over!"

I gathered advice and opinions from many sources. First I went to the peace groups and outlined my plan. Then I got in touch with various social, educational and religious organizations. All expressed interest and even enthusiasm, but had no funds with which to back such a project. However, I was determined. As a start I enlisted the interest of an old family friend, Clement M. Biddle, sturdy Quaker and prominent business man. Then I gained the active cooperation of two well-known New York women, Mrs. Henry Hill Pierce and Mrs. Paul M. Warburg. All through the early spring of 1940, while Europe nervously awaited the end of what was called "the Phoney War," the nucleus of an organization was taking shape.

Meanwhile during those busy months, Rear Admiral Richard E. Byrd, the greatest explorer of our time, and I had been invited by the President of Beaver College, Dr. James E. Mooney, to serve on his college Board of Trustees. And in the Spring Dick Byrd, for whom I had developed the highest respect and admiration, and I received honorary doctors' degrees from Beaver College.

On May 27 I announced the founding of Relief Wings, in an address I had been asked to give at the annual aviation convention of the National Aeronautical Association, held that year in Washington.

The original program was simple enough—to enlist as many private planes and existing facilities as possible for emergency and disaster relief work. We used the Aircraft Owners and Pilots Association as a logical nucleus for mobilizing private and commercial planes. For doctors and nurses we planned to rely on the senior Civil Aeronautics Authority medical examiners in various areas, and on retired airline stewardesses, most of whom were required to have nurse's training.

Author in Beechcraft air ambulance during her organizing tour
for Relief Wings in 1941.

To dramatize the aims of Relief Wings, we decided to stage a simulated hurricane mobilization July 7, 1940, at Greenport, Long Island. Following is a partial account of the occasion as reported by *The New York Times*, under the headline "100 PLANES STAGE DISASTER AID DRILL":

GREENPORT, L. I., July 7—Small privately owned aircraft of many types, of all colors of the rainbow, converged on this town this morning in what is believed to be the first mass flight ever designed for disaster relief. One hundred land and sea planes from six states coordinated their movements via amateur radio operators in solving a hypothetical hurricane problem.

They glided to earth singly or in groups on two adjoining fields on the farms of Mrs. Harrison McCann and Herbert L. Fordham, about a mile and a half north of here. A wide swath cut through the grass provided the runway in each case. The trim pontoons on curving hulls of thirty seaplanes rode at anchor in a yacht basin on Peconic Bay.

The Aircraft Owners and Pilots Association and Relief Wings, Inc., worked out the situation under the direction of Miss Ruth Nichols, one of the nation's best-known flyers. She arrived over the scene in a United Air Lines transport that took off from La Guardia Airport, North Beach, Queens, with medical and food supplies, nurses and doctors.

To set the stage for the demonstration, we had announced an urgent appeal to the Red Cross at dawn, after a make-believe hurricane was supposed to have devastated the northern shore of Long Island, leaving hundreds of persons homeless, many injured, roads blocked and normal communications wrecked. Our purpose was to show how quickly planes could be mobilized and aid rushed to the victims. Amateur radio operators alerted the flyers throughout New York, New Jersey, Pennsylvania, Connecticut, Rhode Island and Massachusetts.

Flight leaders were notified: Tony Little in Norristown, Pa.; J. Starr at Roosevelt Field; H. J. Lentz at Hackensack, N. J.; F. B. Chalifoux in Boston and George Arents, Jr., in Westchester. I was ready to leave La Guardia Field by eight a.m. Accompanying me in the big United Airliner were: Dr.

B. Weiss and Dr. J. S. Sack, both of Brooklyn, as flight surgeons, and two nurses. We carried food and medical supplies. Unfortunately, our director of flight nurses, Gayle Pond, could not be present. She was not only a pilot but had also formulated a fine training program some of which I later adopted for the Civil Air Patrol.

We landed the airliner at Suffolk Airport, and the small private planes ferried personnel and equipment to the supposedly stricken area. We had reached the "hurricane belt" in fifty-five minutes, and thousands of local residents lined the roads watching these maneuvers for their "rescue." We had representatives of the Civil Aeronautics Authority and the American Red Cross present; a Nassau County police plane patrolled the area, and local police, firemen and Boy Scouts stood by for emergency duty. It was a colorful and successful demonstration, ending in a gay breakfast party arranged by Lyle Brookover, a most valuable member of our organization, given in honor of the flyers by the mayor of Greenport. This was followed by a luncheon arranged by Relief Wings at the Shelter Island Casino.

We seemed to be off to a good start, and public interest was lively. Next we were invited to stage a maritime rescue as part of a two-day historical pageant at the famous old seaport of Gloucester, Mass. We sent out notices to the Aircraft Owners and Pilots Association, Aviation Country Club members, C.A.A. doctors and airline nurses. The night before I stayed in Gloucester and sent out the mobilization call for a "sea disaster" at seven a.m., asking seaplane owners and airlines to rush doctors, nurses and medical supplies to rescue two thousand shipwrecked "survivors."

The Gloucester racing schooner *Gertrude L. Thebaud*, representing an ocean liner carrying Americans and refugees from Europe, was supposed to be burning in the harbor. Its call for help was picked up at ten a.m. by amateur radio stations, the seaplanes began arriving from a nearby port and the "rescue" was completed by shortly after noon. Afterward the pilots and other personnel taking part in the operations were entertained at lunch by Miss Natalie Hays Hammond, chairman of Defense Day arrangements for the pageant, which was planned in honor of the dedication of the Gloucester seaplane base by Governor Leverett Saltonstall of Massachusetts. Members of the Relief Wings organization received warm praise from Governor Saltonstall, Rear Admiral William Tarrant, commandant of the Boston Navy Yard, and other officials who were on hand. It was another colorful day of make-believe, attracted wide attention in the press and provided entertainment for the Gloucester celebration.

But I felt that we would be far from ready if a real disaster were to strike. I determined that in the future Relief Wings must have definitely enrolled volunteers trained in mobilization procedure, and on call at any hour, day or night. There would be four divisions: aircraft owners and pilots, flight surgeons, flight nurses and amateur radio operators. We also sent registration blanks to the entire list of C.A.A. medical examiners, ex-airline stewardesses and other eligible nurses.

The real impetus for the serious start of Relief Wings, however, came from the backing of far-sighted airline executives: C. R. Smith, president of American Airlines, William Patterson, president of United Airlines and Jack Frye, president of TWA, each of whom made personal contributions of two thousand dollars. Later, Eddie Rickenbacker, President of Eastern Airlines, joined the major donors. Then C. V. Whitney, chairman of the board of Pan American Airways, presented the organization with a fast, five-place Beechcraft airplane, complete with a fine radio donated by William Lear's company.

Provided with a bank account and a plane, Relief Wings was set to go. We used about half the original nestegg to retain one of the most capable professional fund-raising organizations in the United States and I was joined in the enterprise by two of my best friends, Jane Hyde, staunch comrade of barnstorming days, and Mercedes Ormston, who had accompanied me on the movie promotion flight. Jane was to be "Girl Friday" and Mercedes was to act as general secretary of the organization.

On a freezing December day the three of us sat in our little cubbyhole office planning new strategy, and dismally conscious that our exchequer was running low, as the fund-raising firm needed more underwriting, when in walked an exotically beautiful Chinese girl, trim, alert and smiling. She introduced herself as Lee Ya Ching, and I realized that here was China's most famous woman pilot. She said she had heard we planned to send medical relief planes to China, and she had come to help. This was a project which, indeed, had been under serious discussion, and I had had considerable correspondence on the subject with various agencies in China as well as a luncheon conference in Washington with the Honorable Dr. Hu Shih, the Chinese Ambassador. Jane, Mercedes and I welcomed this new recruit, who seemed to bring with her a brisk air of youthful energy and confidence.

"Why not go down to Miami for the All-American Air Maneuvers next week?" suggested Ya Ching. "I have lots of wealthy friends down there, and we ought to be able to raise a lot of funds."

Now here was a confederate worth having! She was not only beautiful and energetic; she was also smart. The more we discussed the idea, the better it seemed. We could fly down in the Beechcraft, get a lot of publicity by appearing at the Air Maneuvers, and conduct our fund-raising in the happy hunting ground of America's social rich. The only drawback was our slender bank roll, but Ya Ching said brightly that she thought she could get us hotel rooms "on the cuff" at Bernarr MacFadden's new Miami Beach hotel, the Deauville, and we could always eat at Chinese restaurants run by friends of hers.

We had just a week to get the Beechcraft in shape for the flight, including having it painted white, which we thought suitable for a mercy plane. Ya Ching was somewhat unhappily familiar with the plane, while flying it the year before when "Sonny" Whitney had lent it to her for a tour she had planned. The day before we were to start I hastily enlisted the services of a check pilot at Floyd Bennett Field to give Ya Ching and myself final checkups in the Beechcraft. At La Guardia Airport news photographers were waiting, together with the Chinese Consul General and other onlookers. Ya Ching and I had uniforms consisting of gray suede jackets and blue skirts, while Jane and Mercedes had blue skirts and matching blouses—an effective contrast to the gleaming white ship with its red-surfaced wings.

Jessie Chamberlin, President of the New York Branch of the Women's International Association of Aeronautics gave us a most thoughtful send-off breakfast. This organization was founded by another good friend of long standing, Elizabeth Grant McQueen. As we took off the weather was threatening, with low visibility. I was concerned, as I felt the responsibility for three other lives besides my own—quite a different thing from my usual solo flying. Although it was understood that I was responsible for the plane and would make all landings and takeoffs, in the air Ya Ching and I took turns at the controls. The weather got steadily worse. Finally I decided to land at Richmond, Va., hoping the weather would clear by the following day. This proved a wise decision, for although the next morning was still cloudy, the sun finally broke through and we zoomed along in sparkling skies for the rest of the trip, making a somewhat precarious landing in gusty winds before twenty-five thousand spectators at the air races in Miami.

We couldn't have asked for a more auspicious start to what was to turn out as a five-month national tour. We were rushed into a whirlwind round of aviation luncheons, banquets and balls. On next to the last day of the four-day air meet, Ya Ching and I were formally received by the Duke of Windsor, official guest of honor. He seemed genuinely interested in our objectives, and talked informally and amiably. I fastened a

Relief Wings pin on his lapel, and he thanked me with an infectious smile.

A day or so later we were invited to Hialeah Race Track in a party which included Dick Merrill, famous trans-Atlantic pilot, and Daniel Mahoney, managing editor of the *Miami Daily News*. Mr. Mahoney was intrigued by Ya Ching's charm and interested in the potentialities of Relief Wings. As we told him of all our hopes and plans for a far-reaching ambulance plane service, he said:

"You ought to do this thing up right, in a big way. For instance, we might help you give a party in a place like Bill Marden's Colonial Inn, as we did last year for a charity in another famous night club, and raised a tidy sum."

This seemed too good to be true. But Mahoney went on to say his paper would back a "Wings of Mercy Ball" for the benefit of Relief Wings, would guarantee a number of tables and in addition would plan auctions to swell the funds. He even helped us work up a glittering list of sponsors among the socially elect of Miami. The affair, under the chairmanship of Mrs. Dorothy Lee Ward, was a great success (though I suffered all the usual jitters in advance—suppose no one comes, suppose lots of people come and are bored, and so on and on). However, it was described in the newspapers as "one of the most brilliant charity affairs of the season." Such famous entertainers as Harry Richman, Sophie Tucker and Joe E. Lewis generously gave their services, and after all expenses were paid, we netted two thousand five hundred dollars.

Ya Ching and Jane Hyde decided it would be best for them to return to New York by airline after the loose ends of the ball were tied up, accounts checked and everything in order, so Mercedes and I carried on.

We received a number of invitations from various friends, including Annette Gibson Magoffin, a fellow flyer, who asked us to stay with her in her Coconut Grove home while we wound up details of the organization of a Relief Wings unit in Miami. The aviation commissioner of Miami, Al Hanson, agreed to act as sectional director, and we enlisted the offices of the head of one of the city's outstanding flying schools as coordinator of planes and pilots. Dr. M. C. Martin, C.A.A. medical examiner, agreed to take over the enrollment of flight surgeons, and Veronica Forsythe, a registered nurse from St. Petersburg, offered to round up the flight nurses.

Our next stop was Palm Beach, from which we planned to make a swing around the country, organizing units wherever it seemed possible. Our luck in Palm Beach was as fabulous as the place itself, and by the time we left we had raised more than ten thousand dollars, a happy contrast to the eighty dollars in the Relief Wings treasury when we left New York.

Buoyed up by this success, Mercedes and I laid out an itinerary for a westward tour, and stopped at her aunt's home in St. Petersburg for a week while we worked out organization details, had various forms mimeographed, caught up with our correspondence and made plans for publicity and hotel arrangements on the trip.

We started off on a swing through the south, making stops at New Orleans, Dallas, Fort Worth, Louisville and other cities. Our days were filled with speech-making, fund-raising, organizing and giving newspaper interviews and our nights (on more than one occasion until near dawn) with dictation and typing. As we were off the regular airline routes, we encountered various difficulties, much bad weather, precarious landings and other hazards, but managed to come safely out of a number of close shaves.

When we reached Wichita, almost five months after departing from New York on what was to have been a two-week trip, I decided we were due for a breather. So I left the plane at the Beech Aircraft factory, under the capable direction of Walter and Anne Beech, who donated a number of modifications and a better paint job, and with Mercedes boarded an airliner for New York.

I felt well satisfied with the results of our tour. We had set up sections of Relief Wings in six cities; we had the sponsorship of every leader of a large aviation association as well as that of many social, educational and civic leaders; and we had raised a comfortable backlog of funds. On my return to New York I was greeted by a rare honor from the General Federation of Women's Clubs.

I was invited to be their guest at the Federation Annual Convention in Atlantic City, having been selected to share honors with such women as Helen Keller, Secretary of Labor Frances Perkins, the Hon. Mrs. Borden Harriman, Mrs. Eleanor Roosevelt, the Hon. Ruth Bryan Rhode, former minister to Denmark, and others of similar luster. Seated before ten thousand spectators in the packed convention hall, I had difficulty swallowing a lump in my throat when I heard the citation . . . "In recognition of her outstanding success in the field of aviation and of her leadership among the women of the world . . ."

For the rest of that summer and fall I continued the work of Relief Wings, and on the afternoon of December 7, 1941 I was in Santa Barbara, California, motoring along El Ciello Drive, under blue skies, drinking in the breathtaking panorama of the green valley below. Then over the car radio came the announcement of the Japanese attack on Pearl Harbor, ending with those fateful words, *"WE ARE AT WAR."*

As all of us must, I thought first of those close to me. My brother Nick was in the Pacific area already, my brother Bill was still in aviation, employed by an airplane manufacturing company. What would this mean to them? Was Nick already under enemy fire? Was he safe?

My next thought was of the future of Relief Wings. There ought to be even greater need for its organization and services. I obtained permission from the Army to fly the Beechcraft straight to New York, to see what could be done. Overnight the tempo of the country had changed. Everything was accelerated. And it became exceedingly difficult for private planes to fly without governmental permission. I went to

Washington to confer with aeronautics and military officials. Finally, I decided that my plans for rescue flying could best grow under the Civil Air Patrol which had necessary government financing. I had built a strong nucleus in eleven sections of the country covering thirty-six states with volunteer sectional directors, coordinators and enrolled members composed of aircraft owners, pilots, surgeons, nurses and radio stations plus certain needed air ambulance supplies, along with mobilization and training procedures. With this basic structure I made available Relief Wings' assets to the larger, nationally sponsored C.A.P.

19

WINGS AROUND THE WORLD

The war years and their aftermath were for me as for others difficult times, despite the fact that I engaged in many and diverse activities to help serve humanity and my country. I worked as a volunteer Red Cross Nurse's Aide. I gave flying instruction and served for a time as a consultant at the Dayton School of Aviation. My part in the war was no more—and, to me, no less—important than that of thousands of American women; it was a time when we all underwent deep emotional experiences but, for the purposes of this book, it can be nearly ignored.

This was a period of further retrenchment for the Nichols family. Only Mother, Aunty and I were at home, since Nick was serving in the Air Force and my brother Bill lived with his family on Long Island, near the airplane manufacturing plant where he was rendering essential service. So at length we sold the big old family home and moved into a small rented cottage in Rye.

During all this period of adjustment and change, my long-time dream of a world flight for a humanitarian cause remained alive and kicking. While I waited for the opportunity I was seeking, I had many months of precision flying, according to the new tough standards set for those who wanted to teach. I finally secured a Flight Instructor's re-rating. A few years later I obtained a C.A.A. rating for multi-engine aircraft and took further instruction in new navigation and instrument techniques.

The long-awaited break did not arrive until the winter of 1948, when it was suggested that I join forces with the president of a youth group who was planning a globe-circling flight inaugurating a series of youth tours to promote international unity among young people. This was a non-profit organization with a high purpose, and it appealed to me. When it developed that it might be possible for me to act as co-pilot on the chartered non-scheduled air transport which was to carry the group, my interest went into high gear. Perhaps I still might be the first woman flyer to pilot around the world. . . .

Plans and discussions went on during the winter, with the flight set to start early in July, 1949. As I got deeper into the plans, I felt that I should make this flight even more meaningful. The aims of the youth group were admirable, but there were greater needs in the nations of the world. An enthusiastic believer in the work of the United Nations, I conferred with various committees there and one day discovered that a long-time friend, Mrs. Oswald B. Lord, Chairman of the U. S. Committee of the United Nations International Childrens' Emergency Fund, was most enthusiastic over the idea that I should focus world attention on the services of UNICEF. She thereupon appointed me as a Special Volunteer Correspondent. In each country United Nations personnel would meet me and arrange for me to investigate and report the progress in feeding, medical care and rehabilitation for the world's needy children.

Now, I knew, at last I had found the crystallization of my life's desire and training—the use of aviation for a great humanitarian purpose, which I had partially realized in my plans for Relief Wings. Here was a work into which I could put my heart as well as my hands, and for which I could finally unite an adventurer's heart with a Quaker spirit.

Ruth Nichols in cockpit of DC-4 before starting her
world tour on behalf of the United Nations International Children's Emergency Fund, July, 1949.

I felt a new surge of life and joy, a new awareness of myself as a potent entity, with my faculties and deep ideals forged together in an effective instrument to help relieve suffering.

Aunty, still alert and vigorous though in her ninetieth year, was as excited as I was. As next best thing, she pored over maps and cautioned me to take both summer and winter clothing for the high Himalayas.

At the last minute, as usual, a crisis developed. But for me that was routine. This time it came in the form of a new government aeronautical regulation ruling out my serving as a professional co-pilot on the flight. I learned of it twenty-four hours before the takeoff, which certainly fitted the pattern of past experience. It seemed that I hadn't had enough hours in multi-engine flying to qualify as a transport pilot for this type of plane. But I did have a multi-engine rating, commercial and instructor ratings as well as instrument techniques, so after much frantic telephoning I finally was cleared to serve on the flight as a "courtesy extra pilot," though not officially a member of the crew. This suited me fine. It would enable me to assist in operation of the plane on every leg of the global flight.

Shortly after midnight July 9, 1949, we assembled at Bradley Field, Windsor Locks, near Hartford, Connecticut. Our plane was a fifty-six passenger DC-4 Skymaster. Though we did not have the full complement of passengers to fill every seat, we more than made up the difference in luggage, being equipped with bicycles, sleeping bags and camping equipment in addition to the usual paraphernalia. The students, boys and girls, were an interdenominational group, both Christian and Jewish, in addition to one Moslem lad from Kenya Colony. My own most important pieces of equipment were the notebooks I hoped to fill with UNICEF reports.

At 2:15 a.m. the DC-4 took off smoothly through a slight ground haze into the star-studded darkness of the sky, and my heart rose with it. How many years of hope and heartbreak had intervened since I first set my sights on a world flight! I piloted during a good part of the first leg to Denver, experiencing the old familiar elation. Having been accepted in the inner circle of pilots all my life, I had looked forward to enjoying the camaraderie of the ship's crew. But these schooled and scientific young men were a different kettle of fish from the old-timers I had known so well. They were, I found, as different from the old school of pilots as this huge four-engine sky clipper was different from the lumbering Jennies and Seagulls of my youth. To be accepted by this new generation of flying men, I would have to earn my standing.

All right, I said to myself, if that's what they want, that's the way it was going to be. I'd show these fly-boys. I settled down to the concentrated task of watching the various dials and making the delicate adjustments required every few minutes, even when the ship was on automatic pilot control, although many hours that night, as well as on the coming tour, I piloted without the control engaged. The lateral angle of the wings had to be watched, the fore-and-aft longitudinal balance of the long fuselage corrected every time a passenger moved from the front of the cabin to the back. I had to check recession on the directional-gyro and about every fifteen minutes reset it for compass heading. I watched closely the sensitive altimeter, so that our altitude did not vary more than fifty feet during the flight. As I glanced around the cockpit at over a hundred different dials and knobs many of which were tightly arranged on the facing instrument panel, I was thankful I had kept up with the new developments in flying.

When we arrived at Denver, the young pilots seemed to regard me with more respect and by the time we reached San Francisco (after very bumpy mountain convection currents) I was in. They relaxed, included me in their special brand of airman talk, and even started asking questions about how it felt to fly one of those bailing-wire open-cockpit jobs.

"You had to be whacky to fly one of those babies," remarked one. "Funny thing is, Ruth, you seem to do all right on this job, too."

When he called me "Ruth" I felt I was one of the crew.

At San Francisco we switched to a new crew and to another plane of the same type, which was to be ours for the rest of the trip. The flight to Honolulu was made in clear weather. Just before dawn we were flying over gauze puffballs spangled onto a rose pool-like sea beneath. Then the sight of Diamond Head looming ahead brought back all the rapture of my first glimpse of the Hawaiian Islands more than twenty-five years before. From Honolulu we headed for Wake Island, and hit this pinpoint of land on the nose. I realized when I saw it, scarcely more than a dot in the vast stretches of the Pacific, how easy it would be to miss it entirely, and I thought again of the desperate problems Amelia must have had in trying to reach Howland Island.

I was taking regular turns at the controls on each leg of the flight, and having a wonderful time. Before we left New York I had been reading newspaper accounts of a British housewife, Mrs. Morrow-Tait, who had also been attempting an around-the-world flight, accompanied by a navigator. She was traveling on a west-east course, but had met with many delays, having a crackup in Marseilles and another in Alaska. The last I had heard she was bogged down in Chicago, stymied by lack of backing.

On the flight between Wake and Tokyo I flew the ship for four out of nine hours, the other five hours being divided between captain and co-pilot. I was getting more unconsciously the feel of the ship, and establishing that rapport between plane and pilot which is so intangible yet so essential for both complete pilot enjoyment as well as efficiency. As I automatically handled the various knobs and the control wheel, and as the large airliner responded to the lightest pressure, I thought with satisfaction that, as a matter of fact, this was another "first." Women had flown other areas to north and south, but none had piloted this particular stretch. "Jackie"

Cochran during World War II and immediately thereafter zigzagged under most interesting circumstances over a large part of the world including Guam and the Philippines by various means of transportation though largely in Air Force transports. Although we had been alerted to the possibility of a typhoon, none appeared, and we arrived at Haneda Airport in Tokyo without incident and on schedule. We had crossed the International Date Line July 14, losing the day of July 15 completely.

Four days were spent in Japan; from Tokyo to Hongkong we flew over Formosa. Never before or since have I seen the unique color effects of air and water that we encountered on this route. The air was clear, yet somehow opalescent, with a kind of mother-of-pearl iridescence, while below in the blue water there were streams of varied colors, from deepest indigo to exquisite jade green near the milky shoals. These are the moments a pilot stores away like jewels in the vault of memory—the unexpected experiences of unearthly beauty one views from the upper air.

We reached Bangkok Saturday, July 23, where arrangements had been made by UNICEF officials for me to interview Princess Aditya Kob Khaew, widow of Prince Adit, former Prince Regent of Thailand. I was received in her cool, modern summer home, one of her several estates, where the princess, over a friendly cup of tea, talked at length of conditions existing in her country in relation to child welfare, and described both the work being done by UNICEF and her own program for progress.

I learned that one hundred and fifty out of every thousand children in Thailand died before one year of age, and that sixty out of every thousand mothers die in childbirth. Life expectancy of the Siamese poor was only twenty-eight years. These dire conditions were due to the high prevalence of malaria, tuberculosis and stomach disorders caused by water pollution and, in the case of babies' deaths, to unsanitary breast feeding. Princess Aditya headed a dynamic program of relief as chairman of Thailand's drive. In that capacity she had become the first woman to address the august assemblage of provincial governors. As a result she raised sufficient money to aid hospitals, orphanages and mobile units for dispensing medicines, clothing and health education, as well as a reserve fund for emergency relief.

I spent several days investigating various aspects of the status of children in Thailand, held a number of conferences with American UNICEF representatives and was guest of honor at a dinner given by them. Then, laden with notes and photographs, I rejoined my companions of the youth group and after a few more days we took off for India.

On this leg of the flight our benign weatherman deserted us and the monsoon season took us in tow. The torrents of rain through which we flew defy description. I was piloting through a good part of this condition and it was like flying through a solid Niagara. The deluge did not maintain a constant pitch, but swept over us in waves, as if we were battling mountainous seas. Had the decision been up to me, I would have tried for more altitude to try to get above the storm. But we adhered to the usual flight procedure of large modern transports and ploughed straight through it. I didn't care for the looks of the landscape below, for purposes of a forced landing. It alternated between dense jungle and great flooded areas. Over Burma the storm seemed to increase in fury, and there were none of those friendly landmarks so comforting to old-time pilots—those reassuring railroads and highways. We flew entirely by compass and radio navigation.

As we approached New Delhi, there was a sudden break in the clouds, and the Skymaster circled. One of the pilots came back to the cabin, where I had gone for a rest.

"Heads up, everybody," he said. "Got something to show you."

It was a vision of incredible beauty. Through the rift in the clouds a shaft of translucent light picked out the Taj

Mahal, a shining fairy palace beneath us, its white marble perfection lighted up against the surrounding darkness of the storm as if by a celestial spotlight.

Shortly after our arrival at New Delhi, we received word that the entire group would be received by Prime Minister Nehru. We had barely enough time to wash and change after our six-hour flight through the monsoon, and were enjoying tea and cookies at the Y.M.C.A. when the summons came and we set out for Nehru's mansion.

We passed through great wrought-iron gates, across well-kept grounds to be met at the porte-cochere by Nehru's secretary, a smiling, buxom woman in a beautiful sari. She ushered us through spacious rooms, which reminded me of some of our American southern mansions, to the reception hall, where we were not kept waiting. Almost immediately the Prime Minister entered unannounced, dressed in a long white cotton coat and white jodhpurs, he shook hands briskly all around, and suggested that we sit on the floor instead of on the chairs placed formally around the walls.

As fruit juice was served, India's leader regarded us with twinkling eyes and invited questions. The students had been waiting for this, and they fired at him queries on every subject from international relations to politics and from welfare to religion. I was fascinated by watching Nehru's hypnotic eyes and mobile face as he gave his answers, now alert and shrewd, now grave and reflective, now amused and jolly. My final impression was of a highly educated man of genial discipline in living and a sincere interest in people, who showed he had had years of spiritual and political experience.

When the students completed their questioning, I asked Nehru about India's educational program for children, and he replied thoughtfully:

"It has been my experience that neither children nor their mothers are interested in education while they are hungry. In India our greatest need is milk."

It was a two-hour interview, touching on many subjects, but the high mark was a fifteen-minute dissertation on the spiritual and selfless life of Mahatma Ghandi.

That night I jotted down a number of facts and statements in my notebook, and through the following days covered many more pages with data supplied by T. Glan Davies, UNICEF representative at New Delhi, Dr. O. Mani, regional director of the Southeastern Asian Section of WHO, and Col. Barkat Narain, director of health services in Delhi Province. The work being done was fine, but pathetically meager by comparison with the appalling need. For example, I was told that twenty million children needed food.

With Colonel Narain, who held an M.D. degree, I visited a refugee center holding twenty thousand inhabitants living in mud huts, all of them ragged, unkempt and undernourished. Hospital wards were inadequate but relatively clean, though flies were a constant menace in the maternity ward. All the patients looked sad and hopeless, with only an animal instinct for survival.

Though the Colonel did his best, it was impossible to meet the extensive demands for medical care, and as we left one institution he was literally mobbed by women clamoring for advice, help and food. When finally we made our way to the waiting car, agonized faces pressed against its windows—faces that I have never been able to forget.

Our next stop was Karachi, Pakistan's leading city where I made another UNICEF survey, and where our group was received by Begum Raana Liquat Ali Khan, wife of Pakistan's Premier, a gracious lady in a gorgeous blue and silver sari, who talked with friendliness and understanding of the problems of her people.

Karachi to Teheran, over desert and mountains five miles high. Here the United States Ambassador arranged an audience with King Mohammed Reza Pahvlevi, the Shah of Iran, at his summer place. Teheran to Cairo, and a night camping out under the stars in the shadow of the pyramids. Cairo to

Author at Ste. Jeanne d'Arc feeding center near Haifa, Israel, during her UNICEF world tour in 1949.

Cyprus, thence to Israel, where Catholic nuns at an orphanage struggling under shocking conditions, were forced to drag great loads of potatoes from market on little carts, and during an Arab-Israeli battle had had to bury their own dead, in shallow graves in their own courtyard. In the cellar, they cared for the adult insane.

Israel to Istanbul, then on to Athens along the most beautiful island-dotted coastline I had ever seen—and the tragedy of forty thousand orphans of war, cared for in many centers throughout Greece by various relief agencies, aided by UNICEF. I visited as many as I could, and was shocked again by the marks of suffering and malnutrition on little faces too young to be so tragic. The work was going on, and marvels of rehabilitation were being accomplished, but for some of the children the scars of tragedy were too deep to heal. Greece completed all of my official visits since at that time UNICEF had not found it advisable to develop their program in Europe. Therefore from the beginning I had planned to end my UNICEF survey in Athens.

I had been informed at the start of this tour that probably there were twenty million children needing UNICEF help. At its end I realized that the number needing food, medical equipment and simple human kindness was nearer sixty million.

From Athens we flew on to Rome, where the group of youngsters would leave me, to complete the end of their tour by ship, and where I would make arrangements to continue by air, possibly as co-pilot of a plane flying to America.

20

TERROR AT SEA

I was having breakfast in bed my first morning in Rome and looking forward to a leisurely week in Europe when a headline caught my eye in the English-language newspaper delivered with my coffee. The British flying housewife, Mrs. Morrow-Tait, who I thought had abandoned her round-the-world flight attempt in Chicago, had somehow solved her difficulties and had reached Greenland with her navigator-pilot. If luck was with her she could complete her world flight, which had taken her over a year, in the next two days.

Since I had started out with the idea that the first round-the-world flight by a woman would serve to focus attention on the UNICEF program, in addition to the old competitive spirit, I felt I must follow through. My UNICEF surveys were now complete, and I had planned merely to do a little sight-seeing and relax for a couple of weeks before returning home. But with luck I might still complete the globe-circling flight first. In any case I felt I must try.

I cancelled my future itinerary, and then, with the assistance of a kindly UNICEF official, I called one airline after another in a frantic effort to locate a plane leaving for New York that day, on which I could serve as an extra pilot. It took two hours of pleading to solve my problem, but in the end I had clearance to replace one of the two stewardesses in the crew of a non-scheduled airliner departing that afternoon for the United States. I also obtained permission to act as an extra pilot, in addition to the plane's regular contingent of pilots.

During this time I had repacked my bags, sent off various cables to New York and called a taxi. When the big four-engined plane took off at five p.m. I was aboard, somewhat breathless but triumphant. Our schedule called for only one brief refuelling stop at Shannon, Ireland, and arrival in New York within twenty-four hours.

As soon as the plane reached cruising altitude I was called up to the flight deck to meet the crew. They were most cordial, and the captain at once invited me to take over the controls. As I settled down to piloting the big airliner purred smoothly while we surged swiftly through a clear blue sky, over the Mediterranean and onto the southern coast of France. After two hours of flying the four-engined plane, I thanked the captain and went back to the main cabin. I asked the Chief Steward if I could help. He said there was nothing to do, so I settled down to rest and work on my flight log. I must have dozed off, for when I opened my eyes it was dark outside, and as I peered at my watch I realized that we were an hour overdue for the estimated time of arrival at Shannon, and went forward to the flight compartment to check. One glance at the tight-lipped faces of the crew was all I needed. We had overshot Shannon, they told me. We had lost radio contact with all land bases. The captain had turned back, and the question now was—would the gas last? Presumably we were somewhere between Iceland and Ireland.

I returned to my seat and tried to relax. The passengers apparently were unaware that anything was amiss. Most of them were asleep, a few were reading or conversing in low tones. Forty-five minutes passed which seemed an eternity. I now could for the first—and I hope only—time feel the second by second agony of "sweating it out," with no one to talk to and nothing to do. I could only wait and in not one of all my fifty-five narrow escapes, during over thirty years of flying, did I ever have such inner tension. A pilot's ear is tuned to the rhythm of the engines, and my heart jumped as I heard an engine sputter. This great airliner, so swift and powerful in the sky, would sink like a stone in the icy waters of the North Sea.

The First Pilot, poker-faced and brisk, came into the passenger cabin and snapped out:

"Prepare to ditch!"

Some of the dozing passengers, not understanding English, woke up bewildered, frightened by the urgency in his voice. The pretty young stewardess, speaking in Italian, gave brief instructions from the front of the cabin. Her manner was quiet and matter of fact. She apparently intimated that life preservers were donned for usual landings and was informing the passengers as to how they were to be fastened. She then moved quietly down the aisle helping anyone who seemed to be having difficulty with arranging the cinches of their life preservers. There were only two Americans, besides myself; Paul Blake, Assistant to the airline president, and his young wife. I hadn't wanted to worry either with the news until the captain had briefed Paul on the situation.

I tied square knots in the pliable straps of my "Mae West," as I couldn't quickly figure out the correct method of cinching. I took down my briefcase from the overhead rack, crammed with irreplaceable notes from my world tour—my reports on the desperate needs of sixty million children. It would be impossible, I knew, to take the briefcase as my hands would have to be free. If I lived through this, I reasoned, some of the important facts were indelibly etched on my mind. Hurriedly I stuffed four items down the front of my blouse, two of which would be vital to anyone lucky enough to survive and to find themselves in a life raft: my pilot's license, one remaining traveler's check, four codeine pills—and a package of Life Savers. There seemed little hope that anyone could survive when the big airliner, with its tons of metal, finally crashed into the sea. I thought of Mother, my brothers, and of Aunty, then said a silent prayer,

"Heavenly Father, let it be quick!"

The second engine sputtered and died, then a third . . . and the final one went dead. I braced myself for the coming crash, checking my seat belt and that of the Italian who sat beside me.

In those final moments I think most of the passengers mercifully lacked full realization of what was going on; there was no panic, no one screamed, wept or had hysterics. Most of them were unschooled laborers, and they sat in silence.

But what was that noise? One of the engines barked, then roared, followed by the other three. Paul Blake, who had a little while before been in the flight compartment told me that the crew had discovered an emergency tank with eighty gallons of precious extra gasoline. We could keep going for another fifteen minutes. God, this was *truly* "sweating it out."

The reprieve was more torture than the preceding hour of suspense. The First Pilot sat on the floor facing the passengers with his back to the crew compartment door. Again we had to live through the grim sound of each engine going dead . . . one by one . . .

Now complete silence, and we were going, down, down, down, gliding smoothly toward the sea. Outside was a black void. The seconds dragged out . . . As far as I knew, in only one other major open-sea night ditching had there been any survivors. Would it never end? Let it be quick, *please,* God . . .

A long swishing sound. Foam against the windows, white against the blackness. One hard smack, heads thrown forward, then a second lesser jolt. This was IT. All the lights went out. I was shocked at the suddenness—one second being a part of lighted civilization and the next finding oneself in blackness with the salt sea pouring down the aisle.

But we were still alive! It seemed impossible, incredible. I struggled out of my seat into the aisle where the water already swirled up to my knees, and gave a hand to my seat companion. Screams now rent the air. Paul grabbed my hand and said:

"Ruth, you, Sally and I must hold on tight together."

Now clamber through this torrent of water to that open gap in the rear. We must get out . . . quickly, quickly. At the rear of the plane a glow appeared. And my eyes, adjusting to the darkness, saw a ray of moonlight shining down the aisle through a gaping hole.

The plane's tail assembly had been torn off. People were moving toward the hole.

Had the passengers in the rear of the plane been killed or lost? We knew none in the hull were injured, it had been too good a landing for that. Furthermore, since Paul, his wife and I had been in the front seats, we knew that all behind us had moved outward.

Now we were at the hole. Outside, the picture struck me like an artist's conception of turbulent creation—chaos—vapor —matter—half forms, struggling within the vast, overpowering forces of nature.

Then the voice of Paul Blake snapped me back to a still real world:

"Ruth, we've got to inflate this raft. Grab the other end!"

I yanked, but we couldn't find the valve. The plane was plunging violently in the rough sea, sinking lower. Paul yelled:

"Jump."

We pushed the half-open deflated raft over the ragged edge. Paul and Sally dove at the same time to get clear of the plane before the suction drew them down with it.

As I dove out into the unearthly luminous vapor, I wondered desperately whether this was the end of my universe— or the beginning of another?

I hit the water, and as I surfaced, instinctively set out in a steady crawl stroke through the towering waves and away from the sinking plane. Competitive amateur swimming now stood me in good stead. I didn't even feel the shock of the cold water. But soon I became aware of the hampering weight of my clothes and the tremendous exertion of fight—against interminable waves. There, over there, was the life boat I was trying to reach. Old discipline again came into play . . . *stop* and *rest*. Don't panic.

I looked about for other survivors, and saw, far ahead, a crowded raft. But no matter how I struggled to reach it, the distance between us grew steadily greater. The raft was drifting away from me faster than I could swim. . . . I felt the sudden desolation of being completely alone in the vast darkness of an impersonal sea.

With all my efforts directed toward reaching the receding life raft, I had not looked behind me. Now, to my amazement, I saw the raft we had pushed overboard. It had inflated automatically on hitting the water, and other human beings were clinging to it. Weak with relief I turned and made for it. Some distance to the right I saw a man floating on his back, arms folded, making no apparent effort to save himself. I shouted at him and motioned toward the raft. But he only lifted one arm in an apparent gesture of farewell, and made no further move. He was too far away for me to reach him and fight my way back to the raft. I began to realize that I was badly out of condition; my strength was almost gone. If I could reach the raft, perhaps we could paddle it in his direction and save him. I made a final desperate effort, lost sight of the raft in the trough of a giant wave, then was tossed high on its crest—and the raft was within reach.

With my last ounce of strength I reached out and touched the slippery rubber side—but there were no ropes to grasp. The raft had inflated upside down, with the ropes underneath. A number of people had managed to clamber on top of it and were trying to hold on to others, still in the water. Paul Blake and his wife were in the water alongside, clinging to the legs of those aboard the raft. I managed to do the same.

But we could not cling like this for long in this cold, mountainous sea. Even life preservers would not save us much longer. We must somehow manage to clamber onto the raft. Paul, with the help of the Italians on top, was making a desperate effort to get his wife, Sally, onto the bobbing, slippery bit of rubber that was our only hope of survival in the vast desolation of the ocean. At last Sally was hauled aboard. Then somehow I was dragged up, and finally Paul. I collapsed in the midst of a squirming, heaving mass of humanity, and was conscious only of the blessed security of being among living people—warm, breathing, human people. It was comforting to be packed in among them, even to be gouged by elbows and knees and jostled by feet, for they were symbols of . . . life!

As I caught my breath, I remembered the man I had seen floating resignedly in the water, and gasped to Paul:

"There's a man—over that way somewhere—do you think we could reach him?"

As Paul tried to peer into the darkness the raft was spun around by a huge wave, almost capsized, righted itself, and when we could look again there was no sign of a living being anywhere in the sea around us.

Now a new peril became apparent. Fourteen of us were crowded into a raft built for ten. With each impact of a wave, bodies slid and shifted. Even if this tiny bit of flotation gear could stay afloat with such an overload, there was constant danger that it would capsize if too many survivors slid to one side at the same time.

We were piled two or three deep on the bucking, plunging raft, each person clinging for dear life to the others as frigid waves broke over us, and as the frail little raft, time after time, was almost upended at the crest of a towering wall of water. But each time, just as it seemed we must surely capsize, the raft would miraculously right itself. Paul and I tried to motion to the men to move to the other end in order to equalize the load, but they were now transfixed into rigidity with terror. Each person was fighting like an animal to keep from being pushed off by the movement of another cramped leg or shoulder.

As bodies grew numb from the cold, hysteria and fear increased. With each violent pitch of the waves the Italians would be heard moaning "Mio Dio!" "Mama Mia!"

Something must be done to calm them I thought—singing, I had read somewhere, was a great morale builder. So I started out with one of my favorite hymns: "Eternal Father, Strong to Save." Sally didn't think it was peppy enough, so she started off with "Roll out the Barrel." But the devout Italians had made their vows to God and seemed to resent this levity. I tried the beautiful "Ave Maria," which I knew was a sacred favorite and whose melody I well remembered although I had to fill in the forgotten words with a series of "La, la, le, la." For a few moments they forgot their terror in the release of that magnificent song. But it was difficult to sing with several heavy bodies piled on top of you, and with every lurch of the tiny raft threatening annihilation. Moreover, that was the extent of my Italian repertoire.

We were wedged together so tightly that the air was gradually being squeezed out of my life preserver. Paul told me to blow into the little tube to inflate it again. But this turned out to be impossible. Either I didn't have sufficient power or the nozzle was not properly opened.

None of us could see; we could only feel. I had one hand clenched around a man's belt and with the other I clutched somebody's ankle. With each lurch of the raft, the weight of bodies shifted, the moans and prayers rose in volume, cramped muscles protested more fiercely. Paul, Sally and I called back and forth to each other, for reassurance that we were all still there. I tried to calm the men around me, but as they could not understand a word I said I could only hope my voice sounded soothing. It was imperative, but almost impossible, to urge them to keep from sliding toward the low side of the raft.

As the night wore on our energy steadily waned. It was all

we could do to summon enough strength to hang on to each other and keep from being pushed overboard.

Suddenly, I thought I saw a light. Was I having an illusion? No, one . . . two . . . three lights . . . it *was* a boat! It was coming nearer. It was getting bigger. We could see sailors on the low-slung deck of a trawler. Soon it would be here. But its bow seemed headed off course.

"They don't see us," Sally said dully.

Like all the others, I waved and shouted. It was no use. The ship veered off. They didn't see us. We stopped shouting; we stopped waving.

"But they were so close," I muttered. "So close . . ."

"Yeah," said Paul.

I lapsed into meditative revery. I thought of the work of the last few months, and felt a sick emptiness; all my reports for UNICEF were now at the bottom of the sea. I knew that this was the most important work of my life up to now, and as I looked back on events of the last twenty-four hours I thought unhappily that if I had not been so intent on chalking up another "first" for a world flight, I would not now be facing eternity. The race—*any* competition—seemed inconsequential. What could it possibly matter whether I was the first woman to fly around the world or not? Anyway, Morrow-Tait needn't worry about me now! The important thing was the work for UNICEF—and if I slipped off this raft, I wouldn't be doing much good for the world's children. Yet I had a feeling of peace and satisfaction in my heart—I had done my best.

I must have lapsed into unconsciousness, or perhaps the sleep of exhaustion. A huge wave breaking over the raft jerked me back to consciousness, and the sudden despairing realization that I was being pushed off the raft by a sudden shift in the mass of bodies. I cried out to Paul. A strong male voice bellowed a reply:

"Ruth! Let yourself go over the side. Keep hold of the raft and work your way around to this side. I'll haul you up!"

It was the Captain's voice! Sometime during the night he must have pulled himself aboard the raft. It was a wonderful sound. Now we had authority aboard. The Captain would know what to do.

Unquestioning, I let myself slide over the edge, digging my fingers into the rubber of the raft, then cautiously inching my way around it, swimming with one hand, clutching the raft with the other. Then a strong hand came down, caught me under the armpit and heaved me aboard.

"Careful!" cautioned Captain Johnson, as I collapsed against him in blessed relief. "There's an injured man here. Blackwell, radio man. Try to put his head in your lap. He's unconscious."

I gasped out my thanks to the Captain, then gently lifted the head of the unconscious man, feeling the weight of his head and shoulders on my lap. I shifted my body to shield him from the waves that periodically broke over us. Johnson still held my arm, and I heard him groan.

"Are you hurt?" I asked.

"Cramp," he replied. "My legs—while I was in the water. Had to hold Blackwell up. Took more than an hour to get onto the raft."

Another wave broke over us, traveling the full length of the raft, calling forth new cries of terror. Clawlike fingers dug into my back, and I hooked my heels over the edge of the raft to provide a firmer anchor. Everybody had to hold on somewhere.

Paul Blake's voice called, "Are you all right, Ruth?"

"Okay!" I shouted. "How's Sally?"

She answered for herself, a brave "Hi, there!"

"What time was it," I asked Johnson, "when we hit?"

"Two-forty," he replied.

I tried to figure the hours until dawn. It seemed as if we had spent a lifetime in this icy darkness. I moved slightly, adjusting the weight of Blackwell's head in my lap. I was glad it was there. It gave me a responsibility. Everybody needs a responsibility . . .

My thoughts grew fuzzy, got lost in the blackness and the cold. I seemed to see a fire in the grate at home, with Aunty sitting beside it . . . a steaming cup of tea . . . a warm bed . . .

The shock of a wave jolted me back to the raft.

"How's the leg, Captain?" I asked.

"Better," he said. Then— "My name's Jim."

This seemed terrifically funny, for some reason.

"Okay, Jim," I giggled. "Hello, Jim."

"Hello, Ruth," he said, and roared with laughter.

"Fancy meeting you here," I went on.

"Oh, I get around to the best places," he said.

Both of us were lightheaded from exhaustion and cold and strain.

Then his voice was suddenly normal and alert again:

"It's getting light!"

Now that was a poor kind of joke, I thought resentfully. I couldn't see any light. Or could I? Maybe it was a little lighter, out there on the horizon. Yes, it was! There was a definite streak—dark gray against the black. I shivered in excitement. The coming of dawn was a sight I hadn't counted on seeing again.

The quality of the darkness changed, almost imperceptibly. Now I could see the face of the man whose head I held. Now I could see clear across the raft, could make out the huddled figures of Paul and Sally. Now I could look across the leaden water . . .

"Watch for a plane," he said. "They'll be sending search planes. They'll be looking for us. It's getting lighter all the time. A plane will see us."

Of course! Of course they would send planes. A big airliner couldn't just disappear without people caring. Our radio man, the one whose head lay in my lap, had of course sent an SOS. The minute it was light we would see the planes— they would be taking off now—they would find us.

I looked up at the sky, and my heart sank with a thud. Low, scudding clouds were close above us. A plane couldn't get under them. And a plane couldn't see us from above.

The man whose head was in my lap stirred and moaned. I tried to shift my position, to make him more comfortable. But my legs were numb, like stone. I concentrated on this problem, then——

"Clearing," said Jim.

I looked up, unbelieving. It was true. A freshening wind was blowing the scud away, but was at the same time heightening the waves to twenty feet with a six foot chop. There were patches of clear sky through the clouds. Far off on the horizon I thought I saw land. A coastline. Yes, it *was* . . . a thin distant coastline of black cliffs.

In the sky appeared a speck—a moving speck, growing larger. Then there was a faint hum. This was a dear, familiar sound, a sound I knew. I was afraid to say anything. I kept my eyes on the speck in the sky and strained my ears. Now the others heard it, too. There was a scrambling, and incoherent shouting. The raft tipped dangerously. And the plane flew past us, about a mile away. It didn't circle. It didn't come back. It flew on, out of sight.

The raft had sunk deeper in the water. A new hysteria was breaking out among the frightened men. They clawed toward the higher side of the raft.

Another sound grew in the sky. Another plane! We were to have a second chance. Probably dozens of planes were searching for us. This one would see us. It must!

But it flew on, still farther south.

The waves now had foamy crests; it was harder than before to keep the raft balanced and a sudden shift in the huddled crowd threatened to push both me and my unconscious charge into the water. I was not going to have him pushed overboard. He was my responsibility. I braced myself, shoved back, shielding Blackwell's head with my body.

"There's another one," said Johnson, pointing. I peered

upward. Yes, there was a third plane, but it was flying much too high. It passed directly over us, and went on. If so many planes failed to spot us, they would abandon this area to search elsewhere . . . I thought of the time I had joined Harry Rogers in a search for a flyer lost at sea. We hadn't found him.

Why prolong this agony of see-sawing between hope and despair? What was the use? How could we hope that a pilot would sight this tiny pinpoint in all the empty stretches of the sea? Why hope, anyway? How much could the human heart endure?

How often can hope come back to life? I can tell you. Twelve times. Twelve times a plane passed over us. Twelve times it flew away. Then the thirteenth—no, it was the twelfth, flying low, coming back, wagging its wings, then flying on.

"Did he—did he—" I couldn't go on. I gazed imploringly at Captain Jim.

"He did!" cried Jim. "He saw us! I saw the pilot wave! You saw him dip his wings. Buck up. We're okay now!"

The plane was heading toward the horizon, where a trawler soon appeared, a smoky smudge between sky and sea. If it *was* heading for us, its progress seemed so slow, that again the cold, wetness and wallowing of the raft drifted me into semi-consciousness. As time went by, and my mind focused once more on the reality about me, our inverted, over-loaded raft was now almost awash with the water line. I looked out and saw that the trawler was growing bigger. She was heading directly for us, and I could actually see the smokestack and the white bow waves. Only a short time more and the trawler was alongside. Men reached down with strong, dry arms. One by one the survivors were pulled up. When my turn came, I could not raise my arms, so when a big wave carried the raft flush with the deck, a sailor grabbed the coat on my shoulders and pulled me like a wet, limp fish over the rail, plopping me down on my stomach onto one of the hatches.

A sailor came over with a knife and cut the straps of my life jacket, saying:

"Come on, Miss. I'd better get ye below."

With his help I made the forward part of the trawler where we climbed to the bridge and then slid down the perpendicular ladder into Captain A. S. Browne's cabin.

The bunk was occupied by the stewardess and another Italian girl, both of whom had been somewhat injured in the ditching. Sally, very seasick from the severe wallowing of the small vessel, lay on a sofa ledge near the window. I dropped on the sofa at her feet.

Then another sailor brought grog for us all. He saw that my teeth chattered uncontrollably and my arms still seemed paralyzed. So he stripped off my cold wet clothing and slipped over my head a brand new, snowy white turtle-neck sweater of the Captain's and a pair of his pants, and poured grog into my mouth.

Never could I remember such a sense of well-being. After the terror of the night, the hopelessness, the certainty of death, it seemed a miracle to be wrapped in a blanket. We were the last raft to be picked up. We were told it could not have floated with our overload another twenty minutes. Survivors from two others were safely aboard. There were forty-nine survivors, all aboard the trawler *Stalberg*. Nine persons had been lost.

Just before we ditched, our plane had made radio contact with another airliner, a TWA plane enroute to New York from Shannon, Ireland. Its Captain, Charles Adams of Franklin Sq., L. I., was trying to guide us back to Shannon when our fuel gave out. That he dropped flares made it possible to ditch at night. Radio, atmospheric and other conditions had prevented our own contact with Shannon. Our radio man had sent out a stream of "May Days"—the SOS call of the air to alert Air-Sea Rescue Service. It had been tireless, efficient Captain Browne of the *Stalberg* who had seen our plane go down, but couldn't find the rafts during his night search. Our own particular raft had first been sighted by a Pan-American World Airways airliner flying from New York to Brussels. After its Captain, Allen D. Reedy, landed his passengers, as tired as he was, with true humanitarian spirit, he re-fueled in Shannon and then joined the RAF Air Rescue search. When Captain Reedy spotted us, we were told, he was again getting low on fuel. Because of not having the same radio frequency necessary to contact the trawler, his radioed location of our raft had to be picked up by shore stations and then relayed to our trawler. This all consumed critical time.

Doctors, nurses, ambulances and Red Cross workers lined the dock at Galway as the trawler came alongside. All the survivors were transferred deftly and efficiently to a modern hospital for whatever treatment was required. A doctor said I had a slightly congested lung, but I replied that I felt all right and insisted upon leaving after a shot of penicillin. The first thing I did was send a cable home:

"Am feeling fine. Back soon. Ruth."

This was one plane crash from which I emerged uninjured. I counted my blessings. After a few hours rest in the hospital during which I was equipped with a well-fitting green jersey suit, underwear, polo coat and wrapper by the generous Red Cross, I went with the survivors to a hotel in Ennis, a few hours from Shannon Airport, where I met the airline president. There would be a plane in twenty-four hours, he said, with the same courtesy-pilot arrangement for me as before.

We landed at Bradley Field, Hartford, Connecticut at three a.m., August 18. Again, I was greeted by the usual crowd of press and newsreel representatives. I later learned that Mrs. Morrow-Tait completed her globe-circling flight the next day, August 19.

So an old dream had at last been realized, and with it the direction and purpose of my life. All the adventures, all the yearnings and conflicts, all the ups and downs had tempered my spirit for the new frontiers to come.

My notes on the plight of the world's children together

with the precious gift of exquisitely embroidered table covers
which had taken a destitute Greek child weeks to design and
make and through which I had hoped to focus the attention
of America's heart on the world's needy children—all had
gone down in the Irish Sea. I could, however, remember
enough to make a strong and fairly complete report to and on
behalf of UNICEF, which is still today salvaging millions of
young lives for the future.

Nevertheless, I was warmed by the unregenerate glow of
pride and fulfillment when I learned that Captain Carstaff of
our last plane had remarked to Paul Blake:

"You know, that babe sure can fly!"

No one really *wants* to grow up, any more than did Peter
Pan; but, either like Topsy or by long struggle, we finally *do*.
In the process, we learn the need to sever parental domination, as well as the omnipotence of childhood, where every
desire is felt to be a need which can be demanded and where,
if the demand is deprived, or frustrated, there seems to be a
cause for anger, conscious or otherwise, which is often dis-
played in seeking power and domination.

However, to *grow* we must also feel vitally important to at
least one person or to a cause, and we must feel that at least
such a person or cause wants us to assume responsibility for
our own safety, as well as for their future, even though we
may not be otherwise related to each other.

As for the courage needed in these types of life, it varies
with consciousness and conditions. There are many varieties.
Apparently, there are psycho-dynamic reasons why one person has more of one sort of courage than another, or more in
general. Books on psychiatry explain it on the basis of innate
unconsciousness, or even perhaps atavistic (pre-incarnate
animal instinctive) fears such as fear of drowning, water,
mice, snakes, noise, etc. Therefore, either a vivid imagination
or a deep-seated unknown cause of fear may make some
pilots highly sensitive or apprehensive regarding the possibility of danger, such as forced landings, ditching at sea, etc.,

which could mean death, slow drowning or aloneness. Yet this does not mean that a pilot is an unhealthy "Worrier." In discussing temperament with military flight surgeons, one finds that new standards are being set up for pilots who are to fly efficiently the complicated, fast aircraft of today, which require extreme alertness, and sensitivity, as well as lightning coordination. Therefore, some medical specialists claim that a high strung pilot, all other conditions being favorable, is apt to be the safest type for supersonic planes—if he is able, on the ground, to bury, or offset over-anxiety concerning the realistic possibilities involved.

In retrospect, when considering the beneficent effect upon mankind throughout history of individual martyrdom to a principle, many of us are perplexed by absolute applications, yet we have come to certain conclusions.

For instance, when dealing with the problems, conflicts and competitiveness between individuals, economic groups or nations, nonviolent resistance is surely a lofty Christian ideal, in combination with energetic, but permissive education and examples of friendship through the bestowing of bank loans, food, machinery and know-how. However, the question often arises: where does dynamic passive resistance leave off and an aggressiveness begin which will arouse resistance and hostile feelings? For instance, if our country provides material aids and we use that generosity as a bludgeoning lever to enforce our own views and methods, the means destroy the very things we seek to preserve. On the other hand, when understanding the dynamics of human personality, it becomes apparent that we cannot *insist* on a change of viewpoint, or on a way of life. We can only *assist* those who seek help, with gifts to which *no strings* are attached. In the long run that seeming unselfishness pays off—both to individuals, as well as to groups.

To be realistic, such objectivity requires a good deal of general education as well as personal discipline. Until that condition is more prevalent, we may have to evolve an International Police Force through the United Nations, whereby many rights of sovereignty will have to be relinquished in order to keep the current "Bad Child" in order. On the other hand, death itself may not be so forbidding—but rather the warping of personalities in organizing and carrying out the brutality of violent force may well have long range, deleterious or retarding effects upon the spiritual growth of individuals on this earth, as well as during the aeons of life to come.

For to me it seems that *all life flies*—protons, planes or people. Even tiny microcosms experience the instinctive, or electromagnetic propulsion to dart about freely in the ultimate fulfillment of their functions. This is a good force, signifying the propelling energy and limited freedom that the astral self possesses in its growth and progress toward those higher realms that ultimately merge with the Loving All-Soul. Truly you must have *wings for LIFE*, as there is no living without flight . . . You need but to feel the celestial wings in your heart, in order for them to fly you skyward.

21

WINGS FOR TOMORROW

And now at last, I have learned to weld together the warring elements of my inherited nature—my father's adventurous nature and the spiritual urge of my Quaker ancestors—by understanding better our individual rights of self expression, by observing some of the patterns that compel us to such expression and finally by discovering what are some of the most satisfying goals.

Recently a new means has been given me to pursue this basic idea of service through flight. My old dream of Relief Wings again rose into life, with my appointment as "Advisor to the National Commander on Matters Pertaining to Aeromedical Administration" in the Civil Air Patrol. Since the subject of flying ambulances has long been close to my heart, I have found an intense personal satisfaction in this appointment, which grew out of similar organizational work in New York State, and which I was asked to undertake in 1954.

It was then that I resumed active duty in the Civil Air Patrol, to which I had assigned certain assets of my Relief Wings organization at the beginning of the war.

After various conferences with Major General Lucas V. Beau, National Commander of CAP and his successor Major General Walter R. Agee, I learned that no uniform procedure had been set up for recruitment and training of flight surgeons and nurses, or for the medical operation of services pertaining to air evacuation, air rescue and air ambulances.

Lieutenant Colonel Ruth Rowland Nichols, C.A.P., and her brother,
Colonel Erickson Snowden Nichols, U.S.A.F., before making a jet
flight at Hamilton Air Force Base, California, Summer 1955

Thus I found myself launched upon a volunteer organization program which was to start in New York State under the supervision of Colonel Joseph F. Crowley, Commander of the New York Wing. I soon enlisted into the program the advice and services of Lieutenant Colonel Seymour Fiske, M.D., well-known in civilian aviation medical circles, as Medical Director of the New York Wing.

During the organizational stage, I had the opportunity of observing USAF air rescue techniques at Air Force bases. As a member of the Civil Air Patrol, I have various opportunities to pilot a number of different types of aircraft, and was most happy, while spending some CAP briefing time at Hamilton Air Force Base, where my brother Nick was stationed, to pilot another jet—an early prototype of the new sonic space age.

After two years of recruitment and developing civilian air evacuation techniques in my home state, I was able to report a good start in the organization of doctors, nurses and first aid cadets, to be trained in special aeromedical procedures as a medical division for the New York Wing of CAP. It was as a result of this that Major General Agee asked me to formulate a Standard Organization Procedure which could be used on a national scale.

So another dream is coming true, and I have high hopes that, with government interest and support, the civilian flying fraternity may sprout an effective new mercy wing.

Every human being must work out his own goals and methods of attaining them.

There will always be pioneers of the sky, for this is our last frontier. Today's flying frontiersmen are streaking through space at supersonic speeds in planes as different from the lumbering bailing-wire machines of my youth as an atom bomb is different from a penny firecracker.

The pioneer pilot will always be "that daring young man on the flying trapeze." When the most famous of them all,

Charles A. Lindbergh, succeeded in flying across the ocean thirty years ago, his achievement was far more startling than that of the Army test pilot of today who considers it routine to take an F101 fifteen-ton twin-engine turbo jet plane ten miles high at a thousand miles an hour. And the plane he is testing probably is obsolete before it gets into production, as research engineers strive for ever greater speed and altitude.

As I look back on a long series of adventures in the sky, I am grateful to have been able to play a part in the highest drama of our times, the unbelievably swift development of aviation, the new science that has changed the habits of the world and now is setting its sights on outer space.

Sometimes it is difficult to believe that in the span of my lifetime, which I hope still has a long way to go, I have seen air transportation progress from the flimsy, primitive, open-cockpit planes in which I learned to fly to the jet airliners of today. Most of us now take safe, swift air travel so much for granted that we forget how short a time ago it was when a flight from coast to coast rated banner headlines. Even though my early speed, altitude and distance records seem kindergarten achievements compared to our present sky blazers, they were significant and exciting episodes at the time. And they all helped in the development of added speed, load factors and safety in the air.

This development is what, I believe, all pioneer pilots cherish: Every new achievement in the air adds to the sum total of human knowledge on which is based the next big step forward. All of us who flew those clumsy, precarious Jennies and Seagulls so long ago played a needed part in the unfolding air drama of today, and the potentials of tomorrow.

Another fact of which I am grateful is that I am still flying —and I never intend to quit. When life gets too cluttered and stuffy on the ground, I can still take to the privacy and freedom of the sky, and there adjust my sights to distant vistas not yet contacted.

The horizons are flying outward with a speed never known

A group of Ruth Nichols' trophies, medals and mementos in her "sky parlor" at her home in Rye, New York.

before and so too our views must grow swiftly to keep pace with today's world. I have followed with interest the many reports and arguments as to the existence of "flying saucers," and the endless debate as to whether they are psychic phenomena or actual emissaries from other planets. There is too much evidence, from sane and respected men, that some such strange objects have been in our earth's atmosphere to dismiss them all as figments of overwrought imaginations, whatever else they may be. Furthermore, the discoveries in extrasensory perception at Duke University and the amassing of scientifically observed phenomena by the parapsychology groups, along with the even more recent uncovering of life's mystery, show we are on the threshold of a vaster reality.

Thirty years ago a man who said planes would fly at speeds above a thousand miles an hour, directed by electronic equipment on the ground would have been laughed off the map. Anyone who had said that one day we would be able to look at a little screen and follow the course of an approaching plane many miles distant would have been considered an impractical dreamer. And the man who talked of space ships and flights beyond the earth's atmosphere would have been considered likely material for an insane asylum.

Yet in the space of one generation we have seen many such dreams become actualities, taken for granted, and others are imminent.

So I have learned not to laugh off any prediction about the potentials of the air, however improbable. I consider it quite possible that during my lifetime interplanetary travel will become an accepted fact, and that ordinary citizens may plan vacations on the moon instead of at Miami Beach.

Of one thing I am certain—when space ships take off, I shall be flying them, whether in my present bodily form or another.

FLYING ACHIEVEMENTS OF
RUTH NICHOLS

First woman World Pilot—1949 global air tour for United States Committee of the United Nations International Children's Emergency Fund.

First woman in the United States to pilot a twin-engine executive jet (1955).

Standardized in aeromedical procedures, the first state in the Civil Air Patrol (1956).

Earliest-licensed woman flyer piloting in the United States today. (F.A.I. Certificate accorded 1924. 19th woman ever to be licensed in United States of whom approximately five are still living, none active excepting RN.)

Only woman in the world to have held three maximum international records: altitude, speed and long distance. (According to NAA Chronology of International Records, January 1, 1939.)

Has flown more models of airplanes than any other American woman. (As of a survey whose results are dated April 8, 1939.)

HOLDER OF THE LARGEST NUMBER OF FIRST PLACES AND
MISCELLANEOUS PAST RECORDS, OF ANY AMERICAN
WOMAN PILOT FLYING TODAY:

1st licensed woman seaplane pilot in United States. (2nd government-licensed woman land-plane pilot in United States.)

1st woman airline pilot in the United States. (New York & New England Airways 1932.)

1st seaplane to carry air mail out of New York State. Piloted by RN and Webb Schmaling, May 19, 1938.

"1st Lady of the Air" for 1930. Awarded by International League of Aviators.

1st U.S. championship awarded to an American woman by the above International League.

1st licensed woman pilot in New York State (among thirty-five men).

1st non-stop flight—New York to Miami (as co-pilot).

1st woman to attempt a solo Atlantic flight.

1st American woman to assist in remodeling a modern record-setting airplane.

1st plane in aviation history to set maximum records in three totally different categories, piloted by RN.

1st woman to use an airplane radio.

1st aviation lecturer on aeronautical applications of various college sciences by individual seminars and general science lectures on aerology, navigation and aerodynamics.

1st woman executive of a million-dollar aviation corporation— Fairchild Aviation Corporation.

1st Aviation Country Clubs organized by RN and two men.

1st woman officer of an aviation magazine—"The Sportsman Pilot."

1st woman pilot organization, "The Ninety-Nines"—originally conceived by RN and Amelia Earhart.

1st woman airline passenger between New York and Los Angeles on christening flight of American Airlines.

1st "Air Ambassadress" for five million women when making a 3,000 mile good-will tour sponsored by the National Council of Women.

1st woman to land solo in forty-six states and third United States air tour made by any pilots when completing a 12,000 mile flight for Aviation Country Clubs in 1929.

1st flight of newspapers from New York to Chicago—carrying the *New York Times.*

1st woman to set a one-stop transcontinental record, when flying from Los Angeles to New York in 13 hours, 21 minutes, flying time, which surpassed Colonel Lindbergh's flying time record made six months before. (Although Colonel Lindbergh's record had been broken by Captain Hawks before RN's flight in one hour's less time than hers.)

1st woman pilot to fly in Honolulu (1925).

1st American woman to pilot a multi-motored French transport in that country.

1st American woman to pilot across the Irish Sea.

1st woman to set an American altitude record for Diesel Motors, when surpassing Colonel Chamberlin's mark in 1932.

1st woman to pilot a twenty-passenger airplane, while making an educational tour of New England in 1935.

(Record still held: Official National Altitude Record for Diesel Motors.)